THE S.I.S. STORY

THE S.I.S. STORY

HOW AN ACCIDENTAL ENTREPRENEUR FROM BIHAR BUILT A GLOBAL SERVICES CONGLOMERATE

PRINCE MATHEWS THOMAS

HARPER
BUSINESS

An Imprint of HarperCollins *Publishers*

First published in India by Harper Business 2025
An imprint of HarperCollins *Publishers*
HarperCollins *Publishers* India, Cyber City,
Building 10-A, Gurugram, Haryana – 122002, India
www.harpercollins.co.in

2 4 6 8 10 9 7 5 3 1

Copyright © Rituraj Sinha 2025
Written by: Prince Mathews Thomas

P-ISBN: 978-93-6989-719-3
E-ISBN: 978-93-6989-995-1

The views and opinions expressed in this book are the writer's own and the facts are as reported by him, and the publishers are not in any way liable for the same.

Prince Mathews Thomas asserts the moral right
to be identified as the writer of this work.

All rights reserved. No part of this publication may be reproduced, stored in a retrieval system, or transmitted, in any form or by any means, electronic, mechanical, photocopying, recording or otherwise, without the prior permission of the publishers.

Without limiting the exclusive rights of any author, contributor or the publisher of this publication, any unauthorized use of this publication to train generative artificial intelligence (AI) technologies is expressly prohibited. HarperCollins also exercise their rights under Article 4(3) of the Digital Single Market Directive 2019/790 and expressly reserve this publication from the text and data-mining exception.

Typeset in 12/16 Crimson Text
by HarperCollins *Publishers* India Pvt. Ltd

Printed and bound at
Replika Press Pvt. Ltd.

This book is produced from independently certified FSC® paper to ensure responsible forest management.

HarperCollins *Publishers*, Macken House, 39/40 Mayor Street Upper,
Dublin 1, D01 C9W8, Ireland

*A business succeeds not because it is long-established or big.
It succeeds because of the people who live it, dream it and
strive to build a grand future for it.*

CONTENTS

	Preface	ix
1.	The young leader	1
2.	First steps	14
3.	The wandering CEO	22
4.	A bold entrepreneur	30
5.	The secret sauce	43
6.	The boot camp	51
7.	A unique record in industrial relations	62
8.	Shaping the industry	70
9.	A generational change	82
10.	The making of the dream team	94
11.	The boom years	102
12.	A failure and a win	114
13.	A study in deal-making	122

CONTENTS

14.	The audacious deal	130
15.	Getting the deal right	142
16.	Bringing a college project to reality	154
17.	Leading the way during Demonetization	167
18.	The second diversification	179
19.	The tech evolution of SIS	198
20	Going public	211
21	Fighting the pandemic	225
22.	The future	238
	Acknowledgements	251
	Notes	253

PREFACE

Who is the largest employer in India?

The obvious names that come to mind are the Indian Army and Indian Railways. That's correct. The Indian Army has nearly 25 lakh personnel. The Indian Railways, about 12.5 lakh.[1]

Who is the largest *private* employer in India?

Again, if your answer is Tata Consultancy Services (TCS), that's right. It has a little over 6 lakh people on its rolls. Next on the list is another IT giant, Infosys, with about half of TCS's number. In third place is Reliance Industries Ltd, with a workforce of nearly 3.5 lakh. All of these are blue-chip companies with millions of investors. Their chief executives, founders and promoters are among the most followed businesspeople in corporate India. Everything they do, in office and outside it, makes headlines.

If you thought, like me, the next company in the pecking order to be either Larsen & Toubro (L&T) or Tata Steel, it's a logical expectation. Both have a huge geographical and manufacturing presence. Imagine my surprise when I came to know that it's not them but SIS Group Enterprises that comes next. Previously known as Security and Intelligence Service Ltd, SIS currently employs over

3 lakh people as on 31 March 2025. Give it a thought. That's more than what conglomerates like the Aditya Birla Group and the Adani Group employ, with all their companies put together.

Despite its size and over fifty years of operations, little is known about SIS. Chances are that before you picked up this book, you would have heard of the company only fleetingly. It was the same with me until I met its founder Ravindra Kishore Sinha and his son Rituraj Sinha in 2013 for a story in *Forbes India*. By that time, the company had already charted a fascinating journey.

SIS was founded by Sinha in Patna in 1974. It was on the suggestion of socialist leader Jayaprakash Narayan that Sinha, till then a journalist, started helping out retired army jawans and officers get jobs as security personnel. 'It was a social service. I had no intention of making a business out of it,' Sinha would say. That's understandable. The 1970s were not a time for capitalist ambitions. But over the years, Sinha took decisions that seemed to be pulled right out of management books, just that he didn't have an MBA. What he had were the street smarts of a rustic entrepreneur, eye for detail and a connection with people.

Look at some of the decisions he made. In November 1984, SIS started a training institute for security guards, something no one had thought of doing in the security business. Not just in India, but globally. Two years later in 1986, the company added a graduate trainee officer program. Today, the same training programme, now conducted in twenty-two training facilities across 14 states, is the bedrock of SIS's growth. Also, SIS was among the first, across any industry, to bring in computers—in 1989—to manage organizational processes. It was around the time that then Prime Minister Rajiv Gandhi brought in the computer revolution to India. That early introduction of technology is seen in SIS's operations today, which are based on artificial intelligence and machine learning. SIS now has its own IT team. This includes 59 engineers who produce a suite of proprietary products custom made for business requirements.

In the early 1990s, just as the domestic economy was opening up amid a slew of reforms and private enterprise was taking off, Sinha expanded SIS beyond eastern states and entered major urban markets like those in Delhi and Bengaluru. And then, just after the turn of the century, as the information technology-led tech boom was taking off, Sinha did something uncharacteristic for a first-generation entrepreneur.

He took a back seat and handed over the business to Uday Singh, a childhood friend who had a successful corporate career with stints in Indian and multinational companies. Second, he brought in his twenty-two-year-old son Rituraj into the company, in an unexpected generational shift in SIS's leadership. Handing over the reins of the business to his son and a professional who would also double as the youngster's mentor was a rare decision for a first-generation entrepreneur. No entrepreneur really lets go of his company. Sinha did. And it turned out to be a masterstroke. Few business families in India, including the biggest ones, have managed such transitions.

SIS scaled from 14 branches to 100 by 2012. With Rituraj's youthful vigour, risk-taking mentality and out-of-the-box ideas, coupled with the disciplined professional in Uday Singh who couldn't stress more the importance of processes, training and quality, SIS grew vertically and horizontally. Just like McDonald's created a cookie-cutter model that became a template for its exponential expansion across the world, SIS did something similar to get to over 300 branches today. It developed a replicable business model for a simple service to be delivered with quality standards, consistently.

Each of these threads make for fascinating business case studies. The *Forbes India* story from 2013, however, was on an audacious investment that SIS had done in 2008. It acquired insurance giant

Chubb's security business in Australia that was seven times its size. That made it an even more high-risk bet than Tata Steel's acquisition of the five times bigger Corus a year earlier. Neither did SIS have the money nor did it have the backing of a 'parent' like Tata Sons that Tata Steel had. Yet, not only did it pull off the acquisition, but SIS turned the operation around and converted Chubb into its cash cow, fuelling more acquisitions and joint ventures. The *Forbes India* article was on the turnaround of this high-risk acquisition.

Now, let's come back to SIS's workforce. In 2013, SIS had a staff strength of 65,650. This was after three decades of accelerating growth and a mammoth acquisition. So, what did it further do to add over 2 lakh more people in the next twelve years?

As it turned out, Rituraj was just starting off. Over the next decade or so, Rituraj led SIS to thirteen more acquisitions. Four were done in 2019 alone. This helped the company's diversification into cash management, through a joint venture with Spain's Prosegur, and into facility management, riding on its partnership with ServiceMaster Corporation of the US. And then there was the pest management partnership with another US multinational, Terminix. Each of these companies were the biggest in their fields, and bringing them to India was no small feat. The expansion was international too. Through acquisitions, SIS entered New Zealand and Singapore, after Australia, making it one of the global market leaders. In between, SIS also raised growth capital from marquee investors such as D.E. Shaw and C.X. Partners.

In 2017, SIS was listed on the National Stock Exchange. This was a big milestone. SIS was the first from the security industry to do so. It was also a big personal milestone for Sinha. The significance is well explained by U.K. Sinha, the former chairman of market regulator Securities and Exchange Board of India (SEBI). 'There are thousands and thousands of companies from Bihar that are registered and some of these were listed on the exchanges. But, over the years, they had stopped trading. So, as a person from Bihar, I used to encourage, even through the state government and other entrepreneurs from Bihar, that why don't you try and do something so that we don't have a situation where not a single company from Bihar is listed on a national stock exchange. Sinha took this challenge very seriously. Right now, I'm very happy to say that SIS is among the few companies registered in Bihar and which is also listed on the two national exchanges.'

In all, these are remarkable milestones, especially so for a company from the security industry. Though their people are all around us, few security companies have managed to break the shackles to become a name to reckon with. Just look at where SIS stands today, around fifty years after it was founded.

SIS had revenues of Rs 13,189 crore in the 2025 financial year. Its operations are spread across 62,000 sites and 343 branches in over 700 districts of India, serving 22,000 customers. It's the largest security services provider in India. It's also the largest facility management provider and the second largest in cash logistics. It's the largest security provider in Australia, third largest in New Zealand and fifth largest in Singapore.

These impressive numbers apart, Sinha and Rituraj have had a similar impact in the industry. Sinha set up industry platforms that have been catalysts in promoting best practices and quality standards. He also took the lead in ensuring the security industry was formally recognized by the government in the form of the Private Security Agencies (Regulation) Act, 2005. Later, during Demonetization, SIS, now led by Rituraj, played a pivotal role in getting back cash to ATMs across the country. Three years later, when COVID hit, Rituraj convinced the government to make security and facility management an essential service, a decision that limited the deadly disruption caused by the pandemic and saved lakhs of jobs.

For all these achievements though, what do Sinha or Rituraj point out as SIS's biggest accomplishment? Its culture.

Seeded by Sinha and nurtured by Rituraj, SIS has a unique 'family culture' that has been the glue that holds together its employees. Old-timers talk about how Sinha and his wife Rita Sinha did the kanyadaan in their weddings as their own families were opposed to it. Others fondly remember the khichdi that Sinha would cook for the guards when he visited their barracks. Or the innumerable instances when Rituraj asked senior officials to personally visit families of deceased employees, making sure that last rites were held, while also providing financial security to the family.

Amit Garg, founder of MXV Consulting that worked with SIS on its transformative journey, recalls a similar meeting with Sinha. The SIS chairman had gotten a call from a guard. He listened to the guard, noted down the feedback and made sure that his colleagues got back to the guard. 'This was rare. That a guard is empowered to call the chairman of the company and share his problems, and for a chairman to leave everything aside and address a guard's concern,' recalls Garg. And there's something Sinha told him. 'We have no labour union in SIS. You know why? Because every guard in this organization has my phone number. What can a trade union guy do that the chairman can't?' Indeed, SIS is probably the only security company in India that doesn't have a trade union problem.

SIS's success has brought wealth to Sinha and his family. He has been ranked in *Forbes*'s list of richest entrepreneurs in India. But it's not just the founder and his family. There are scores of stories of exponential personal growth in SIS. The company's rise has mirrored that of its employees. Many of its present presidents and vice presidents had started off as young graduate trainee officers. Even before SIS launched its IPO, hundreds of its frontline employees had been given employee stock option plans (ESOPs). Being a lifer in SIS is such a common trait in the organization that present chief executive officer, and successor to Uday Singh, Dhiraj Singh quips, 'Even after eleven years, I feel like a relative newcomer!'

In short, SIS's fifty-year journey has many layers:

1. It is a time travel through India's modern economic history. SIS evolved even as the Indian economy did.
2. It's a story of an entrepreneur from the interiors making it big in the mainstream India Inc.
3. The scaling of its service business is a lesson in management and entrepreneurship.
4. Leapfrogging with M&A and partnerships
5. Importance of market leaders taking ownership and shaping the industry
6. In times when the startup era embodies the triumph of the individual over the collective, SIS's culture proves collective growth and success are possible.
7. Through R.K. Sinha and Rituraj Sinha, SIS is a lesson for their peers on how to handle generational change, and how to overcome the odds that confront family businesses—nearly 70 per cent of family businesses fold up in the second generation.

Yet, there is something more. 'Beyond the data, I believe this is a story of very ordinary people achieving extraordinary results. What Infosys is to the IT industry in India, I think SIS is to the security industry and outsourced services. If you look at the bottom of the pyramid, there are the unskilled rural youth whom we have trained. We have over 3 lakh people. Now with the 40–50 per cent attrition rate in the industry, we must have trained close to about 2 million people in this journey of fifty years. If each family has an average of four members, we have been responsible for 8 million mouths to be fed as well. That's a social transformation nobody recognizes, though everyone looks at EBITDA [earnings before interest, taxes, depreciation, and amortization] and growth numbers. That is like providing security and safety to the most underprivileged people,' Uday Singh says.

That sums up why SIS's growth is remarkable. Most companies do social good through their corporate social responsibility (CSR) arms. In SIS's case, enabling the unskilled and the underprivileged is core to its business. Remember, Sinha had started off with a simple aim: to provide employment. In the process, he, and later Rituraj, built an extraordinarily successful business. And that's what SIS is today—a fifty-year-old multibillion-dollar enterprise.

I've scarcely come across a business story as rich as this in my twenty-two years of writing.

1

THE YOUNG LEADER

Nagendra Nath couldn't believe his eyes. In all his years as an officer of the Indian Administrative Service (IAS) he hadn't come across a scene like this. Standing outside his office door were a group of school students. It looked like a procession. In the front was a boy, presumably thirteen years old. 'I am in the ninth standard,' he answered when Nath asked him. He spoke confidently, standing right at the front, and clearly was the leader of this motley group.

What were he and the rest of his friends doing at the office of the Director of Education in the middle of the day, instead of attending class, Nath asked.

The boy went on to describe how an incident had taken place in his school, Patna High School, and the principal had suspended a few students. 'It's not correct. The future of these students will be in question. We have come here to request you to take back the decision,' the boy said.

Nath was unimpressed. This was gross indiscipline, coming to a government office and requesting action against a principal's decision. The IAS officer dismissed the boys and ordered them to immediately get back home. 'Otherwise, you will be the one wondering about your future,' he threatened.

An incensed Nath called the Patna High School principal. 'This is poor behaviour by the boys. These protesting students shouldn't be left lightly, otherwise it will set a poor precedent. They should be rusticated,' Nath told the principal. And then, he asked, 'That boy who was leading them. What's his name?'

'Ravindra Kishore Sinha,' replied the principal. 'He is a good student, but yes, he does get into these kinds of activities. He came to you without permission. That is wrong too. But he doesn't deserve to be rusticated. Perhaps, we can transfer him to another school.'

With much persuasion, Nath agreed. Ravindra Kishore Sinha was transferred to Patna's Kendriya Vidyalaya. The move hurt the young boy but it didn't rankle too much. His passion for people was intact, as was his confidence and fearlessness. Looking back at the incident decades later, a much older Sinha would say, 'I agree that was a case of indiscipline. My view was that children should be well taken care of and shouldn't be suspended for one mistake.'

At home, no one—parents, siblings or friends—were surprised. 'From a small age, he showed immense passion and confidence in his beliefs,' says childhood friend Uday Singh, who would work with Sinha decades later.

That passion and belief, and the nerve to lead a procession to a senior government servant's office, was beyond what was typical for a thirteen-year-old. There would be such episodes later in life where Ravindra Kishore showed a similar conviction in his beliefs and passion for people. Some call these qualities a gift from God, the oft-cited reason in India when one can't explain or rationalize genius. Perhaps, a part of who Ravindra Kishore is indeed God's gift. The rest could be traced back to the environment at home.

Ravindra Kishore was born in Patna in 1951 to Suraj Prasad Sinha and Annapoorna Sinha. Suraj Prasad was a promising government official, erudite, fluent in English and well versed in the Vedas. He had topped the entrance exams, and got a posting in the coveted commercial taxes department. Coveted because an official could easily supplement his official income with some help under the table. Just that Suraj Prasad was not one of those. In fact, he abhorred it. He would constantly write to the chief secretary of the state, requesting a transfer. 'This is a very corrupt department and I can't sustain myself in this kind of atmosphere,' he wrote.

As it happened, Bindeshwari Prasad Verma, the first speaker of Bihar's assembly in independent India, was translating the Bhagavad Gita into English. He wanted help from somebody who knew English and Sanskrit equally well. One day, he called the chief secretary and asked if he had anyone who could do this. The secretary immediately thought of Suraj Prasad and said, 'Yes, there is a young man who keeps writing to me that he doesn't want to remain in the commercial taxes department, and his English is very good. In a few of the letters, he has quoted some shlokas from the Bhagavad Gita also. I think I will send him to you.'

Suraj Prasad happily moved to the state legislature. In the assembly, his reputation grew as someone who was excellent with parliamentary affairs. Senior politicians would come to him for tips on how to ask questions in the assembly, how to participate in debates or how to introduce various kinds of motions. At home too, he began getting visitors from all walks of life, including monks. They used to come either for spiritual discourse or help with editing their writing.

The young Ravindra Kishore was deeply influenced by his father and by the discussions he had with his visitors. In between serving tea and biscuits to guests, Ravindra Kishore would hover around, listening to his father explaining the finer details of a law to a politician or discussing the philosophy of a shloka with a sadhu.

Suraj Prasad also led a disciplined life. He would wake up at four in the morning, performing the Vedas and other rituals. Ravindra

Kishore and his siblings would accompany him. There were eight of them, four brothers and four sisters. Ravindra Kishore was the fifth child. The government quarter they inhabited was a modest three-room house. Often, guests would stay overnight. Suraj Prasad, Annapoorna and the children would sleep on the floor, keeping the beds for the guests.

As much as Ravindra Kishore soaked in the atmosphere at home, he was equally influenced by what was happening in the country.

The mid to late 1960s were years of soul searching for a young, independent India. The death of its first Prime Minister, Jawaharlal Nehru, in 1964, left a vacuum. His successor Lal Bahadur Shastri had ably led the country in the victorious war against Pakistan in 1965. But he soon passed away, paving the way for Nehru's daughter Indira Gandhi to head both the Indian National Congress and the government at the Centre.

She may have stamped her authority but Indira Gandhi continued to face opposition within the party and outside. The 1967 general elections saw the emergence of the Bharatiya Jana Sangh, the political arm of the Rashtriya Swayamsevak Sangh (RSS). The Jana Sangh won thirty-five seats and emerged as a significant alternative voice. Unemployment, inflation and scarcity of food were serious issues. On the other hand, the RSS's doctrine of discipline and nationalism provided an identity to several youth, including Ravindra Kishore. He was a regular at RSS's shakhas and was among its most active volunteers. 'He was one of the leaders, sometimes holding classes and even attending RSS officers' training camps,' recounts his younger brother, Satyendra Kishore Sinha.

A 1966 RSS camp held in Bhagalpur in particular had quite an influence on the teenager. It lasted for forty-five days, during which time he came across three influential personalities. The first was the RSS's second-in-command Madhav Sadashivrao Golwalkar, who is known to have first suggested the idea of Sanskritik Rashtravad (cultural nationalism). While at the camp, it became a ritual for Ravindra Kishore to make tea for Golwalkar, half a cup nearly every half an hour. Later, Ravindra Kishore came to know that Golwalkar had been suffering from cancer at the time and used to have tea to relieve his pain.

The second was Pandit Deendayal Upadhyay, one of the most recognizable faces of the Bharatiya Jana Sangh. During his sessions, Ravindra Kishore caught the national leader's attention with questions on rupee devaluation, something that Prime Minister Indira Gandhi was forced to do to avert a financial crisis. The country's financial distress was similar to the one that it would face years later in 1991. As ever the curious student, Ravindra Kishore peppered Upadhyay with questions on the monetary action, much to the irritation of others but to the delight of the senior leader. 'At least there is someone who's asking questions about devaluation,' the leader said. Impressed, he asked Ravindra Kishore to join the Bharatiya Jana Sangh. Ravindra Kishore did so, in 1966 itself.

The third person at the RSS camp that left a lasting impact on Ravindra Kishore was Baleshwar Agrawal, a senior functionary of the RSS and also managing editor of the Hindustan Samachar news agency. Hindustan Samachar provided news in ten languages. Later, in 1975, it would merge with the Press Trust of India, the largest national newswire.

Impressed with the young boy's unusual interest in subjects ranging from economics to religion, Agrawal made him an offer. 'If you pass matriculation in first class, I will give you a job in my agency.' It was unexpected but Ravindra Kishore was delighted. At home, he could see his father struggling to manage the needs of a large family with his meagre government salary. Ravindra Kishore could make a difference.

He scored distinction in all subjects in his matriculation exams. Promptly, Ravindra Kishore went to Agrawal with his mark sheet.

'This is fine. You can join us and start working,' the senior journalist said. In 1967, at the age of sixteen, Ravindra Kishore landed a job even before he got admission into a college. The salary was a handsome Rs 25 a month. Other benefits? A samosa for lunch.

Now that he had a job in hand, he needed a college seat. With his results, Ravindra Kishore could have gotten admission at Patna College, one of the most premier educational institutes of the time, and the state's oldest. It was also a family tradition. His father, elder brother and cousins had studied there. But Ravindra Kishore had other ideas. He needed to get into a college that had early morning classes. That would leave him with enough time for his job at Hindustan Samachar. So, he chose Anugrah Narayan College, also known as A.N. College, which offered him a monthly scholarship of Rs 50. His father and his father's friend and Patna College's principal Mahendra Pratap tried persuading Ravindra Kishore to change his mind. Pratap offered to match the Rs 50 a month scholarship that A.N. College had promised. 'You are too young to work,' Suraj Prasad said. Nothing worked. Saying 'It's important for me,' Ravindra Kishore stuck to his decision.

At A.N. College, Ravindra Kishore quickly formed a routine. Classes began early in the morning. He commuted on a cycle, donning a crisp and clean white kurta pyjama. He carried books and a diary. In the kurta pocket was a small notebook he used to jot down his notes, both from his classes and reporting. Classes got over at 10.30 a.m.

Ravindra Kishore Sinha, the student, then became Ravindra Kishore Sinha, the journalist. At 11 a.m., he would be at the Hindustan Samachar office for the editor's morning meeting. He started off writing on the education beat, later moving on to crime and, even later, political reportage. Ravindra Kishore was busy. He had few friends in college, but for one, Kurian aunty. She was the wife of IAS officer Kurian Abraham, who was among the senior most government officers. It was an unlikely friendship but one they both treasured. They exchanged history and political science class notes when the other would be absent. Ravindra Kishore became friends with her son Michael and was often invited to the Kurian household. And that's where he first had the Kerala delicacy, appam. 'She was my aunty. Like my mother. She had a profound impact on me with her kindness. She would cook food for me and bring it to the college,' Ravindra Kishore would reminisce years later.

Things were going to become even more interesting and adventurous for the young journalist. In 1971, Indira Gandhi decided to intervene in the Bangladesh Liberation War in East Pakistan. The provocation was Pakistan's preemptive strikes on eight Indian air stations. It was a short war. India entered the fray on 3 December 1971. Thirteen days later, on 16 December, Pakistan's military capitulated and surrendered. Nearly 1 lakh Pakistani soldiers surrendered, which to date remains the second largest surrender of personnel after the Second World War.

Ravindra Kishore, all of twenty years, was the only journalist from Bihar to cover the war. In the months that he spent in Bangladesh, he sent daily reports through telegrams made available by the Indian Army. While witnessing a historical moment play out in front of his eyes was a life-changing experience, the young man was much pained by the loss of human lives and destruction. The completion of war brought relief and a memorable experience for Ravindra Kishore, when Sheikh Mujibur Rahman, the founding President of Bangladesh, hosted journalists.

This was also the first time Ravindra Kishore came in contact with Indira Gandhi. She had returned to power with a massive majority in the 1971 elections and nationalized the nation's banks, which underlined the socialist policies that governed the country's economy at the time. Ravindra Kishore admired her tenacity but identified more with the other side of political philosophy. And that would shortly change the course of his life.

Politically, India was in a flux. Issues such as food inflation, land rights and lack of jobs led to protests along the length and breadth of the country. Among the first to mobilize were the Naxalites through the Naxalbari-Maoist insurgency, which had seeds in the Naxalbari uprising of 1967. International incidents like the Cuban Revolution and the Vietnam War had given way to uprisings influenced by leftist ideology.

In India, the movement which had begun in the Naxalbari block of Siliguri in West Bengal soon spread to nearby states such as Bihar. In 1971, the kidnapping of two Gandhian volunteers by Naxalites in Mushahari in Bihar's Muzaffarpur district sent shock waves across the country. It was seen as a personal setback for Jayaprakash Narayan Srivastava, popularly known as JP. He had started off as a leader in the Congress and was deeply involved in the Independence struggle. Later, he left the grand old party and built a reputation as a socialist reformer who caught the nation's pulse during the tumultuous 1970s.

As JP rushed to Mushahari, Hindustan Samachar sent its brightest young reporter to cover the leader's movements. For the next six months or so, Ravindra Kishore closely tracked JP, spent several hours with him talking, discussing and debating social and political issues, and shared meals prepared by the leader's wife Prabhavati Devi. Once back in Patna, Ravindra Kishore kept in constant touch with JP, visiting him whenever the leader was in town. The relationship between the two developed to that of a mentor and disciple, with Ravindra Kishore sharing developments in his professional and personal life with JP.

The political turmoil in the country had become even more intense in 1974. There was the railway strike by 17 lakh workers led by George Fernandes, the union leader who would later go on to become a defence minister. Indira Gandhi responded with an iron hand but it still led to a widespread breakdown of the important transport system. It was around the same time that the Bihar movement, also called the JP movement, took place.

The spark came from the western part of the country, from Gujarat. Students and people from the middle class had protested against alleged corruption and food inflation. It was a successful movement that led to the dissolution of the state government after chief minister Chimanbhai Patel was forced to resign. It ignited similar protests among students in Bihar. Corruption was again the main issue. Adding fuel were the student wings of the Bharatiya Jana Sangh (Akhil Bharatiya Vidyarthi Parishad) and Samajwadi Party (Samajwadi Yuvajan Sabha), as was the Lokdal, which later merged into the Janata Party. Student leaders involved in the agitation included future Bihar chief ministers Lalu Prasad Yadav, Nitish Kumar, and future Union minister Ram Vilas Paswan.

JP, who had supported the protests in Gujarat, made a similar move in Bihar. His involvement made the movement in Bihar stronger and participation even wider. He called for Sampurna Kranti, or Total Revolution. The seasoned politician used the momentum to unite opposition parties from all over the country against the Union government.

These were busy days for Ravindra Kishore. He would furiously work his pen, bringing alive on paper the discontent on the streets. His words were sharp and an instant hit with readers. But, for his editor, they spelled trouble. Ravindra Kishore had moved on to work at *The Searchlight*. At the time, publications across the country were under pressure from the government. It took brave editors and owners to take an objective view and publish fearlessly. Few managed. Shortly, and not unsparingly, Ravindra Kishore got a call from his own editor.

Ravindra Kishore went to a hotel in Patna to meet the editor who treated the young reporter to a hearty lunch. He said, 'You write very well. But *bahut teekha likhte hoon* (you write very harshly). And if you continue this—you know Indira Gandhi is a very whimsical lady—within no time the Birla Group's sugar mills in Bihar and UP will be closed. And thousands of workers will be unemployed.' The Group owned *The Searchlight,* and later *Hindustan Times.*

Ravindra Kishore got the message. 'Because of my writing, if your Bihar and Uttar Pradesh mills are closed down, then thousands of people will become unemployed. I don't want to be responsible for that.' He resigned from the job later that day. Disappointed, he sought the company of his mentor JP, who was in town. One look at the dejected young man and JP understood what had happened.

'Has the Marwari fired you?' he asked.

Ravindra Kishore recounted the meeting. JP agreed it was indeed a touchy situation for the editor. 'What will you do now?' JP asked.

Fortunately, given his exploits as a journalist, Ravindra Kishore wasn't without options. He already had an offer from Dharamvir Bharati, the renowned Hindi poet and author who also ran the weekly magazine *Dharmayug* from Mumbai. There was another offer from Alok Mitra of Maya Press.

'Are you considering their offers?' asked JP.

'No, I won't leave Patna. I will take up freelancing work,' Ravindra Kishore replied.

JP asked him to do that. At the same time, he also suggested his mentee could do something that would make a bigger impact. 'Every month, hundreds and thousands of soldiers retire from the army. They get a pension. But that's not enough. All of them are looking for jobs. They didn't understand security. It's important that we provide them with employment. Can you help them?'

Ravindra Kishore said he would.

The army had a system in place to help its personnel find jobs post-retirement. This system in the army unit in Patna got a boost after Ravindra Kishore got in touch. In the last month of service, as the jawans got busy with documentation related to their retirement benefits like pension and gratuity, Ravindra Kishore suggested adding a training programme that would help them get jobs in industrial units as security guards.

Thus, in 1974, an idea took shape that later would become the Security and Intelligence Service, or SIS. In the initial years, Ravindra Kishore did not charge for his services. But this work wasn't enough to feed a family. Two years after starting his voluntary work, Ravindra Kishore married Rita Sinha in November 1976. He now needed to make a living. With the help of his brother Satyendra Kishore, he founded an advertising agency.

'The local telephone department were coming out with a telephone directory. One of the department's senior officials was known to us. He asked my brother if he could get advertisements for the directory. That's how, for the first time, we got into the ads field,' says Satyendra Kishore. R.K. Publicity Private Limited had a mixed run. It helped Ravindra Kishore get in touch with more people, mostly in the government and industry, the biggest ad spenders. But those were not years of consumerism, and getting advertisements was not easy. On the other hand, Ravindra Kishore was beginning to get more inquiries for security manpower from industrialists. One of the biggest referrals came from JP himself. JP would direct any businessman who went to him with a problem—and almost everyone in those days had problems with labour—to Ravindra Kishore. 'He will solve your problems,' the leader would promise.

But there was a problem. Providing manpower also meant adhering to local regulations, including laws on minimum wages and provident funds. Ravindra Kishore needed a formal setup, a company. Otherwise, he risked being pulled up by the labour department. The push also came from one of his clients, Hari Krishna Budhia. The owner of Bihar Foundry and Casting Limited had already taken help from Ravindra Kishore to hire army personnel for firming up security in his facility at the Ramgarh industrial area of Bihar (now a part of Jharkhand).

'I'm having labour issues at my factory. I need to tackle it with more security personnel. But before that, you should set up a firm. Let's have a formal agreement to comply with labour laws,' Budhia said. He was a first-generation entrepreneur who had returned from the US after completing higher studies to set up Bihar Foundry and Casting along with his brother. But lack of security and law and order and endless labour unrest were making his life difficult. He needed Ravindra Kishore's help.

Ravindra Kishore himself was keen to move on after the middling performance of the ad agency. He was keen to start on his own. Not that he had any big ideas, say like an Elon Musk had to disrupt the four-wheeler industry. Nor did he have a product, something that Steve Jobs had with his Macintosh and later iPhone, that could create a niche for itself. Alas, Ravindra Kishore didn't even have money or come from a business family, like Marico founder Harsh Mariwala, who had started off in his family's trading business.

But what Ravindra Kishore, through his native intelligence, understood was that there was a need, and there was a market for providing security. In the last six years, countless businessmen had come to him asking for guards. What convinced him the most, however, was an altruistic reason.

'It [the business] came to me from the blessings of JP and I felt that it will help other people. It will be for the betterment of other people. It was there in my mind that it should help the needy because I had been a needy person since childhood. I had faced all the troubles of life but there was no one to aid my betterment. So, I decided I would do something for the betterment of other people when I was capable of doing so. Social enterprise was in my mind from the beginning,' he would explain much later. This calling would remain at the core of SIS's growth over the next 50 years, playing a vital role in how the company grew, and also of the culture that defined the organisation.

Fortunately, setting up a security company didn't need much. The rest, he made up with his gumption and street smarts. He set up Security and Intelligence Services as a proprietorship company on 27 December 1979. Less than a month ago, on 29 November, his son Rituraj had been born. How did the name SIS come about? Satyendra Kishore, who was then studying at Jawaharlal Nehru University, suggested something rhyming with the School of International Studies, a well-known department. 'I liked the sound of it,' says Satyendra Kishore. Using this template and keywords related to security, the name was decided. The dot over the 'I' in SIS represents the sun, designed to honour their father, whose name 'Suraj' means 'sun' in Hindi.

Budhia, the first customer, helped design and print the logo. 'He was also instrumental in setting up our salary and the cost structure that is shared with clients. This includes the benefits for the security guards. Minimum wages, plus ESI [employees' state insurance], plus provident fund, plus gratuity, plus leave benefits. And then comes supervision and inspection charges,' says Ravindra Kishore of the security business's financial model. Till date, industry uses similar structure.

SIS's first customer? It just had to be Hari Budhia's Bihar Foundry and Casting Ltd.

2

FIRST STEPS

After the success of Indian IT behemoth Infosys and American social media giant Facebook, and recent startups like Zomato and Ather, it has become a norm to celebrate businesses that started off from garages or modest one-room operations. The beginnings of SIS were similar.

In the first few years of its life, SIS's address was 94, Patliputra, Patna. Officially, this was the residence of Ravindra Kishore. But for all practical purposes, it was also his office. He lived upstairs on the first floor with his family, including his parents. Downstairs were two rooms that became SIS's office. If there were too many people to accommodate, the veranda would become the office's extension. On the back there was a garage, which in later years would hold a kennel for dogs that were trained and deployed on customer sites.

On Sundays, 94, Patliputra would become a recruitment centre. The house had a lawn that would be filled with a steady stream of youngsters hoping to land a job. They would fill up their forms and wait for instructions from U.N. Singh, one of Ravindra Kishore's earliest hires. On his instruction, the young men would stand in a queue and their height and weight would be measured. Each candidate needed to be at least 5'7" tall and weigh a maximum of 70 kg. A physical test would be done.

Once a candidate cleared these rounds, he would be asked to go inside one of the two rooms on the ground floor for the interview. The interview panel was headed by Ravindra Kishore himself. Accompanying him would be retired army generals, senior bureaucrats and police officers. Once selected, a candidate would be given a kit that included his uniform. He would have to report for training for a month and then be deputed to a customer site.

Some of SIS's senior most executives of today started their careers from that very lawn. This includes Arvind Prasad who would go on to become the chief financial officer, Vinaya Srivastawa, the future chief executive officer and A.K. Singh, who would head multiple ancillary ventures. Not all of them started off as security guards. Arvind Prasad was in the accounts department, Srivastawa in stores. But all of them attended job interviews and got their offer letters right there.

The line separating home from office was blurred. At meal times, whoever was present, be it employee or client, would sit down with the Sinhas to have food. More often than not, Rita, Ravindra Kishore's wife, would be in the middle of preparations when an employee came with a message: 'Sir is coming with six people. They will also have lunch.' How does one manage to feed twenty people if the food was being cooked for only twelve or fourteen? Was it possible to quickly cook more? If not, what adjustment could be done? For Rituraj, and later his sister Rivoli, the first lessons of people management probably were learnt right from the kitchen of their home.

As the family held the fort at home, Ravindra Kishore focused on the business. He had taken the entrepreneurial plunge with the security business. To grow it, the business needed a push and a shove as often as possible. In the first few years, Hari Budhia's Bihar Foundry remained SIS's biggest customer. It became Ravindra Kishore's own training ground even as the industrial landscape of Bihar in the 1970s evolved, throwing up opportunities for a startup like SIS.

Erstwhile Bihar is a state of paradox. It was naturally gifted. It had coal, iron ore, bauxite, limestone and several other minerals (much of these mineral-rich regions are now part of Jharkhand that was carved out of Bihar in 2000). This is what had led Jamsetji Tata, the founder of Tata Group, to come to Bihar in search of iron ore and set up Tata Iron and Steel Company (TISCO), better known today as Tata Steel. That was in 1907. Jamshedpur, the company's headquarters, became one of the first industrial hubs in the whole of India. The city is also an example of a modern planned urban place, with better civic amenities than most of the other cities in this part of the country.

Going by Bihar's immense natural bounty, the state should have had many Jamshedpurs by the late 1970s when Ravindra Kishore set up SIS. To be fair, it did attract the likes of Hari Budhia. The Ramgarh belt had huge deposits of coal, one of the two critical ingredients along with iron ore used to make steel. Many more companies, like Bihar Foundry, came up in Ramgarh's industrial area. Similarly, aspiring entrepreneurs like Budhia also set up cement companies to exploit the rich limestone deposits in the region.

Yet, they had a problem: labour trouble. Tata Steel had a long history of tussles between its management and labour union. Budhia also faced a similar problem at Bihar Foundry. A manufacturing facility like this involved movement of different kinds of raw materials and products, either transported from mines or being shipped to customers. These moved in trucks in and out of the premises. Security was needed in nearly every part of this movement—at mines, gates and where the loading and unloading of materials took place. These industrial units employed hundreds or even thousands of labourers, mostly on contract. Supervising them and their movement—these were days before security cameras and drones—was a difficult job. Unions made the job of supervising even more difficult. While it would be unfair to characterize all labour unions with the same brush, it was not uncommon for unions to develop links with local mafias or enjoy political patronage. Company owners and their management would hesitate to directly intervene when cases of pilferage cropped up, fearing an industrial unrest by the unions that would have an even worse impact on operations than the theft itself. Owners like Budhia depended on their security personnel to keep an eye on the movement of manpower and material, and also the other on the unions.

Security came in the form of a chowkidar and a darbaan. They had little to no training. This meant they didn't understand the demands of the job. Worse, many couldn't read and write properly, a requirement to check documents at entry and exit gates. Were they trained to take on physical demands of the job, including facing off with unwanted elements? Rarely. Worse, in many instances, these very security personnel would join hands with the unions. This would make the union and their leaders even more powerful.

With no respite, businessmen would approach politicians who had clout and influence with the unions and local police. As we know, those who approached JP for help were directed to Ravindra Kishore. In SIS, Ravindra Kishore had the opportunity to change how the security manpower business worked. Listening to Budhia and the problems he was facing, Ravindra Kishore understood the requirements: bold and honest security personnel who could read and write, were fit physically and were trained to understand and address their client's needs.

Ravindra Kishore found the solution in the resources that were available—retired army officers and soldiers. These ex-servicemen were the only ones who had exposure to a life in uniform and work experience that centred around security. 'They were disciplined, followed commands and were aggressive,' says Vinaya Srivastawa. They also became officers, supervisors and trainers. Among the most influential ones in those early days was U.N. Singh. He had retired as a subedar from the army, and Ravindra Kishore made him SIS's first officer in the manager rank. Singh had a registration number of 5001—all officers in the company had their numbers starting with 5. He was not posted to a specific site but managed people, planned recruitment and training and even sanctioned leaves.

Like ex-servicemen, Ravindra Kishore also roped in retired police officers and bureaucrats. Retired police officers, like army veterans, had also led a life in uniform and specialized in providing security. They responded well to training, and again, understood recruitment. These police officers, like bureaucrats, had another attraction. They had influence with local administrations and former colleagues at police and government departments.

The bureaucrats, army and police officers also came with years of experience in administration. As brigadiers, heads of government departments or as superintendent of a city, these professionals had managed people, budgets and offices. They knew how things worked. Ravindra Kishore, a young entrepreneur, grew to understand the importance of systems from them. And they were the ones to set up SIS's first systems and processes. Quickly, Ravindra Kishore developed a flair for it. If anyone suggested a new practice or method, Ravindra Kishore was quick to understand if it would work or not. If it did, he was equally swift in implementing these in SIS.

Today, there are computers and software to create systems. Back then, it was all on paper. The bureaucracy's penchant for paperwork turned out to be a blessing for SIS, which had several retired bureaucrats on its payroll or as consultants. The documentation of work at SIS was unprecedented for a company of its size and time. There was a duty register that would arrive from every site each month. It contained a detailed duty report of every guard. Each guard's report was signed by him. It included a summary of his work, the client and the nature of the job that was required at the site. These documents came in handy every time there was a dispute, either with an employee or, crucially, with a client. There was always a signed document to go back to. P.R. Mehra, a retired deputy superintendent of police whom Ravindra Kishore had brought in, would read through these reports with an eagle eye and leave his red and green markings. The red mark, unmistakably, was for something that needed to be corrected.

Each guard had a dossier. Right from the moment he got selected on the lawns of 94, Patliputra, a document was formed in his name. The set of documents would later become a file that would be updated every month, providing details of his monthly performance, good or bad. Within the first three years itself, there were about 300 dossiers. It was the responsibility of the filing department to oversee the process and maintain the documents.

'It was a very different type of business. None of us had any experience in running a business. Yet, we set up a system of monitoring each contract as a separate business. That has survived till today,' says Arvind Prasad. Each client had a separate profit and loss statement (P&L). For instance, if SIS was deploying guards at ten sites in Patna, each of those sites was treated as a separate business and had a P&L of its own. This was required because each contract had a different rate, requirement and varying sizes of manpower and wages.

Even the payroll was by hand. Getting the salary documentation right for 200 to 300 people would take three days. On those days, the staff would work till three in the morning, rest for two to four hours and then get back to their desk. Arvind Prasad's accounts office would have three people working on huge rolls of sheets spread out on a table. Inevitably, there would be errors as the work was complex and the mind was fatigued. Still, it set the groundwork for a sound practice.

Overall, SIS had developed a sound manual system. It helped set the foundation for the business to grow and handle its growth. Years later, when technology first came in the form of computers, inevitably

SIS was among the first in the industry to embrace it. It didn't take much time for Ravindra Kishore to understand why computers were the way forward.

'The system orientation of the company is something which Mr Sinha believed in and he built a team to support that system, mainly from governmental sources. The foresight to get bureaucrats paid off in multiple ways. That was very relevant,' adds Prasad.

Put together, this group of men and their foot soldiers looked like a confident, formidable bunch when compared to the chowkidar and darbaan that entrepreneurs like Budhia were used to till then. From a business point of view, this differentiation was important for Ravindra Kishore to command a better rate for his men than the chowkidars and darbaans got.

This is how the security business worked. If a company asked for a security officer, guard, supervisor, armed guard or a dog handler, SIS would charge them a supervision or inspection charge that would be 5 to 10 per cent of the total cost. These jobs were called billing positions within a security company as the client was billed for the security personnel it had hired. The others were the non-billing positions in the company. These were employees who did the administration work—SIS paid them directly. It was thus important that the billing positions made enough money and more to cover non-billing seats and other expenses. It wasn't easy to convince company owners and promoters to cough up more money. A security agency was a new concept in the 1970s. 'We had to go and make the customers aware about a security company and its benefits,' recounts Vinaya Srivastawa.

There were two big benefits for clients that Ravindra Kishore would stress on:

1. Freedom from unions. With security personnel sourced from an outside vendor like SIS, the unions would find it difficult to

influence guards whose salaries, and loyalties, lay elsewhere. 'In bigger companies, the security personnel were paid as well as any other employee. But they wouldn't take orders from the management, only from the unions,' says Srivastawa.

2. Second, the ease of working with an outside vendor. Management wouldn't dare to take action against an erring security guard lest they invite the wrath of the union. With an outside vendor, however, his interactions and rapport with unions could be controlled. If a guard was getting too friendly with the unions, he could be moved to another site.

These were all good reasons. But it was still not easy convincing the owners. Even though the management would understand the logic laid down by Ravindra Kishore and could see the benefits, senior officials would dither over a decision. One concern was about increasing costs. A bigger reason: 'We not only had to convince the owners, but also the officers down the ranks. And in some instances, we had to even face off with union leaders or convince them to allow security guards to be employed from outside,' says Srivastawa.

It was eventually down to Ravindra Kishore on how SIS went about growing its business. In these first few years, he had established some of the most important tenets of the business—systems, an employee-first culture and setting standards instead of following the prevalent practices of an industry that was highly unorganised. What started off as an altruistic-driven initiative, was slowly taking form of a business. Technology was absent, and thus SIS was not a typical startup of today that uses tech as the enabler of their business. Ravindra Kishore didn't have any angel investor either. What shone through—and made up for the lack of other resources—was his entrepreneurship. One aspect that stood out, was his penchant to hit the road and get on with his business.

3

THE WANDERING CEO

By the 1960s, the concept of management by wandering around had been made famous by two business partners—Bill Hewlett and David Packard. Their company, Hewlett & Packard, which later split into Hewlett Packard Enterprise and HP, is one of the biggest manufacturers and sellers of computer hardware in the world. One of their favourite ways to monitor work, mingle with employees and get feedback was to wander around their workplace, from offices to work floors. Every time they flew to a unit of HP, Bill and David would walk around, engaging in small talk with employees or in deep discussion with engineers on a product. This random act grew as a proven management tool for entrepreneurs and managers in the years to come and has been documented in management books.

Ravindra Kishore hadn't read any of these. He was yet to hear about Bill Hewlett and David Packard or their astonishingly successful company or their penchant to travel to meet employees and clients. But the SIS founder understood the need to keep a tab on his company's operations. Sites manned by SIS guards were beginning to spread out. Jharia was over 300 kms from Patna. Kharkharee, another industrial area, was on the way. There were officers to supervise each site. And there was the reporting system that came with a lot of information on how his men were performing. But that was not enough.

He needed to see for himself how his men were doing. Not just check their performance, but also understand their wellbeing. Was there anything they could do better? Could the practice of one site help another? Did the client have anything to say? Maybe a complaint or a suggestion? Ravindra Kishore needed information. There were no phones or emails. Getting into his rickety Ambassador car and moving around and meeting his people was the only right thing he could do. It had another advantage. Ravindra Kishore would use these trips to form acquaintances with local businessmen and government officials.

Unsurprisingly, Rituraj and Rivoli's earliest memories are about accompanying their father on these trips. For impressionable young minds these rides were an adventure trip, going along narrow, potholed roads and through dusty villages, waiting for cattle at innumerable places to cross the road and finally reaching the destination—not a resort or a hotel, but a mine, foundry or cement plant. 'That was our holiday. We used to sit in a car, drive for hours, stop for lunch somewhere, stay in a guest house. Papa would go to work, we would just roam around. Also at night, Rituraj and I used to have this huge hobby of catching hold of guards who knew horror stories and staying up at night, through late-night sessions of listening to their village stories and getting spooked,' Rivoli says.

It may have been an adventure for a child, but travelling for hours is no child's play. It was not everyone's cup of tea. Satyendra Kishore accompanied his brother on one such trip to Ranchi from Patna and was left astonished at his brother's enthusiasm. 'He had a very high energy level. I still remember that it was in the 1980s, when road conditions were very bad. It used to take around twelve to thirteen hours to reach Ranchi from Patna. We had an Ambassador car. I was sitting in that and I was having a very bad time. I was very tired by the time we reached our destination.'

They lodged at a local circuit house, the official accommodation for senior government officials. Ravindra Kishore planned to meet the local district commissioner. To Satyendra's astonishment, his brother washed up, got ready and was immediately on his way for the meeting. 'He didn't need any break. Whereas I decided I couldn't do such a trip again,' says Satyendra.

SIS personnel would look forward to their chairman's visits. Few had heard of company owners taking the time out to travel hundreds of kilometres to meet security guards on the ground. Not just that, Ravindra Kishore would sit down with the guards for dinner. Often, he himself would cook khichdi for everyone present. Or, it would be another local favourite—litti and mutton curry.

This was the opportunity for the guards to bond with their chairman and share their experiences, their working and living conditions. 'He would come to our barracks in Ranchi every few weeks. We would speak to him for hours. He would ask about our duties and people would give their opinion. Some would talk about the delay in salary payment, others would wish for better living conditions,' says A.K. Singh. In one such visit during December, when winter was at its peak, the guards, who were living in tents, asked for sheds as accommodation. 'He cleared that immediately,' says Singh. But come the next summer, the same tinted sheds made the accommodation even hotter. The guards brought it up on Ravindra Kishore's next visit. The SIS founder heard them out and promised to fit fans. At the same time, he cited an instance when Hari Budhia—one of the richest entrepreneurs in the region—rolled up his sleeves to help repair a furnace that had broken down. For context, a furnace is extremely hot and just standing close to one is extremely uncomfortable. Budhia never complained of how hot it was but got on with his work. The guards took the cue.

'The chairman listening to us and taking us seriously made him very respectful in our eyes. We reciprocated likewise. He was like a fatherly figure and you know that respect comes if you view someone as a father not as a boss. I always respect him as a father as he's a godfather for us. So that's the feeling we have for him, and it was very emotional,' says Dinesh Gupta, who joined SIS in 1993 and went on to become an executive vice president. 'I will never forget this. Whenever I eat khichdi, I remember that first khichdi I had with the chairman.'

These interactions were informal. Yet 'How's your family doing?' wasn't a casual question from Ravindra Kishore. Instead, he would ask the guard about his wife, children, parents and siblings. Remarkably, the next time the chairman visited—it could be months later—he would meet the same guard and follow up on his family. 'How is your daughter doing now? Has your brother finished his studies?' This exceptional memory and ability to remember names and details left SIS employees in wonder. They also appreciated that the chairman was making an effort.

'He would know you personally. He knows your parents' name. He knows your sister's name. And if you had any children, he would know their names and which grades they were studying in,' says Narayan Lenka, Chief Operating Officer, Security Solutions at SIS. It was in one of these interactions that Lenka shared something that was bothering him with Ravindra Kishore and Rita. Lenka was in love with a woman who was from a different faith. Both wanted to get married but their families didn't agree. Ravindra Kishore promised to help. 'Neither of the families attended. But it was Chairman Sir who attended and helped us conduct the wedding,' says Lenka.

He further shares an anecdote of Ravindra Kishore visiting his unit in Tata Steel's iron ore mines in Khondbond in Odisha. The unit was deep inside the forest. On an inspection visit, the unit was suddenly attacked by elephants. While they escaped unhurt, Ravindra Kishore realized the risk his men were facing in these areas and, in order to motivate them, announced an 'elephant allowance'. This became a norm for all guards who opted to be in units at inhospitable locations, all of them got an elephant allowance.

Meeting the guards and spending time with them was first of the two major priorities for Ravindra Kishore during these trips. The second was to visit prospective customers. If there was an industrial unit close to a customer's, Ravindra Kishore would drop in and meet the senior most executive present. He would take notes on what the customer needed and what kind of security was required at the site. Once the day was over, Ravindra Kishore would prepare a document, dictating notes to Ashok Prasad, who worked directly under him and who accompanied the founder on most of these trips.

'How much ever late it was, Ashok Prasad would then type out the whole thing, and I would help iron out the draft. In the morning, the chairman would again take a look and the report would be ready,' says Arvind Prasad. At the prospective customer's site, the senior most executive whom Ravindra Kishore had met the previous day would be surprised to see him back so quickly. 'The customer will be very impressed. "You all came in one day and the next day you have come up with a security report for my organization," the customer would say,' recounts Arvind Prasad.

Arvind Prasad further explains how SIS would get its contracts. 'There were basically two aspects to this. One is where you have some referral for the customer. And then there is cold calling.' Ravindra Kishore's passion for meeting prospective clients and making presentations was a kind of cold calling. Arvind Prasad also cites examples when referrals worked.

B.M. Prasad was a retired officer of the Indian Police Service (IPS) that Ravindra Kishore had hired. Prasad was a fantastic footballer in his heyday. Tata Steel was one of the few corporate names of those times that spent heavily on promoting sports as part of its corporate social responsibility mandate. Football was one of the sports it funded. Its managing director Russi Mody himself was a football fan, and it was over this common passion that Prasad and the Tata Steel top leader had become friends.

That was the opening that Ravindra Kishore needed. Through Prasad, SIS got an introduction to relevant executives. 'There were a number of visits, negotiations, several project reports and finally we got the order to provide security to Tata Steel,' says Prasad. 'What worked in our favor was obviously that somebody so high up in the organization knew somebody from our organization on a personal note,' he adds.

On the other hand, in Tata Motors, Ravindra Kishore and his men tried several ways. Cold calling, sending letters and innumerable visits to Tata Motors facility and offices. 'We were literally not allowed to enter the gate. It was as bad as that. Nobody would give us an appointment in Tata Motors,' recalls Prasad. The breakthrough came when a serving IPS officer, who was well known to Ravindra Kishore, quit his job and joined the Tatas. On one of his visits to Patna, the SIS founder confided in him that his attempts at Tata Motors had made no inroads and requested his help. The IPS officer, now a senior official at Tata, obliged. 'That was how we landed our first appointment. So, unless you know somebody, it was difficult to land an appointment and create an opening for a sales pitch,' says Prasad.

Overall, the growth has been '90 per cent brownfield,' says Prasad. 'We never went to a place where we didn't have a presence. We will first get work then build a presence in an area. It has never been a green field, where we set up an office and then look for order. It's not that we will decide, okay let's go to Gujarat and set up an office there even though we have no business in Gujarat.'

The simple reason behind this was that the company didn't have the money to invest in a 'greenfield' office. Once SIS would hoist its flag in a market and build the business to a decent size, an area office would be set up and the target would be to get more orders and deploy more guards. There would be just one or two officers to start with. The operations would expand and more people would come in when orders started flowing in. The area office would then become a full-fledged branch. And the branch would itself become a whole operation with its own separate teams for payrolls, administration, operations and so on.

Ravindra Kishore had moved out of Bihar and shifted the SIS headquarters to Delhi in 1989. Delhi, unlike the eastern markets, was urban and clients there had requirements that were markedly different. The government-owned ITDC was one of the earliest clients and one which convinced Ravindra Kishore it was time to branch out of his home state. The ITDC contract was big in scale and spread across locations. In one go, it led SIS to multiple new sites in different cities. The ITDC operated a hotel chain under the Ashoka brand. SIS won the tender but had little experience with the soft skills required for security personnel manning hotels.

Ravindra Kishore did something ingenious to make up for that. The moment SIS won the contract, which marked its entry in the Delhi market, he convinced an ITDC veteran, L.D. Verma, to shift sides. 'I won't be able to run this contract on my own. You come over and take the responsibility,' Ravindra Kishore told Verma, who agreed after much convincing.

That was crucial. As Arvind Prasad points out, SIS guards who were otherwise quick to square off against goondas and mafias were intimidated by the sleekness of a five-star hotel. 'All the guards were of rural background. They had never seen a five-star hotel in their lives. They were even scared of drinking water in such a hotel. So, how do you prepare them for a job like this?' Arvind Prasad explains. Verma understood the nuances well. While SIS didn't have much time, a boot camp was set up in Mahipalpur to train the guards.

Verma taught the SIS guards some of the basics of the hospitality business. The guest is always right. The basic principle of Athithi Devo Bhava. 'If someone was coming to Ashoka Hotel and staying there or throwing a party, then they must be very rich people. So on how you need to handle those guests, Verma used to give shift-wise training to our people. We used to do three shifts of eight hours and in every shift, there was training on how you need to handle the guests, how to greet them, how to open the gate, etc.,' says Sanjay Pandey, one of the employees transferred to Delhi for the ITDC contract. The men were even trained on how to take care of a guest who had had one too many drinks! 'It was on-the-ground training. Gradually, people became trained in that work and then they trained the other people,' says Pandey.

The positive outcome pushed SIS's case in the Delhi NCR market. Already, by 1990, the expansion in the region had taken SIS's overall headcount to 1,000 people. Ravindra Kishore began delegating more functions to his senior colleagues. Till now, he would be directly running functions like sales, marketing and administration. Finance was headed by Arvind Prasad. With the move to Delhi, he expanded his administrative staff too. Ratna Sinha, who had joined SIS as a telephone operator in Patna, also moved to Delhi and was moved to the administration, working closely with Ravindra Kishore. The office in the capital was in Safdarjung Enclave, which again was a residence-cum-office arrangement, similar to the one Ravindra Kishore followed in Patna. Later, the Delhi team moved to a bigger space in Nehru Place, where they had two floors to themselves.

While these organic, brownfield expansions continued, SIS's reputation as a bold, daring organization grew. This perception also showed another aspect of Ravindra Kishore the entrepreneur, underlining a key principle of entrepreneurship: it is never a straight line. And the security industry was not one for the faint-hearted.

4

A BOLD ENTREPRENEUR

If hitting the roads and constantly calling up his employees and clients helped Ravindra Kishore expand his business's length and breadth, there were also instances when he worked out of the box to solve sticky and often dangerous situations. These were not exactly within the purview of a security agency that is responsible for providing safety within the premises of a company. But then, this is how entrepreneurs go beyond the norm. In doing so, the entrepreneur takes on risk, even physical, and is rewarded for doing so.

B.P. Jain was known as the koyla king, or the coal king, of those days.[1] He is said to have controlled over nearly two dozen coal mines in the rich coal belt of Jharia in Bihar. As was the norm then, and maybe even now, running a coal mine was impossible without giving a hafta—extortion fee—to the local strongman. These were the coal mafia. One of their biggest and most feared leaders was Suryadeo Singh.

Singh started off as a bodyguard who later on became a coal mafia leader. His rise was aided by political patronage. In 1977 he won the Jharia constituency in the Bihar assembly elections. Though Singh won as an independent candidate, he is said to have the support of the Janata Dal party. Interestingly, Singh was known to be a close associate of a senior politician from the state who would go on to become India's Prime Minister in the 1990s. Singh had several murder charges against him, was arrested on multiple occasions but always managed to get away scot-free.

It so happened that Jain, who had till then paid the monthly hafta to Singh, now refused to do so after differences cropped up between the two. In response, Singh asked his men to put out a notice on Jain's factory gates: 'Vacate these premises, otherwise you and your people will be at risk.' Worried and running out of ideas, Jain approached Ravindra Kishore. Jain's company had been using SIS's services to beef up security in its sites. But now, the coal king's need was different.

'Can you help me?' he asked Ravindra Kishore after explaining the threat from Singh.

The SIS founder was never one to turn away a customer. But this needed a solution of a different kind. Ravindra Kishore did something most would baulk at the thought of. He went straight to the doors of the mafia leader himself. As a member of the state's legislative assembly, Singh lived in the government quarters in the MLA colony in Patna's Bailey Road. As expected of a mafia political leader, security arrangements were heavy outside Singh's house. There were a dozen men, some with firearms, manning the entrance. Ravindra Kishore informed the guards the reason for his visit. He was let in and led to Singh's bedroom. The strongman was lying on his bed. He had been unwell. Even inside the room, there were four men keeping guard. Ravindra Kishore came to the point straightaway. 'I'm not carrying a gun or anything. Your men can check me. But can you ask them to leave the room?' Few had made such a request. Intrigued, Singh asked his men to step out.

'You have given a notice to B.P. Jain,' Ravindra Kishore continued. 'I'm here to inform you that they are not going to leave the place.' Amused, Singh again looked at the young Ravindra Kishore. This time more closely. 'Who are you?' Singh asked. Ravindra Kishore explained. Singh thought for a moment and said, 'Since you run a security firm, I will give you other contracts. I know a lot of people around here. You just vacate B.P. Jain's facility.'

'I won't do that,' Ravindra Kishore said fearlessly. 'Jain trusts me and he has given me work. I can't be disloyal to him. You have so many security guards here. Many of them have guns on them. You trust them with your life. What if one of them cheats you?'

Singh wasn't used to such plain speaking. He was used to people falling at his feet and agreeing to his conditions. He was challenged here. Yet, he wasn't angry. There was a candour and a spark in the youngster that he instantly liked. He repeated his offer of more work and clients for SIS. Ravindra Kishore didn't budge. Instead, he stood up and folded his hands in a namaskar. 'It's okay if you do not agree. I am leaving but it will harm you a lot,' Ravindra Kishore said. That riled Singh. He became incensed. A near nobody had come into his bedroom and threatened him on his face. Though he was unwell, Singh stood up and went close to Ravindra Kishore. 'How dare you say that! What do you mean it will harm me?'

Calm and composed—just like he was as a student years ago in the office of director of education—Ravindra Kishore explained. 'You charge Rs 1 lakh a month as hafta from B.P. Jain and all other industrialists in the region. I know if we don't vacate, your men will attack us and they will open fire. They may manage to injure some of my men. But we will be prepared. We will also have the protection of being inside the four walls. You may hurt four of my men. Your men are sharp so they will kill my men. I will take care of their families. But even if two of your men are hurt or killed, the Rs 1 lakh a month that you get will be gone forever. It will dent your name in this area. Nobody will pay you, not even a single penny.'

Singh was startled. He couldn't fault the logic that Ravindra Kishore had employed. He hugged Ravindra Kishore and said, 'This is the first time in my life I have met a brave man like you.' Singh agreed to step back and take back the notice against Jain. Singh would be one of the hundreds of admirers—some of whom also became friends—that the entrepreneur would make thanks to his innate understanding of people and his ability to engage with them.

Jain was thankful. SIS had ensured a lifelong client. The impact went beyond cementing one client. An episode like this couldn't but become the talk of the town. Every mine owner or promoter of a foundry and cement plant needed bold, fearless security men who didn't mind squaring up with the local goondas. The episode with Singh led to a sudden surge in calls and enquiries and contracts for SIS. Among the new ones were several cement companies. The biggest was Japla Cement Works. Japla, in Bihar's Palamu district (now in Jharkhand), was a cement manufacturing hub thanks to its rich reserves of limestones, the key raw material to make cement. The contract in Japla started on 1 January 1983. No guessing who the owner was—B.P. Jain. It was SIS's biggest unit then. Ravindra Kishore deployed 100 guards who were supervised by five officers. 'I don't remember all of them. But there must have been at least six cement plants we were serving by the time I joined,' says Vinaya Srivastawa, who became a part of SIS in 1984. There was another reason why 1 January 1983 was a special day for Ravindra Kishore. His daughter Rivoli Sinha was born the same day.

What Ravindra Kishore did that day with Singh also emboldened SIS's guards. With the founder showing the way, the guards on the ground got the message to be equally tough when facing an adversary, be it a union leader, local contractor or mafia leader. 'If someone slapped us, we would slap them back. We knew that if we had a problem, the whole organization would be behind us, supporting,' says Arvind Prasad.

Unsurprisingly, over the years, SIS guards would build a reputation of being physically fit and deft in defence and, when needed, in attack too. Vinaya Srivastawa had a gun pointed at his chest in front of his family. Local goons have slapped SIS guards. There have been violent face-offs and showdowns. In one instance, SIS men were responsible for controlling stray cattle in Jamshedpur, a potentially sensitive communal issue that could flare out of control. Each time, SIS guards and supervisors took inspiration from their chairman and handled the situation knowing that the organization backed its men in any situation.

Similar instances would play out in the coming years—in far off places, from the urban jungle of Gurugram to the iron ore mines of Bellary. These two need a special mention. First, let's look at the DLF incident.

One of the biggest cases of urban development in India happened in Gurgaon, the National Capital Region of Delhi that officially lies in Haryana. Today, the land of high-rises and premium housing colonies that coexist with unreliable infrastructure that hit a low during monsoons is called Gurugram. It was in the 1990s that the construction of much of the Gurugram that is known today started.

The primary builder was India's largest real estate company, DLF. It had bought land from farmers to convert the region into an urban megapolis. Many of these farmers and landowners remained, staying back in the land they had retained. Though they had sold much of their holdings, that didn't stop them from venturing into the area now technically owned by DLF. It could have been by habit, or knowingly, one can't say for sure.

'The locals continued using the area. They would park their vehicles. Sometimes, construction material would go missing. The local people even continued to use some of the open area for their basic needs,' recounts Sanjay Pandey, Vice President, Logistics in SIS. He had joined the company in 1991.

Pandey was one of the seniors who had been asked to move to the DLF site. It was a big contract for SIS, which was providing security for phase 1 and 2 of the Gurgaon development project. One of their main tasks was to keep trespassers out of the property that belonged to DLF. That was turning out to be a tough job, as the local villagers continued using the area. 'Once a truck came in without permission. Our guards stopped the driver and refused to let the vehicle go. Incensed, the driver punched one of the guards. Not to be left behind, the guard hit back,' recounts S.S. Ojha, President, Security Solutions of SIS, who had joined in 1989.

The minor altercation sparked a wider face-off. Resentment had been growing among the villagers. Some weren't happy about the money they had received for their land. Others didn't like being restricted in their daily movements. Though their anger was towards DLF, it was the SIS guards who felt it. The driver had backed off after being hit by the SIS guard who was accompanied by his colleagues. But now, the driver, a Jat local, was back with his own people.

First there were ten, and then as the word spread, a whole lot started gathering. 'There were nearly 1,000 of them in no time,' says Ojha. As this was one of its bigger sites, SIS too had about 300 of its men. While the Jats were strong, SIS guards were also well trained in combat skills. 'It was like a war. They were armed with rods, sticks and some even had swords. We also gathered what we could,' says Pandey.

The clash, which had started in the evening, lasted late into the night. It was only after the local police came that the locals dispersed. 'Our motorcycles were burnt. We had trained dogs with us. One of them died. Many of our men were injured and we took them to Safdarjung Hospital,' says Dinesh Gupta, one of the commanders stationed there.

The following days were full of tension. 'But we continued speaking to the locals. We got in contact with village elders and made them understand. Slowly, with time, things settled down. The DLF management was appreciative of our work,' says Pandey. It was one of the biggest fights involving SIS guards in the history of the company.

The episode marked SIS's presence in Delhi.

If the DLF episode pushed SIS's brand equity in the Delhi market, a similarly explosive situation had the same impact down in the south.

It was in 1993 that R.K.—as Ravindra Kishore was now being known as in the industry—first opened a branch in Bengaluru, their maiden presence in the southern regions of the country. The Karnataka capital was yet to make a splash nationally and internationally as the country's IT hub but changes were already visible. Thanks to its pleasant climate, many service-oriented multinationals were beginning to make Bengaluru their base in India. Beyond the urban market of Bengaluru, SIS also set its flag in the industrial hubs, including in mining centres.

From the early 1990s, Bellary was beginning to make its reputation as one of the biggest mining centres in India. Sajjan Jindal had just set up JSW Steel's first plant in the region to make the most of Bellary's ample iron ore mines. JSW would go on to become the largest steelmaker in the country, toppling Tata Steel.

One of the biggest iron ore miners in Bellary were the Baldotas. They had already hired SIS for guarding their mines. Ojha, who was one of the officers present during the DLF episode, was the senior most SIS executive stationed in the mines owned by the Baldotas.

One summer night, close to 12 a.m., as Ojha was finishing his dinner, he got a call from Narendra Baldota, the family patriarch. 'There are two or three people who have come here and they are abusing me. They want to kill me and want to break the gate and get inside my bungalow. Can you come as soon as possible?' a scared Baldota pleaded.

Now, SIS wasn't responsible for Baldota's personal security or for keeping his residences secure but Ojha didn't think for a second. 'I will be there in two minutes,' he assured Baldota.

Ojha asked one of his staff to accompany him. When they reached the Baldota residence, greeting them were three strapping youngsters, inebriated and threatening Baldota to cough up money or face dire consequences. They seemed to be members of a local mafia. 'Please don't make noise here. Can you please go back and come back tomorrow and we can discuss the issues peacefully?' Ojha tried consoling them with folded hands. Instead, the three turned more violent.

'How dare you come in front of us, one of the three shouted back. The second guy suddenly lunged forward and punched Ojha on the face. The third slapped Ojha's colleague. Realizing quickly that requests and pleas wouldn't work, Ojha and his colleague counter-attacked. Seeing their fearlessness, Baldota's lone security man who had been hiding till then also came out and joined Ojha and the other SIS guard in thrashing the three drunk men. The situation changed immediately. Now, it was the youngsters' turn to ask for forgiveness. But Ojha's colleague was so incensed by the curses pelted at them, he took a huge stone to crush one of the drunk guy's head. 'What are you doing? You will kill him, move away,' Ojha shouted, pushing him back.

The three guys, now licking their wounds, ran away. But Ojha sensed the disturbance wasn't over yet. He quickly asked his colleague to call the rest of the SIS guards who were there on site. Fifty of them came in no time. Ojha asked the men, armed with sticks, to station themselves in various parts of the Baldota bungalow. The idea was to surprise the enemy in case they returned. Meanwhile, Baldota had called the police.

As expected, the three men came back. This time in two dozen vehicles and with nearly a hundred more men. They broke open the gate, vandalized Baldota's cars, including a Mercedes and an Audi, and called out for Ojha. Fortunately, the police, including the local superintendent, came in time with enough forces to deter the local mining mafia. 'Initially, they refused to listen to the police but later calmed down. In the following days we were careful, in case they attacked our office. Fortunately, they didn't,' says Ojha.

Baldota was relieved and happy with SIS's help in a sticky situation. He was confident that as long as SIS men were around, he would be safe. 'He trusted us more after that incident. Four of our guards would accompany him. Baldota even offered me a job as his private security officer. I declined. Our salary was not very high, and often it was delayed, but we were loyal to our chairman,' recounts Ojha.

The incident spurred SIS's operations in Bellary and Hospet, the adjoining mining district. Mine owners preferred having SIS men secure their properties and often trusted the guards to be more swift and agile to their requirements than the police. 'I got many calls from mine owners and we landed quite a few contracts. Hospet became the single largest branch for SIS in the south,' says Ojha. He later came to know that the local mafia man he had beaten up that day in front of the Baldota residence was a criminal who would later go on to become a local MLA. For obvious reasons, we are not naming him here.

The bottom line: R.K. showed the way in pushing the envelope and going beyond contract terms in helping and serving his customer. His philosophy was absorbed by SIS's rank and file. This struck a chord with customers. SIS expanded in the east, north and south.

SIS had a marginal presence in the west. Its first unit in the region was in Pune in 1999, in a multinational's paper mill unit in the city's outskirts. Group 4, the world's largest security firm, was the security provider but their forces were unionized. The general manager of the mill wanted a change and contacted SIS. To ensure he had the right people, he came down to Patna to choose an officer and fifteen guards from SIS. It was Narayan Lenka who then moved to Pune to man the mill, which is spread over hundreds of acres. It had no boundary, which meant nearby villagers would often encroach inside the premises. The SIS men, led by Lenka, managed to make an impact despite the presence of the union and multiple skirmishes with local people. Even though it took a while to stabilize the unit, says Lenka, 'We managed to increase the number of our men to 150 there.'

While the Pune contract was managed skilfully, the expansion in the western markets had to wait. R.K.'s attention, as much as it was on expanding the business, was also continuously on keeping the company's internal infrastructure as robust as ever.

A major step towards this end was introducing computers in SIS in 1989. Computers was an uncommon sight. Even televisions hadn't yet become ubiquitous and affordable. Computers still sounded like an invention straight out of science fiction books. As they were rare, they came with a heavy price tag. R.K. didn't see that as a hindrance. It was through Vinod Singh, the younger brother of his childhood friend Uday Singh, that he was first introduced to computers. Vinod Singh worked for HCL, the Indian IT company. 'I thought since we have been handling human beings, every person is data. If we do not maintain it properly, you cannot do big things in the long run,' says Ravindra Kishore. Data was an unusual focus for a small company from Bihar. But the SIS founder always had his ears on the ground and a watchful eye on technological advancement. His focus on preserving data was on the dot.

Arvind Prasad had to ensure the company had saved up enough to buy computers. It had. Vinod Singh held classes for SIS employees on how to use the high-tech equipment. 'We used to gather in a crowd to watch it,' says Vinaya Srivastawa. Some were more fascinated by the video games in the computer, and that made the machine quite popular! The fact, however, is that the organization benefited. The processing of wages, which used to take over a week by then, became much quicker. It was easier to account for the several wage components, and getting data—as Ravindra Kishore had envisaged—was no longer an insurmountable task. Errors went down. SIS employees were among the first in Bihar, and the rest of the country, to get comfortable with computers. A few years later, V-SAT, a satellite communication system, was introduced so that all branches of SIS could access internet.

It was the same when pagers and mobile phones came into the market and revolutionized communication. The handsets were costly. Tariffs were even more expensive. Yet, SIS's leadership were given mobile handsets, even though they were mindful to limit calls within two minutes to keep the monthly bill in check. SIS employees became the centre of attention wherever they went. Vinaya Srivastawa recalls an incident in an airport when a curious fellow passenger approached him after he had spoken to someone on the phone. 'Whom were you speaking to? There was no one with you,' asked the bewildered person, half concerned about the SIS senior executive's mental health!

In 1992, R.K. also set off the ISO 9001 certification process. The company was awarded with the quality certification in 1995. A year later, SIS also implemented British standards BS 7499 and BS 7858. These were the codes of practice governing static site guarding and mobile patrol service, and secure screening of security. It was unusual for an Indian security company to take such initiative but R.K. had understood the importance of these certifications in his sales pitches to clients. They added a layer of credence and a stamp of confidence to the company's operations.

These steps also became an imperative with the entry of a giant in the Indian security industry, Group 4. It was founded back in 1901 in Denmark and had grown to be the world's largest security firm. Later, in 2001, it would merge with the British Securicor to become

G4S. In 1989, its entry was big news for the Indian market. For the local players, including SIS, it was an additional challenge. Given its legacy and experience in developed markets, the company came with a proven track record and highly standardized operations. It had excellent marketing and sales teams and, with deep pockets, could afford the latest in security equipment. That made G4S a formidable threat for SIS, which had just made its entry in the urban markets. The European peer had a natural advantage and it could command higher margins for itself in contracts.

'Actually, Group 4 showed they were superior to us. They were focused and took away big contracts. We didn't have those businesses but they built and got the contracts. Their entry in India was a big thing for us. They showed the rest of us how to serve an urban client. Their guards had good communication skills and smart uniforms. They were serving some of the best customers, the most elite of them,' says Arvind Prasad.

What G4S didn't have was the pluck of an entrepreneur-driven organization like SIS. R.K. understood the system, had built a network and now was expanding. But was that enough?

If R.K. was bothered, he didn't show it. Instead, he kept on traveling, meeting his staff and expanding his clientele. Every time R.K. came back home from his trips, he would use the learnings to make changes in the business. 'He used to sleep very little. He used to travel all the time for work. If he was sitting in the office, then he used to look after the work. At that time, we didn't have as many facilities as we have now. If we wanted to draft a letter, then there were stenographers and we dictated and then they typed it. Then there were some errors in it and we had to correct it with pen and it was retyped with a manual typewriter,' his daughter Rivoli says.

Much of these notes were about changes required in training of the guards. As SIS expanded beyond the industrial belts of Bihar and moved to urban markets that had modern commercial establishments and residential colonies, the skills that a guard required also changed. A mine's requirements will be different from a cement factory's. Similarly, a hospital's requirements will differ from that of an IT company's or, as we have seen in ITDC's case, that of a hotel's.

R.K. was mindful of these needs. It was for this very reason that he had set up something that proved to be pathbreaking in the security industry. In fact, in later years, it proved to be the critical difference between SIS and G4S.

5

THE SECRET SAUCE

The founder sets the culture of a company. The founder's personality, how he engages with colleagues right from his senior most hire to the junior most one on the ground, his interactions with clients, working style and even the hours he keeps, all of this is absorbed by the staff around him. His behaviour rubs off on theirs. And this, over the years, forms the core of the company's culture. Management studies have said 80 per cent of a company's culture is shaped by its founder.

Some of the most successful companies around the world share this feature. Apple's customer centricity and obsession with detail is thanks to the tough high standards founder Steve Jobs set. Richard Branson's colourful and fun-loving personality is what his Virgin Group, including its airline, espoused. Back home in India, it was founder Jamsetji Tata who set the core of the Tata Group's philosophy—philanthropy—and that has influenced the way customers, vendors and the general public perceive the conglomerate.

At SIS, that 80 per cent was probably higher.

R.K.'s handling of the coal mafia set a high standard for the guards. The requirements of the job were clear—be bold, you have the backing of the organization. In the service of the client, there were no limits to cater to their requirements. If something requires an out-of-the-box solution, so be it. Most of all, the founder showed the way when it came to valuing an employee. One of his most used adages, and now often quoted in the corridors of SIS, is this: Take care of your people, they will take care of your business.

It was not just another pleasant-sounding and smartly worded phrase that made for good content in brochures or signboards in office rooms. It wasn't a hollow sentiment, like we have seen in some recent examples with corporations. Modern business history has seen many companies that provide swanky cubicles and workspaces, gourmet dishes and foosball facilities in offices. The very same companies don't bat an eyelid to lay off employees at the first signs of distress in the business or in the economy. In fact, a unicorn startup founder famously boasted of having fired his top team after the firm listed on the Bombay Stock Exchange. The reason? They had become complacent. Startups continue to report the highest attrition rates.

At SIS, R.K.'s style of management instilled loyalty in its ranks.

'In a lot of companies that I find today, people are working for CTC [cost to pay] and are not working with passion. They will immediately quit and move on if somebody gives them a 15 per cent hike. It happens in banking, in manufacturing. The IT industry is the biggest culprit,' says Uday Singh.

That's not the case, he promises, in SIS. 'I have not seen this amazing passion as I see it in SIS,' says Singh, who has worked in multinational companies such as Praxair Carbon Dioxide Private Limited and with big domestic names such as JSW Steel. 'You give an extra bit of work to an SIS employee, whatever the work may be, they don't say no. If you tell a supervisor it's Diwali season, and apart from his routine work in the office site, he will also need to distribute sweets, he will say, '*Ho jayega*, sir. I will do it.' The supervisor has many other responsibilities but he will still do it, that's the passion.'

Years later, the passion would be played out in two of the most disrupting phases in Indian and global history—Demonetization and the 2019 COVID pandemic.

That passion and loyalty is in response to R.K.'s employee engagement. Up to the year when he stepped back a little due to ill health, R.K. would be present in the most important events in his employees' life, from weddings to funerals. 'He would be there personally, he would fly in and make sure all arrangements were done. He would travel whatever the time and often at the cost of his health. That's the kind of culture he cultivated in the company,' says Arvind Prasad. Few founders show such commitment. And that's one reason why SIS has survived in an industry that has no entry barriers—there are over 30,000 security companies in the country.

As in any other company, unfortunate events occurred. R.K. ensured the organization backed the deceased employee's family. 'Whenever a guard died, the company would ensure his body is taken to his native place, whichever corner of the country it may be. The family is given Rs 1.5 lakh within forty-eight hours to help manage expenses. Apart from this, there are many benefits that the company provides the family,' says Vinaya Srivastawa.

He narrates his own experience when he suffered a stroke that left him partly paralysed. 'Chairman Sir was in Singapore at that time when he got the news about me. He booked a ticket from there and they took me to Delhi for the treatment. I was there for fifteen days for the treatment. I got well too. They looked after me and my needs. If they are doing so much for me, it's my duty to work for my company. We have guards who have worked for years and have got ESOPs from the company. They got a very good amount of money and we also got it. Our owner cares for us and that's the reason we are working for the company. We have employee satisfaction.'

R.K. created what is now popularly called the family culture of SIS. 'He has a talent of spotting potential in people, it is amazing.

That some of the people who are working from the early days are still with him, and these were people who were not so qualified and they didn't have the right background, but he could spot talent. And once he spots a person, he grooms them,' says Uday Singh.

R.P. Singh, head of recruitment and training at SIS, recalls several instances of R.K. making an impact on his work style. In the early 1990s, SIS had an office in Delhi's Safdarjung Enclave. R.K. would often visit the city as the market was a growing one for SIS. 'He would be in office till late at night. And we would be waiting for him to finish. And then suddenly at 12 in the night he would finish his work and tell us, "Bring the car, let's go for a night inspection." These checks would then become a class for us,' says Singh.

If a particular branch was having issues, R.K. would weigh in. Like the time when R.P. Singh's unit was having difficulty in getting payment from a steel company. 'We would keep sending them reminders and they would just stall us,' Singh told R.K., who immediately offered to help. The two went to the steel company's office at Delhi's Bhikaji Cama Place. 'We went to the office and Chairman Sir just told them, "Please clear the cheque so that I can pay the salary of my staff."' The company executive, surprised to see R.K. in the office for a cheque, promised to do it soon. To their amazement however, R.K. wouldn't budge from his seat unless the cheque was actually issued. They had no choice but to hand it over. 'He was very polite the whole time. Yet firm. It was a good way to understand how to deal with tough clients,' says R.P. Singh.

Interestingly, on the way to the steel company's office, R.P. Singh got another lesson. New to the city, Singh didn't know how to operate a lift. The lift and its several buttons were intimidating. R.K. sensed the hesitation. As the lift started towards the floor where the steel company was housed, the chairman schooled Singh on the basics of using a lift.

'It's difficult to get this kind of mentorship in today's world. Just by looking at a person he would understand where this person was getting stuck and the training they need. He would teach everybody in this manner,' says Singh. 'He is like a jeweller who understands the quality of the gold by taking one look,' says Narayan Lenka.

Unsurprisingly, mentorship also brings loyalty. An organization culture of this kind elicits commitment. People stay because they connect with the founder's vision. And they don't leave. R.P. Singh didn't. Aditya Birla Chemicals, which had a facility near SIS's Garhwa training centre, approached Singh with a job offer. Singh would be a vice president, in charge of the whole administration. He turned down the offer. The executives at Birla kept trying. It so happened that when the executive called next, Singh was having dinner with R.K. 'I told him I was with the chairman. Surprisingly, he asked to speak to Sir. I handed over the phone,' says Singh.

'Sir, we want R.P. Singh in our company and we are ready to offer him a job with a lot of benefits. If you give permission, we would like to give him an offer,' the Birla executive said. It was a touchy moment. R.P. Singh was one of SIS's brighter prospects. R.K. didn't want to lose him. But he needed to handle this sensitively.

'It's a matter of pride for us that a person whom we have trained is being offered a big job by the Birla group. It's a proud moment for me. You do the process and I will ask him to join. But before doing any of these, just ask him if he himself wants to leave and take up a new job,' R.K. said. And he handed over the phone to Singh. 'Sir,' Singh told the Birla executive, 'I came to my senses at the age of twenty when I came to SIS and I will retire from SIS only. This was my first job and this will be my last job, I can guarantee you that. Come what may, I cannot think of leaving SIS.' The senior Aditya Birla Chemicals executive finally got the message.

This devotion to the company is remarkable given SIS's financial condition. In fact, it has not been easy for an SIS employee. A security business generates little cash and is always at the mercy of its clients to get payments. Some are prompt in their payments; many—like the steel company—need repeated calls and follow ups. This meant that SIS often ran out of cash to pay its guards. Sometimes, guards wouldn't be paid for a month, sometimes for five months at a time. Often, officers would have to wait even longer. 'We have seen many ups and downs. People had many opportunities to take up other jobs. But few did. We had faith that our salaries wouldn't go anywhere. If not today, tomorrow we will get our salary. We had so much faith that the salary will not go anywhere, we felt instead of keeping it in the bank, it is better that it remains with SIS. We had faith in Chairman Sir,' says Singh. This may sound too good to be true. Yet, scores of SIS employees echo Singh.

How did R.K. develop this culture? Was it intuitive or was it a model that he realized was the best for a company that employed a lot of people?

'I'm quite clear it was not accidental. It was very strategic to develop a culture around the theme of a family. You remain part of a family in good times and bad. So, when employees were not being paid for months because there was no money in the company, they stayed, didn't leave,' says Uday Singh. They didn't leave even when competition came in the form of multinationals like G4S. 'I don't think we have lost more than one or two managers to some of our biggest competition,' says Singh. In fact, quite a few moved on to SIS's boat.

What does R.K. himself say about this culture that he inculcated in his company?

'As a human being, it doesn't matter where one is coming from. What matters is his grooming, his training and the opportunities he gets. If your grooming and training is proper and you get an opportunity, he also can become whatever you want.

'For the success of any uniformed force, the most important thing is their good morale and, for good morale, connection is important. Until and unless you dine with them, the connection will not be there. As much as you identify yourself with them, they will agree to your leadership. As much distance as you maintain, they will not bother about you.

'Technically, they are my employees but, if we look at it another way, they are stakeholders of the company and its future in exactly the same way as I am. No difference. If I am a boss, they can become a boss too. We do not have a product, they themselves are our product.'

Now, being people centric is one aspect of SIS's culture. The scale it achieved in later years was much because of this employee centricity. But that wasn't all. There is another critical part to the SIS culture—the founder's mentality.

A concept that has been rigorously discussed and propagated by leading global investment firm Bain Capital, founder's mentality is made of the core strengths and values that helped a company grow, disrupt its industry and emerge as a leader. In a Forbes article, Bain's Partner Chris Zook points out three elements to the founder's mentality—a clear 'insurgent mission,' a front-line obsession and the owner's mindset.

Companies start off as insurgents, nimble and thinking out of the box. But this typically wears off as they grow in scale and become big. That's when they tend to lose the founder's mentality. In fact, Bain's research shows that one in nine companies that had a sustained, profitable growth are those who have managed to retain this founder's mentality.

At SIS, R.K. was adamant about inculcating this founder's mentality in his officers. Each SIS officer who went on to manage branches, was expected to lead a branch as its chief executive. Just like in the Bain definition, the founder's mentality in SIS also had three parts—an owner's mindset, challenging status quo and frontline obsession. It's often referred to as 'Chairman's mindset' within the SIS corridors. This includes:

1. Customer advocacy. Don't complain about the demanding nature of customers. Go beyond contract.
2. Leadership traits like aversion to bureaucracy, cash focus, being a self starter in this highly dynamic industry.
3. And most importantly, thinking big, setting audacious goals—having growth appetite, changing the industry (this is what enabled SIS to take risks that no one had dared to, including acquiring a company that was seven times its size). To ensure that this founder's mentality was ingrained in each SIS employee, who was also SIS's main product as a service company, R.K. did something no one else had.

6

THE BOOT CAMP

With his ears firmly on the ground, R.K. realized early on that the biggest product in his service business were the guards. 'They are our product and the production process is their training and grooming,' he says.

That brought him to another realization. He couldn't depend exclusively on the pool of ex-army men, especially when it came to SIS's increasing requirement of well-trained guards and officers. 'These army officers have just retired and are mostly looking for a part-time job. In other words, they were not desperate for a job as they got pension from the army,' says R.K.

Also, most of the retired army men wanted to work close to their homes. They had been away from home for years and had been posted all over the country. Life had been unsettled. So, after retiring, they wanted to stay with their families, look after their properties and farms. 'This meant that we didn't have enough guards to send to sites,' says Arvind Prasad. 'So, Chairman came with the idea to recruit freshers in Bihar as the state was a fertile ground for recruitment because jobs were scarce.'

The retired army men had also been hardened and trained in a specific environment. That made them excellent when it came to providing security to the nation. They were disciplined and fit. But they did not have any knowledge of industrial security. Often, they struggled to see the point of view of the customer. What is the expectation of the customer? What does the customer need? These were questions that they were not trained to address. What they were trained for, however, was to respond in the time of crisis.

This was among the first serious challenges for R.K. While he had immensely benefited from the wisdom of the retired officers from army and police, and the retired bureaucrats, their job in SIS was their second innings. They lacked the gusto and the appetite that was needed to build and expand a young business. They were trained as reactive forces. If there is a situation or a development, they know how to respond or reply. They were not preventive forces.

Whereas, SIS's core work was more of prevention and not much of reaction. 'That's why we started the training centre and then took on young men, recruiting them to be officers and supervisors,' explains R.K. To understand the customer and their requirements, you need to be trained. And this training has to come early in the career of a guard. And that's why SIS got into training, says R.K.

This also ensured the trainees were exposed to SIS's culture right from the day they started at the Garhwa training centre. From learning martial arts to defending themselves on the ground to picking up nuances of their work, the training was geared to servicing the ever-changing needs of the customer, and doing so while adhering to SIS principles.

It's not that training was new for SIS. Right from the start, SIS had a training programme. But it was rudimentary in the early days and soon outlived its use. Though the opportunity to set up something bigger came by accident, R.K. immediately caught hold of it.

By 1983, one of SIS's biggest deployments was in B.P. Jain's cement plant in Japla in Bihar's Palamu district. There were over 100 guards and five officers manning the facility. A little over 50 km away from the cement plant was an ashram in a newly formed district called Garhwa. Jain had given the ashram to Jain monks. But in recent years, the region had become a hub for Naxalites, who soon began asking the monks for money and ration. Unable to keep up with the demands, the monks deserted the place. Given its idyllic location—the river Koel flowed next to the ashram—the Naxalites started using the place and eventually took it over. The local police weren't happy. 'The ashram is turning out to be a law-and-order problem. Please provide security arrangements for it, otherwise the police will take over the place,' the police said in a letter to Jain. Worried, Jain called R.K. 'You take over the place and provide security,' he told R.K.

This was the time when the SIS founder was trying to find a solution to his human resource problem: the requirement for trained manpower within a predictable time period and scale. Arvind Prasad, his close confidante, had already suggested the idea for a formal training organization. When Jain asked him to take over the ashram in Garhwa, R.K. saw the opportunity to plug this hole in his operations. In November 1984, the SIS training centre began operations in Garhwa. Two years later, R.K. added a graduate training officer (GTO) programme. Now, the centre trained and churned out both guards and officers.

For young hopefuls, a training centre led credence to their job. A guard's work was still seen as that of a chowkidar or a darbaan. It had little social acceptance. 'I told my father and he was not happy with me that I was going to do a watchman's job,' says S.S. Ojha, who was from the fifth batch of GTO. 'When my family told others that their son is doing a security job, people say, "Oh, he is working as a watchman?" Even after they clarified I was an officer, they would tease, "Oh, so he is a senior watchman?" I used to feel a little odd that people thought that I work there as a watchman,' says Ojha.

Yet, youngsters looked at the opportunity differently. P.K. Singh, for instance, wanted to join the army but his mother wouldn't let him. Later, he had the opportunity to join the Border Security Force but says he needed to grease hands to land an opportunity. 'My father offered to pay money. But I said if I get a job after paying money, my only aim will be to make money out of my job, and I will not work loyally,' says Singh. But the wish for a job in uniform didn't go away. He jumped on the opportunity when he came across an advertisement to join SIS's GTO programme. The script is similar for many others including Prakash Binjola, who would go on to become a vice president, and Narayan Lenka, President, Security Solutions, all of whom started their careers in the training centre in Garhwa and then climbed the ladder in SIS.

To get an entry into the training centre itself wasn't easy. Some of the eligibility criteria remained the same as it was in the days the recruitment was done on the lawns of R.K.'s house in Patna. To be eligible to write the entrance test, a candidate should be at least a tenth pass (graduation for the officer trainees), be at least five feet and seven inches tall, weigh not more than 70 kg and be anywhere from sixteen to thirty years of age. In recent years, the upper limit has been increased to thirty-seven years and the weight to up to 90 kg.

R.P. Singh remembers being one of the 5,000 boys who had written the entrance test in Patna. The tests, which tested the hopefuls' math and general knowledge, were carried out over three days. There was a physical examination too—3 km run, high jump, long jump and a few more such exercises. Those who cleared the written and physical tests progressed to the next round. This included group discussion and public speaking. The last would be the interview by the board, which included R.K.

Of the 5,000 who attended the written test, only 99 remained at the end, says R.P. Singh. And then, they headed to Garhwa for the three-month training. Many of the 5,000 would have come from outside Bihar. Like Narayan Lenka, who grew up in rural Odisha, and submitted his application at Birla Tyres' Balasore unit that was being manned by SIS. The application was then sent to Patna, where it was accepted. Lenka got a call to appear for the test in Patna.

The training centre itself took on a regimen right out of an army boot camp. In the early years, the centre had one building and something 'like a shed,' says Lenka. It looked like a tent. It was winter when he joined the course. Beds were made of gunny bags. There were no toilets, instead they would dig pits. The Koel river was where they took baths. Later, a dormitory kind of structure would come up where rooms would be shared.

Life would start early in the morning, at 4.30. First up would be running and then a session of martial arts. From 9.30 a.m. to 1 p.m. there were classes that touched upon the requirements of the job, including on how to do documentation, write letters or understand basic English and Hindi. After a short rest period it would be time for another round of drills and games. That would be followed by dinner and then it was time to hit the bed. 'This was the routine for six days a week. Sometimes, we would have activities on Sundays too,' says Singh. The martial arts classes, mostly karate, would be intense and physical. 'People broke their arms and legs. Many would drop off, not being able to keep up with the intensity day in and day out for three months,' says Singh. Karate was introduced partly thanks to Arvind Prasad, who himself was trained in the martial arts. 'It was important to make guards strong and also make them bold and confident. You can frighten one or two people of SIS but you can't frighten the whole group. That culture has been built,' he says.

Training for both officers and guards was equally intense. The difference was qualitative. Officers would be taught supervisory skills, basic accounts, marketing and sales. These were skills they needed to know to manage the operation of a branch. For many of these trainees, this was the first time they had ventured out of home. Lenka didn't even understand Hindi well, let alone English. 'The only thing I could say in English was, "Can I have a glass of water?"' His mates would pull a fast one and teach him wrong Hindi. Once it was in front of the chairman, who had come on one of his visits, that he blurted out something wrong in Hindi. R.K. promptly put him under a teacher to learn Hindi.

Three months of training done, the boys—now hardened men—would be sent on internships to several parts of the country. 'Depending on our performance at the end of this period, which could last up to a year, the decision would be made where to deploy us. Was he more suited for mines or a manufacturing facility? A monument or a hotel? Accordingly, posting would be done,' says Singh. The newly minted officer would join a unit as second-in-command to a senior officer.

Today, the fortieth batch of GTO is undergoing training in Garhwa. Till date, the centre has churned out 1,085 officers. Of the 150 branches at SIS Security, 65 are manned by officers who passed out of the GTO programme. There is little doubt, 'The GTO programme is the backbone of SIS,' says R.K.

In today's world, a training centre may sound like a natural thing to have for a company that needs a huge workforce. But not in the 1980s, at least in the security personnel business. Not in India, and probably very few globally. It was a rarity even for G4S, the largest security company in the world that entered India in 1989. 'Ravindra Kishore had no training himself. He had no formal education in security, engineering or management, but he had a tremendous flair for systems. If you suggest a system to him, he will never say he wouldn't implement it. It if adds a little of value also, he will support you all the way in the system being built,' says Arvind Prasad. 'Now we see that people are brought from anywhere and are sent to the client's location and duty is started. As you can understand, I am the witness that thirty five years ago the chairman had the conviction that "Without training not even a single guard should go to the client's location to do duty",' he adds.

The training centre was a good example of R.K.'s foresight. The Indian security industry hadn't seen a similar setup before. 'I first went to Garhwa as a young boy. My father was invited by Mr Sinha and I tagged along. As my father was from the army and I had seen army establishments. The training centre at Garhwa looked right out of an army-run operation. Mr Sinha had a great vision,' says Sanjeev Paul, managing director, Scientific Security Management Services Ltd. His father Lt Col. Jaswant Singh Paul was a contemporary of R.K. and had founded the company in the 1970s.

Scientific Security Management itself set up a training centre later in Delhi. But it's not easy running and maintaining a centre. 'It's a huge expense to have a training academy in Deli. First of all, you need land. Then the costs related to training itself, which is huge. The centre doesn't make any money and you just need to keep pumping money to train people and also to scale it. That's a huge cost,' says Paul.

One could argue R.K. got lucky by getting the ashram from B.P. Jain in a remote place like Garhwa, which wasn't very expensive to run. But the entrepreneur that he was, R.K. had a different outlook. The training centre had to sustain itself to last. And to last, it had to make sense commercially and not become a drag on the core business, which was chugging along but wasn't throwing up too much cash to spare for a training institute. To make it commercially viable, Ravindra Kishore decided that the Garhwa training centre would charge a fee. Right from the first day, even though in those days there were challenges to attract youngsters for a security job, SIS charged a fee. 'It was the only model that worked. The day we stop it, the training institute will become an elephant,' says Arvind Prasad. In return, SIS committed to train the recruits well enough to enable them to go anywhere and work efficiently. 'As long as you deliver, people will pay a price. If you don't, people will say, "Honest *nahin hain*,"' says Arvind Prasad.

R.K. was always keen to see how the trainees were progressing. Garhwa was about 250 km away from Patna. He would take a train every fortnight. Often, Rita, Rituraj and Rivoli would join him. It used to be a picnic for the children, given that the training centre was next to a scenic river. The family would stay in the bungalow and it would be as a family that they would interact with the trainees—sitting with them, playing with them and sharing meals. Ever a people's person, R.K. would use these interactions to connect with the trainees and share his experiences about the work entailed as a SIS guard or officer. He'd also take note of those who made an impression on him. These interactions would be in the classroom, on the ground or at the dinner table.

Some of these interactions would be forever etched in the minds and hearts of the trainees. Like in the case of Prakash Binjola. He was in the fifteenth batch of the GTO programme. At the time, the training went on for six months. His birthday, on 6 January, fell during the training period in 1996. Coincidentally, R.K. and his family were on the campus. In the evening, Binjola got a call and was asked to meet the chairman. Bewildered and nervous, the youngster presented himself at the door of the chairman's office. It was not the chairman but Rita who received him. She had an arati plate in her hands. Somehow, they had come to know it was Binjola's birthday. She did arati, prayed for him and gave him sweets to eat. 'I was nobody. There was no reason for them to take note of my birthday and do arati for me. But Sir and Madam did. It was and it remains a very emotional moment for me,' says Binjola.

R.K.'s influence was palpable in the training curriculum too. 'Right till today, what we teach in Garhwa, the study material, the way the courses are designed, much of these have come from Chairman Sir,' says R.P. Singh. It was common to see faculty at the centre teaching out of photocopies of notes handwritten by R.K. He would write down these notes on his visits to the centre and these were subsequently handed over to the faculty. 'The processes that we follow at the centre have come from Sir's own writing. If we have any confusion as to how the centre should run, we go back to the notes. Some of these notes are from the 1980s and 1990s,' says R.P. Singh.

Interestingly, even the customary sharing of meals with trainees at the centre became institutionalized with time. R.K. began the custom of holding bada khaana, which literally means the big feast. This was an annual event at the centre, where everyone would come together in preparing the meal, serving it and enjoying it. More often than not, the star of these meals would be the quintessential Bihari dish litti and mutton, which was also the chairman's favourite. The chairman himself would take the responsibility of ensuring each part of the bada khaana, including the menu, the logistics and the guest list, was taken care of.

In the initial years, the bada khaana would also coincide with something like an annual conference. Senior executives of the company would travel to Garhwa and spend a couple of days in the training campus. 'Chairman Sir would speak about the year gone by, citing important milestones. It was also the time to announce pay hikes for those who performed well,' recounts Ratna Sinha, who worked in the chairman's office. 'There was no HR department, and everything was handled by the chairman's office,' she adds.

Over time, both the bada khaana and these conferences were scaled as SIS expanded its reach. 'In Delhi, it would be an opportunity for those people whom father knew and were from the city to come over and enjoy litti,' says Rivoli. This included bureaucrats, police officers, politicians and even artists. In Mumbai, the guest list included a similar profile, though given its commercial and entertainment connect, there were many from the corporate world and the cinema-entertainment sphere who would land at R.K.'s Bandra house for the bada khaana. And there was also a bada khaana that was held at the family abode in Dehradun. R.K. built a school there, Indian Public School, his answer to the anglicized Doon School where his son had gone. Later, Rituraj would rebuild a palatial and historical bungalow right next to the school. The bada khaana would be held around New Year and would see people from all walks of lives from the neighbourhood coming in, including the devotees of the Shiva Temple nearby that was built and maintained by R.K. The other bada khaana of the calendar was in Bihar's Bahiara village, the ancestral place of the family. R.K. and his family would not only attend these, but also actively participate in organizing them. This was an extension of R.K.'s own passion for people and the common love for food, which he enjoyed immensely. These feasts would have a lasting impression on those who attended—employees, guests and people from the neighbourhood.

The annual conference went on to scale up in a similar fashion. After the systems and processes came in at the turn of the century, these meetings were no longer about handing over hikes in salary. It became more about presenting business reviews, taking stock of the business and pitching plans for the coming year. The highlight would always be the same—the address from R.K. 'It started being held across the country. For instance, in 2007, this was held in Bhopal and had about fifty to a hundred people attending,' says Natalie Hansda, who works in Rituraj's office. The number of attendees would steadily increase with SIS's expansion nationally and, later, internationally.

In recent years, the annual conference has become a two-day affair with nearly 1,000 people attending from across the country and abroad. The event has become so big that it needs the space of Yashobhoomi, the convention centre in Delhi's Dwarka that is said to be among the largest of its kind in Asia. The planning starts six months in advance, and the logistical needs are complicated and intense. 'There are many different companies in SIS Group now, and they all give their reviews and then next year's planning starts. The main thing on the agenda are reviews and planning,' says Ratna Sinha.

Interestingly, this event has been used by Uday and Rituraj to showcase the company and its growth prospects. They would invite prospective investors, bankers and fellow industrialists to the annual conference.

In short, the impact of the training centre was immense and went way beyond its primary function. Through the years, the training at SIS has scaled up. Today, apart from the centre in Garhwa, SIS has twenty-one training centres, spread mostly in the east, north and western parts of India. Nearly 400 young men are being trained at Garhwa alone at any moment. In total, over 4,000 trainees pass out of these training centres every month.

The key thing about the training centre is that it's a tangible testimony to SIS's deep commitment and investment in people, and its culture around people focus.

7

A UNIQUE RECORD IN INDUSTRIAL RELATIONS

The discipline of a trained guard coupled with the culture that R.K., his family and the rest of the top brass perpetuated had another big impact on the organization. The company, despite being heavily dependent on manpower, never really had a labour union issue.

It's not that the company never faced union trouble. It did when it would take over new contracts in companies that already had labour unions. In later years, it had to sort out labour unrest in one of the companies it acquired. But there was no instance of a labour union being formed in the company in its fifty years of operations. R.K. managed to keep union interference out of his workforce. That was an incredible achievement, given that even a multinational like G4S had to face several hurdles related to labour unrest in its units in India.

When asked how SIS managed to have no union and kept the company insulated from political interference, R.K. had a common refrain: "Union ki kya jaroorat jab main hi union hoon" (what's the need for a union when I myself was the union). The SIS owner had himself become the voice of the frontline, his people skills coming to the fore when he would meet them and understand their issues. It eliminated the need for a platform like a labour union. This culture seeped down the ranks.

Arvind Prasad puts this down to a culture where supervisors take an active interest in solving the issues of guards. He cites an example from the early years, that of a Lajjan Singh. He was an officer running a few sites in Chasnala, in Dhanbad, Jharkhand. In the 1980s, this area amounted for at least 20 per cent of the company's total deployment.

Lajjan Singh had a monthly ritual. Once a month, he would go down to the SIS office in Patna to sort out issues with his branch. These ranged from inaccuracies in accounts to getting budgets cleared. Those were the days when much of the document filing was done manually. 'Every month, he would land in my office with a bunch of applications from his men. One by one, he would discuss each of the applications with my colleagues in the finance section. And he would not leave my office till he got an answer for each application. Sometimes, he would come with over fifty applications to be sorted within a day,' says Arvind Prasad.

Lajjan Singh and Arvind Prasad were friends, and Singh knew which door to knock if things weren't working out. Fortunately, the accounts team was not bureaucratic. 'In his entire career in SIS, I can't remember a month in which Lajjan Singh didn't solve at least twenty problems his men faced. Now, if there is such a culture among supervisors, and the men on the ground know that their problems will be heard and solved—and this is the culture that drives the company—then they will not have strikes, they will not have union problems,' says Arvind Prasad.

However, it hasn't all been smooth sailing. One of the first markets that R.K. branched out from Bihar was in the neighbouring state of West Bengal, in its capital, Kolkata. He had put S.S. Ojha in charge of the market. Despite losing its place as India's commercial capital to Mumbai, Kolkata still had hundreds of industries and Ravindra Kishore knew there was immense scope for a new security agency to make a mark. But there was a big stumbling block—unions. West Bengal has always been a state where Communist parties got immense popular support. This also meant that the unions belonging to the Left parties were powerful and had immense say in the industrial relations of the companies.

Ojha was not having it easy, and R.K. knew it. Before he was to visit Kolkata, R.K. teasingly asked him if his branch was making enough money to spend for the chairman's visits. SIS had bagged a contract from ICI Paints, one of the biggest businesses that emerged from the eastern metro and one that had a British legacy. Nearly fifty guards need to be stationed inside the ICI facility. But there was a problem. The existing security staff, belonging to a multinational, weren't ready to move out and were refusing to let any other personnel enter the premises.

In his sales pitch, Ojha had convinced the ICI deputy manager, responsible for the administration of the facility, that SIS would be able to handle the situation. The deputy manager was happy that Ojha had agreed to do the work. The union had made things difficult and the company had lost many working hours because of labour unrest. The deputy manager even offered Ojha Rs 5 lakh to take care of the expenses to execute the order. But when he saw the extent of the resistance from the union, Ojha became unsure. He confided in R.K. The chairman immediately offered to help. He even invited the ICI official to Ranchi to discuss the issue. They decided upon a novel approach. Instead of deploying a fresh unit in the ICI facility, SIS would absorb the existing security employees. The employees would be sent to Garhwa for training for three months. But who would bear the training costs? Also, the men would need to be paid their monthly salaries too for the three months. ICI offered to take care of the expense, realizing that they needed to do their bit to ensure SIS took over the security responsibility.

And so, it was done. SIS took over the unit and absorbed the men, who dropped their resistance the moment they realized they would be keeping their jobs even after the change in the security provider. They were sent to Garhwa and went through the training regimen for three months. And then R.K. tweaked the script. Instead of sending all of them back to Kolkata, the guards were deployed to different parts of the country. That was a masterstroke. Not only did it ensure that the earlier security team at ICI didn't continue, these men were also pushed to new locations and responsibilities. They now had new colleagues and soon shed their union tendencies.

The deputy manager was pleased with SIS's work. 'We continue to have them as our client,' says Ojha. ICI, which owned the popular Dulux brand, was later acquired by Dutch giant AkzoNobel in 2008. The success here set up SIS well to attract more clients in Kolkata. The next time R.K. visited Kolkata and asked Ojha if the branch can handle the costs, the latter happily answered in the affirmative. 'I paid the hotel bills on his behalf and I told him that it's my wish that he come here quite often. He felt very happy for the first time, knowing that Kolkata's unit can bear the responsibility.'

'One cash logistics company that we bought had union members among its ranks in Kerala, Chennai and Maharashtra,' says J.K. Akash, senior vice president at SIS. There were instances where the members of the union would surround a branch office and threaten strikes if their demands were not met. 'It took time. We kept talking to them, hearing what they had to say, their issues and problems. It was a different experience for them because now they had a management that was listening to them. Earlier, the complaint was, "*Koi humara sunta nahin*" (no one listens to us). Now they had a voice.' With clear communication lines, a barrier had been broken. 'We were able to remove all unions from the company that we acquired,' he adds.

Employees knew that the new management was not only willing to listen but also address justified expectations. However, there was no place for threat, coercion and politicising issues.

SIS also constituted a reward and recognition programme. The senior management of a specific market would have a day-long meeting with the employees of a branch or a region. These events also included the guards' families. The highlight of the event was senior executives handing over recognition letters from the chairman, along with cash rewards. 'Initially, the cash used to be just Rs 1,000. But it was still valuable because they were getting recognized for their hard work. That meant a lot,' says Prakash Binjola. This has now been institutionalized.

The company also provides a wide safety net. This includes benefits that the guards are due as per statutory compliance. Beyond that, SIS provides them with insurance and goes the distance when a guard or his family fall on tough times. On a guard's demise, the family is immediately supported financially. SIS officers are among the first ones to reach the hometown, and arrange and stay back for the last rites.

Interestingly, one of its biggest rivals very early in its stint in India noticed the impact SIS was having with its training centre. Its officials even visited the Garhwa training centre in the late 1980s. The company also set up a training programme but it was markedly shorter than the SIS course in Garhwa, lasting for only three days. The efficacy of a three-day training programme became a relevant question when, in later years, the multinational faced several run-ins with unions across its sites. This is despite the reputation this company developed in the industry for the welfare programme it offered its employees. The made-to-measure shoes and smart uniforms of their security guards caught a lot of attention. Yet, the union problem persisted.

That came to bite when it came to rotating guards. It was a common practice among security companies to transfer men across sites. 'This prevents familiarity. In our experience, familiarity often led to staff dropping their guard, becoming friends and sometimes even getting involved in corrupt practices,' says Vinod Advani, president, Security Solutions at SIS. This would impact the service efficacy, hurt the company's reputation and come in the way when the contract was up for renewal.

SIS follows a policy of moving its personnel every six months. That's possible because there is no union in place. 'Otherwise, for every transfer, one would need the approval from the union. That would slow down business and impact the overall performance of the company,' says Advani. That SIS didn't have this problem was a big plus when it would pitch for new orders as companies were keen to avoid any kind of union problem.

The family culture of SIS had obliterated the need for a union. The biggest factor of all was the direct access that guards had to R.K., who would freely share his personal contact number with the guards. When a guard called, R.K. would give him a patient hearing and ask his administrative staff to note down the complaint or the request. When word went around that calling the chairman helped, it became a big rallying point for the ranks. They hadn't heard of a company where a staff member on the ground could directly call the owner and have his needs addressed. Later, those with leadership roles took the cue from R.K. and would similarly engage with the workforce.

And it was not just R.K. Rivoli cites an instance where her mother Rita came across a SIS guard at a fashion store in a shopping mall in Noida. When she inquired about his well-being, he complained of having been transferred recently from Delhi to Noida, which fell under the state of Uttar Pradesh, where the wages were lower. Even though his expenses had remained the same, the wages had gone down. 'On the way back home, she spoke to several people in the company inquiring why the guard was transferred and if the supervisors weren't aware of the change in wages,' says Rivoli. Not only was the guard's complaint addressed, but it also resulted in a change in the company policy of transferring people within the NCR market.

The impact of the family culture that R.K. imbibed within the organization, coupled with the standards he has set at its training centres, meant that SIS had a lower attrition than the rest of the industry. The impact of this on the guards' lives was immense.

No one describes the impact better than Uday Singh:

'That's why I always keep on saying SIS is a story of ordinary people coming together and giving extraordinary results. They were not extraordinary people. They became extraordinary,' says Uday Singh. 'If there's an IIT or IIM graduate who has done something great, what's so great about it? He anyways belonged to the top 2 cent of the population when it comes to talent. It would be a shame if he didn't deliver.' On the other hand, explains Singh, 'these people in SIS were hardly properly educated. Most were village folks whose only ambition in life was to get a government job or a selection in the army. If you are rejected there, you try the police force. If you get rejected there too, you have nothing to do but join SIS as a GTO. Now, there has to be a teacher, a culture and an atmosphere to change these ordinary men into extraordinary achievers. And this is what SIS has done under Ravindra Kishore Sinha.'

The social and economic upliftment of SIS employees was remarkable. Take Sanjay Pandey, the Vice President for Fleet, for instance. He was the third of six brothers and was among the first to get a job. But their father passed away when nearly all the siblings were studying. 'I was the only sole earner. It was Chairman Sir who then helped and supported the family. Today one of my brothers is settled in Europe, another in Southeast Asia. My whole family is well settled. It's thanks to Chairman Sir,' he says.

For someone who had a profound impact on those around him, it was inevitable that R.K.'s influence rubbed off on the rest of the security industry in India too. His role changed the way the industry was perceived.

8

SHAPING THE INDUSTRY

There are many barometers of success. One is personal wealth. Some of the most successful entrepreneurs are also the richest—for instance, Kumar Mangalam Birla and Anil Agarwal from the old economy sectors and Nithin Kamath and Falguni Nayar from the new emerging ones. Another measure is the prosperity that a business spreads among its wider stakeholders. The story of Infosys white collar employees becoming crorepatis is legend by now. Reliance Industries' stock was a favourite among institutional and retail investors. Dhirubhai Ambani's annual address to his shareholders used to fill stadiums.

But how about an entrepreneur who did well for himself, his stakeholders and also for his competitors? That sounds unusual. Is it even possible? Maybe not, especially going by the common logic that one can grow only at the expense of the other. But R.K. proved it could be done. He may not have done it consciously. Yet, his drive to hear, observe and learn, and then to implement what he picked within SIS, had a larger impact on India's security industry. Through him, the security industry got a voice that for the first time reached policymakers.

R.K. was under no illusions. He was new to the security business. He didn't have an MBA and wasn't aware of the basics of running an operation. He wasn't from a business family and didn't grow up listening to discussions about profit and loss and business strategy at dinner tables. But he had an inherent curiosity and hunger to know more. This was fuelled by the conversations his father would have at home with politicians and bureaucrats. A similar zest led him to the various workshops of the RSS. And when he started SIS, the keenness to know more led him to all corners of the country and the world. He learned by listening to others, be it at home or in a foreign country.

It started with his trips from Patna to the sites where SIS men were posted. Over time, his travel crossed several boundaries within and outside the country. The first time he attended an international security conference was in the late 1980s. That was in Florida, US. After that, he would attend similar conferences every year, sometimes twice or thrice a year, in the US, Europe and Asia. Many of these markets had a more mature security industry than was prevalent in India. The technology, processes and practices were much superior. 'I would attend seminars in these countries. I spent lakhs of rupees because I wanted to train myself, because I did not know so much about it. So, I needed to know,' says R.K.

After a while though, he began to realize these seminars didn't address specific issues he himself faced as an Indian businessman or while doing business in India. When he did ask questions to speakers and experts in these events, it wasn't always welcomed. 'They wouldn't like discussing the security industry in India, Indonesia or Malaysia. Probably because these markets were insignificant for these speakers who were from the US or Europe. Only the Japanese would get an ear. Not us,' says R.K.

Second, the workshops conducted in these events—and R.K. would make sure to attend nearly all of them—were mostly based on local laws in the US and Europe. There was some relevance for an Indian entrepreneur but not enough to justify the cost.

And these seminars were costly. 'On an average, you end up spending $1,000 to $1,200 a day. Not to talk about hotel accommodation and air travel costs,' he says. That was big money, very big money in the 1990s for a fledgling security company and its founder.

The disconnect bothered R.K. early on. 'I thought that a platform is required where we should be able to work properly, cost should be less, quality should be good and orientation should be Indian.' The thought stayed with him. The opportunity to do something towards this arose by accident.

The India security industry, as we have already reiterated multiple times now, has always been dispersed. The need to consolidate was felt early, as early as 1981 when the Maharashtra government issued an ordinance banning private security agencies under the Maharashtra Private Security Guard Board Act. The step was challenged in courts and some security companies managed to get exemptions. Yet, the industry realized it had to get together the various companies in the sector and make its presence felt.

A year later, in 1982, some progress was made during the annual conference of the World Association of Detectives. Attendees mentioned the developments in Maharashtra the year before and called for a central act that would regulate the security industry across states, all over the country. A central act would remove the uncertainty that comes with state-level regulations. This was important because security companies were beginning to expand beyond their home markets, and the differences in regulations was making compliance a tough task.

It so happened that the chief guest of the opening day was senior IAS officer P.P. Nayar, special secretary in the Ministry of Home Affairs and chairman of the Joint Intelligence Committee. It was R.K. who had managed to convince Nayar to be the chief guest and inaugurate the conference. Nayar paid heed to the demand for a central law. Later, he helped the industry representatives meet with Ram Dulari Sinha, the then Minister of State for Home. In the meeting, she accepted that private security agencies should be regulated by the Ministry of Home Affairs and not by the labour department of respective states.

That set the ball rolling for a new law to regulate the industry. That was crucial for the security business to be recognized as an industry and come under the purview of government agencies. This meant the industry could make its voice heard with policymakers. Also, uniform standards could be set across the industry.

A steering committee was formed. R.K. was among its youngest members. He and the rest of the industry executives would regularly meet and lobby with bureaucrats and ministers, pushing for the act to come into effect at the earliest. It looked on track until a setback came in the form of the assassination of Prime Minister Indira Gandhi in 1984. As the country sank in grief, and in violence in the aftermath of the assassination, focus moved away and the file on the security industry gathered dust in government offices.

The next time the movement for a new law gathered pace was six years later, in 1990. Thanks to the constant lobbying by the security industry, the Home Ministry called a meeting. After listening to everyone, Special Secretary P.P. Shrivastava said while the government recognized the relevance and growing importance of security agencies, he asked the industry itself to take steps and 'standardize the profession, make their services professionally effective and useful and self-regulate the profession like the Bar Council of India or the Chartered Accountants Institute of India'.

That left everyone disappointed. They had thought that Shrivastava would give the green light for the act. Instead, he was asking them to form an association. But not R.K. He saw a glimmer of hope in what the senior bureaucrat had suggested. He immediately sought a meeting with Subodh Kant Sahay, Minister of State. 'Yes, you should start an organization as suggested by Shrivastava. We will provide all help,' the minister said. 'Will you be the inaugural chairman?' R.K. asked. Getting a central minister to head the industry organization would be a big win and help push the case. Sahay readily agreed.

That was what led to the formation of the Indian Institute of Security and Safety Management in 1992. Its name was later tweaked to the International Institute of Security and Safety Management, or IISSM. 'IISSM set the ball rolling for the industry. The security industry now had a public forum and this grew to such an extent that the industry was able to engage with different governmental departments. The policymakers realized the importance of private security,' says Gurbir Singh, an entrepreneur who was among the first to bring in new-age camera technology to the security industry in India in 1980s.

Around this time, R.K. was instrumental in bringing another platform to the industry. The American Society for Industrial Security was one of the world's largest associations and included security practitioners and professionals based in the US. It was an association that attracted interest from the global industry because, like in most sectors, the American market was ahead of the curve and set standards for the rest of the world. The society was founded in 1955, and its seminars and events have been an attraction for security industry entrepreneurs and professionals from across the world. Today, it is better known as ASIS after it spread globally and opened chapters in several countries.

R.K. was one of the many who had attended ASIS events. And when a chance came, he convinced the society of setting up a chapter in India. 'He was instrumental in convincing them. They had a rule that to open up any chapter, you got to have fifteen members of good standing. Then you can move an application to open up a chapter,' says Gurbir Singh.

R.K. managed to convince his peers in India on the benefits of joining a global organization like ASIS. 'He called me and I said yes. I had heard of this organization while I was in the US and it was good to have it in India,' Gurbir says. One of the first chapters of ASIS was set up in Patna. 'Today, we have about eleven or twelve chapters in India of ASIS and we have close to over 2,000 members.'

Of the two, it was IISSM that was closer to R.K. He was closely involved in expanding its reach in India and overseas. It was right up his alley. The entrepreneur had exceptional networking skills and could strike conversations easily with people from any walk of life. Holding an event was a natural extension of this. At the same time, these events were not easy to organize. They were expensive. While SIS was beginning to do well, having expanded beyond its home market of Bihar, it was not a highly profitable operation. There was little cash and salaries were still delayed. The rest of the industry wasn't in a much better position. R.K. used his good offices with government officials and bureaucrats to get the best deals and sponsors for IISSM's events. But, in the end, it was up to him to ensure IISSM's functioning, including its annual events, didn't feel the pinch. To make this happen, he would go to any lengths.

One particular year, the financial squeeze was especially telling. But R.K. had to hold IISSM's annual conference, which was to be in

Bengaluru. To cut costs, he changed tack. Instead of booking flights from Patna to Bengaluru for him, his family, senior SIS officials and admin staff, they hit the road to the southern metropolis. That's a road trip of over 2,000 km. The contingent included half a dozen cars, including R.K.'s Contessa and two Ambassadors. Once the group reached Bengaluru, the same vehicles were used to ferry guests to the event and back. R.K. and Rita would make it a point to receive each and every delegate themselves. Often, they would be at the airport to welcome the overseas guests. The whole idea turned out to be a big money saver. 'After the event, we went sightseeing in the south,' recounts Rivoli. Even that was not without purpose. Many of the monuments, including those in Mahabalipuram, had SIS as their security vendor, and R.K. used the opportunity to check on his people and clients.

Never one to limit his vision, R.K. helped IISSM go international. For both these events, R.K. sent Dinesh Gupta, Executive Vice President at SIS, to prepare the ground. One of Gupta's fondest memories is of having khichdi in Mauritius in 1996. And who cooked the khichdi? R.K., who had come visiting to check the preparations of the IISSM conference that was held there. 'It was a roaring success with 200 participants from eighteen countries. The seminar was inaugurated by the Prime Minister of Mauritius. In the following years, annual seminars were also held at Kathmandu, Nepal, and Penang, Malaysia,' says Gupta.

One of the highlights of the early years of IISSM was convincing an American professional to conduct workshops in India. Dr Norman Spain, a Professor of Criminology in Eastern Kentucky University, received a Fulbright scholarship to come to India for six months. Among other things, he also wanted to study IISSM's activities. 'It was a big opportunity for us. We utilized Dr Norman Spain in the best possible manner and organized several three-day workshops on security and loss prevention,' says R.K. These workshops were held in Delhi, Patna, Shimla, Nagpur and at the training institute in Garhwa. Even companies such as Tata Steel and Coal India Limited hosted Dr Spain.

This was a PR coup for the time. Unlike now, it was rare to see an American professional in India, let alone in smaller cities like Patna. These workshops created buzz and were covered by local newspapers. Not just that, several courses that IISSM offers today go back to the workshops conducted by Dr Spain. 'Many of these [setting up associations and conducting workshops] was thanks to Mr Sinha. He had a wide network and knew how to maintain a relationship. Irrespective of the social, political or economic standing of a person, Mr Sinha was very respectful and nurtured his relationships with people. This helped bring together people from all walks of lives for these events,' says Gurbir Singh. Today, we have a robust network of associations which are running across the country and most of them have Mr Sinha as their starting point. He played a pivotal role in all of them.'

Setting up these associations, bringing the industry together in annual conferences and seminars and having bureaucrats and politicians as chief guests and members of these industry platforms eventually helped in doing something that was probably the top priority for R.K. and his work in the industry: get the law, which was first thought of in 1982, passed. 'Mr Sinha was very instrumental in telling the government that there's a law which is needed to license the guarding companies,' says Gurbir Singh.

Progress was slow. Indian administrative and legal systems are notorious for the time they take. Sometimes, it's decades before a legal case concludes. It requires perseverance, patience and a huge dose of self-belief to keep track of and push a case. Getting a law passed is especially tough. Governments change every five years. Sometimes even before. The change often comes with differing views on issues. If not that, a change in a minister or a bureaucrat can also set back timelines. R.K., given his upbringing, journalism and networking with officials from the army, police, bureaucracy and political parties, very well understood the nature of this beast. If others from the security industry lost hope, he never did.

He used IISSM as a platform to push the industry's case. A breakthrough came in 1994, during IISSM's annual conference in Delhi. Union minister Rajesh Pilot, who attended the conference, asked the industry to send suggestions to the government. IISSM promptly set up an expert committee headed by a former director of the Central Bureau of Investigation, Raja Vijay Karan. The committee sent its recommendations to the government, but again it got lost in bureaucracy.

It was not until the turn of the century, in 2000, that the industry managed once more to get attention from the policymakers. It mattered that R.K. served as an advisor to the Ministry of Human Resources for five years from 1999. His frequent visits and familiarity with the corridors of power helped him push the industry's case. In the next few years, there were several rounds of discussions between several arms of the government and the security industry. And finally, in 2005, over two decades after the seeds were sown, the Private Security Agencies (Regulation) Bill was taken up in Parliament. To push the matter, and wary of their file again getting stuck on government tables, a Joint Action Council of Security Industry (JACSI) was set up to liaison with the government, which was then headed by the Congress-led United Progressive Alliance (UPA) coalition. Interestingly, the opposition parties at the time were boycotting Parliament, and the bill was pushed through by the government. And it finally got the signature of President A.P.J. Abdul Kalam. 'By 2005, the government realized the need to regulate the security industry. Some of the critical sectors like banking were dependent on these security agencies for important parts of their operations,' says Sanjeev Paul. 'Also, there was a need for the industry to get formalized, and then be more organized, because the demand was there,' he adds.

Among its many regulations, the new act stipulated every agency must obtain a license before starting operations. Every year, there would be checks on its practices, including training of its manpower and the welfare of its employees. This was a big moment for an industry where there were many hole-in-the-wall operations, with little regulation in terms of employee benefits. Training was nearly absent, except for a few like SIS.

JACSI, interestingly, was converted into the Central Association of Private Security Industry, or CAPSI. And R.K. was its founder chairman. Today, CAPSI claims to represent 'the wider interests of 10 million guardsmen and women and 35 thousand private security agencies operating pan India'.

IISSM continued playing a pivotal role in the rollout of the new act, which took another four years to be implemented across the country. It was IISSM that helped prepare modules for training, pushed standardization of minimum wages and, later on, was instrumental in getting MBA institutes to include a module on the Indian security industry in their courses. Overall, the platforms R.K. helped establish continue to have a lasting impact on the industry. The SIS chairman was now also a well-recognized and widely accepted leader of the security industry.

R.K.'s leadership changed the way the industry was perceived. His relentless pursuit, ably supported by the other stakeholders, transformed the image of security company promoters. From chowkidar ke thekedars (contractors of guards), entreprenuers from the industry got their due as an established business that employed more than a crore people and generated revenues of over Rs 1 lakh crore. The mix of several industry associations and regulations gave the industry a formal recognition that was missing earlier.

By the turn of the century, R.K. was juggling two significant roles. SIS was expanding, training more, hiring more and opening more sites. Many of its earliest employees were now senior executives responsible for critical functions. But the company was still a founder-driven operation, requiring much of R.K's attention. At the same time, he was also spending an equal amount of time in public life. It was no secret. Since his childhood he was interested in issues political and social. Through SIS, which by 2000 had 5,000 employees, R.K. had already made a deep impact in society by providing employment in a state where jobs, other than government ones, were hard to come by.

Now, R.K's attention was on the political landscape. His association with RSS had continued even during the years he was busy building SIS. The rise of the Bharatiya Janata Party (BJP), the political wing of the RSS, in Bihar and nationally, also saw his involvement increasing in the party's activities. Given his reach with businessmen, policymakers and politicians, R.K. was an important person in the political landscape of Bihar. He may not have been the most visible of faces but his contribution was undeniably growing.

In the coming years, R.K. wanted to accordingly manage his time and resources. His natural inclination was to spend more time in the social and political spheres. Yet, he couldn't let SIS go rudderless. He needed someone who could lead the company even as he himself took a back seat. Of course, he would be on the board and wanted to be involved in every big decision that was to be made but he realized it was time for someone else to take over the day-to-day operation of the security company. The decision on who this was would be crucial. The world around was changing, and the Indian economy was beginning to attract attention. He needed someone who understood this and could lead SIS through such an eventful period.

There were also his children, Rituraj and Rivoli. After completing his schooling from the Doon School in Dehradun, Rituraj moved to the UK for higher studies. He seemed to have a liking for the banking industry. Likewise, Rivoli had completed schooling from Mussoorie International School. She was interested in hotel management and had decided to shift location to Switzerland to pursue her interest.

How could R.K. manage his own personal ambitions and at the same time ensure SIS would continue to grow as it had in the last twenty-five years, not to mention the generational change that was inevitable within the promoter family itself?

9

A GENERATIONAL CHANGE

Nine out of ten first generation entrepreneurs don't let go of their companies. It's obvious why. The company is their idea, a risk that they chose to take and then went on to build upon against all odds. To be fair, it should be theirs as long as they want. It's just that time never stops for anyone. It's best to be prepared, otherwise the very business they painstakingly made goes to pieces.

Indian corporate history is replete with examples of family businesses that broke after the first or second generation. The doom is especially stark once the business makes the transition from the second to third generation. The biggest of corporate names, right from Reliance Industries to branches of the Birla family and famous names like Mafatlal, Kirloskar, Modi and Singhania, have split bad blood in public. The impact nearly always is on the business, the very business that their first generation had built brick by brick. Those who have seen *Succession*, the popular TV series on a business family, would appreciate the various factors and interests that come into play when a family patriarch decides on his successors.

That's why a lot of focus in recent years has been on the importance of succession planning, ensuring the interests of the promoter family don't take priority over the interest of the company. More and more entrepreneurs are beginning to realize the importance of having a sound plan on leadership transition once they take a step back. Family constitutions have become a handy tool to set the guidelines and principles.

But that is succession in the conventional sense. What R.K. had in mind, and what he executed, was different. He was just fifty-two years old when he did so. Rarely do first generation entrepreneurs move away from their company at that age. By going against the trend and giving up control of his company, R.K. was forging a new path. The arrangement that he eventually decided upon was one of the most unique ones seen in an Indian company. Again, he didn't go by any rule book. Instead, he made a decision based on what SIS required at that moment. While this one decision set up SIS for the heights it would reach in the next twenty-five years, at that time, SIS was going through a bit of a crisis.

With R.K. wearing many hats within and outside the organization—in the larger industry—the management bandwidth at the company was spread thin. This was also the time when SIS was expanding in the east and in the north. This needed constant supply of cash, which wasn't there. What further complicated the situation was the loss of some marquee clients, including some of the Tata group companies and the contract from ITDC. There was a need to recoup these setbacks

It didn't help that G4S was growing as a rival. The aspirational MNC brand was setting new standards in the industry and clients were ready to shell out the money for the company. Its leadership was decisive and sharp and it grew aggressively. On the other hand, SIS was stagnating, unable to break out from a revenue range of Rs 18-20 crore.

Thus, there were multiple parts to R.K's succession plan. It was not just about a leadership change, but a move to transform the whole organization itself.

R.K. professionalized the management—including the top leadership—something that first time promoters hesitate to do. This was now a must for the business and its survival. Second, he timed the succession within the family perfectly. Again, many promoters keep it late. Often, the succession is forced through a legal route, or is not built on values. But R.K. got it correct.

There are two names that he brought to make this arrangement work: Uday Singh and Rituraj Sinha. One, a hardened corporate professional. The other, a youngster brimming with ideas. Few gave this a chance.

Keen to give more time to his public life, R.K. had looked around for a professional who could take on the responsibilities of running SIS after him. There were the retired army generals and IAS officers who had held top positions in the government. They had excellent experience in administration and had a sound knowledge of systems and processes. But could they handle a security business? Did they have enough industry knowledge or understanding? Without a business mentality, their focus on systems and processes would turn any company into another bureaucracy bereft of nimbleness and growth. No, he couldn't hand over SIS to someone like that.

There were professionals from the industry. Held top positions, worked overseas. But R.K. didn't know them well enough to trust them with his business. How much ever he searched and thought about the best candidate, his thoughts came back to one person, Uday Singh.

The two knew each other from their childhood. R.K. had four brothers. So did Uday Singh. Both studied in the same Patna High School. Singh was a couple of years older, and it was his younger brother Vinod Singh who had been friends with R.K. when they were children. As Ravindra Kishore went on the path of journalism and then entrepreneurship, he had kept track of Uday Singh's career as a corporate professional. Singh spent considerable time in companies such as the Metallurgical & Engineering Consultants (India) Limited (MECON), JSW Steel and Praxair. He was among the earliest in the country to gain expertise on ISO standards and was one of the leading advocates of standardization and total quality management systems (TQMS).

The two would meet whenever Singh was in Patna. After SIS branched out of its home state and spread out to the south, the two would meet periodically in Bengaluru, Singh's base. R.K. would be in the southern metro to visit one of the SIS branches. He enjoyed catching up with Singh. 'He was always a good friend. He was quite knowledgeable and a brilliant team leader and had considerable experience in the corporate world, and was part of industry organizations like the Confederation of Indian Industry. He was also into consultancy, especially regarding ISO standards,' says R.K.

In other words, Singh brought in the experience that Ravindra Kishore himself lacked. That's why R.K. admired Singh and understood the value that the professional brought to the table. He would often ask Singh to take a session for his senior executives. Singh would be unprepared and hesitant. 'What will I tell them?' he would ask. 'Tell them about management,' R.K. would respond. Singh enjoyed these classes. He could see R.K. was building a company with great culture. The employees reflected the same kind of zeal to learn and passion for the job as their founder.

It was sometime in 2000, after Singh had turned a consultant, that R.K. asked him for professional help. That was the time when the SIS founder was contemplating his future steps with regards to SIS and his own social and political commitments. 'You are a professional. You are a management consultant. Why don't you study SIS and tell me about the future prospects of the company and the industry?'

Singh accepted the assignment. There was little data on the industry. He took help from Arvind Prasad, who shared as much detail as was available. Singh studied SIS's account books and examined the competitive landscape. 'Tops Security was the biggest Indian security company in the country. It was being run by a second-generation entrepreneur. It had big clients in Mumbai and the movie industry,' says Singh. There was the international giant G4, which was expanding fast. The company had a definite advantage. As foreign investment grew in India, a lot of multinational companies were more comfortable hiring services from G4, which was also their partner in other countries. As India opened up, G4 was beginning to expand fast in local markets, especially in the cities. Singh studied their numbers. After crunching the numbers, Singh was ready to make his presentation to R.K.

The presentation was held in Bengaluru. R.K. had got his top team in town. He also asked Rituraj, who was studying in University of Leeds in the UK, to fly down. R.K. wanted the youngster to hear for himself how the family's business was placed and its prospects.

Singh talked about the industry, Tops, G4 and finally SIS's own space in the market. 'I talked about vision and SIS's relative position. I showed them that in the large fragmented security industry, SIS was a dot. And given the competition that was out there, unless SIS evolved with time, the dot will shrink while others like Tops will grow,' recounts Singh.

There was another aspect. R.K's own equity, or his personal brand value, was separate from SIS's. Given his leadership in the industry, R.K. was now a well-regarded entrepreneur. 'Mr Sinha's brand value was very high. He was running SIS, he had helped create platforms like IISSM. He gave training to others. He was considered the guru of security in India,' says Singh.

Singh's conclusion was straightforward. Going by current trends, R.K's brand value would grow. But not SIS's. It was a small operation (around Rs 18 crore in 2000). It was profitable but was always short of cash because of the nature of the business. SIS needed to grow.

R.K. heard Singh out. He couldn't agree more with his childhood friend. SIS now needed someone to guide it to the next phase of growth. It couldn't be a retired general or a bureaucrat. It had to be no one else but Uday Singh himself. He ticked all the boxes. Was a proven business leader. Was known to R.K. for years. Both grew up in similar circumstances and shared a similar culture. R.K. could trust him. Also, both gave equal importance to an organization's people focus and, service and growth orientation. In fact, these three—trust, people-centricity and the orientation—were the 'core values' of SIS.

R.K. did what he thought was the best thing to do. He formally asked Singh to take over the reins of SIS. Singh was taken aback. In all his years of corporate life, he hadn't come across an entrepreneur who was willing to hand over his entire business to a professional. The offer also made him nervous. Singh was new to the security industry. He was more comfortable in a manufacturing plant than in the security business. R.K. calmed his fears. 'You are not just a steel executive. You are a professional, a knowledgeable leader. You are right for any people-oriented business and you can run any business.'

R.K. was also matter of fact. 'I won't be able to match your CTC. But there is something else. I have known you since childhood. You care about the poor. SIS employs some of the poorest of the poor and by training them and enabling them to make a livelihood. By running SIS and growing it, you will get the opportunity to take care of the poor. That will be a bonus.'

Years later, looking back at this exchange with R.K., Singh would admit that the SIS founder had understood him well and given him the perfect reason to join the company. R.K. had struck a chord with Singh, again reflecting his ability to understand people.

What helped Singh in making up his mind was a tough decision awaiting him at his own workplace. The company had wanted him to move countries and take up a position on a more global level. It was prestigious but Singh wasn't keen to move out of India. Now, R.K.'s offer would give him a reason to stay back. But he was still not able to make up his mind. He confided in a close friend and mentor. 'What should I do?' he asked. The mentor, someone who has led steel companies in the past, said, 'The time has come for you to be a big man, albeit in a small company. You have a lot of passion, energy and knowledge. How long will you continue to run companies that are dictated from the US or elsewhere? You need to build a company.' At the same time, the mentor added, 'A lot depends on your trust level with the promoter.' Singh had no uncertainty about that. 'I have complete trust in Ravindra Kishore and he has complete trust in me.' That almost sealed the decision for Singh. But he had one more question to ask R.K.

Singh went to his friend. 'I have always wanted to excel in my work. And I want to be successful. I have my own plans and ideas of running a company. It shouldn't happen that you have another opinion or see things differently. I fear something like that happening. I will lose a friend and won't gain anything professionally.'

R.K. was pleased with Singh's forthrightness. 'The day you walk in SIS, I will walk out,' he said. R.K. went on to share his political ambitions and his plans to increase his involvement politically and socially. 'I will be focusing on a political career. You can focus on SIS.'

Uday Singh agreed. He joined SIS in 2002 as Executive Vice President. In making this happen, both R.K. and Singh had shown two great qualities that help build a sound professional relationship: communication and trust. The importance of the two can't be stressed enough when talking about a company's promoter and its professional leader. For the two childhood acquaintances turned friends and now professional colleagues, this is what would make all the difference in the coming years.

Now that R.K. had executed the first part of his succession plan, it was time for the second.

Rituraj has always liked to be organized. He would set a target and then work towards it. He joined Doon School from the seventh standard even as his parents and sister Rivoli moved base from Patna to Delhi. The school had a merit system that awarded students for excelling in studies, sports and extracurricular activities. Excellence in each field was awarded with a coveted blazer at the end of an academic session. Rituraj was good in all the three fields but not outstanding. Yet, he wanted to get those blazers and went about attaining them in a planned, structured way.

Rituraj represented the school in debates, was part of the expedition to scale Imja Tse in the Mt. Everest range in Nepal and also went to the US for the Round Square conference. He was a school prefect. By the end of the academic year, it was not a surprise that he bagged the blazer for excellence in academics called the Scholars blazer and extracurriculars (called Duke of Edinburgh Award), missing the third one—for games—just by one point.

Growing up, it was with the same focus and lucidity that Rituraj always knew what he wanted to pursue as a career. His earliest memories were of his father conducting recruitment of guards on the lawns of their Patna house. As R.K. was influenced by the conversations around him at home, Rituraj was equally exposed to what was happening around him and that gave him a 20k feet view on several issues—in the early years of SIS, R.K. was operating out of the family house. 'SIS was his first child. We were second and third!' Rivoli would quip half-jokingly. And as SIS grew, the family travelled together to different sites, to Garhwa and also to IISSM events.

'Dad used to organize the security industry conferences since 1991. These were mega conferences and hordes of foreigners used to come—Americans, Brits, Israelis—and it was like a big family party for three to four days. A lot of business was getting done but you were also getting to meet very successful people from not just India, but overseas. I think it was very helpful because you become at ease with business and subconsciously, I'm sure it has helped [in shaping me],' says Rituraj.

Things changed for a while when he moved to Leeds for higher studies. For the first time, he saw up close how a First World country, and its economy, functioned. The businessmen, professionals and overall corporate culture was markedly different from what he had seen back home. He was especially fascinated by the workings of the banking world, and investment banking in particular. Rituraj decided he wanted to get a taste of this world and see what was in store for him. After graduating from Leeds in 2001, he joined Halifax, a well-known British banking company.

Back home in India, R.K. was happy with his son's progress. He had let Rituraj decide for himself his career and future plans. If he wanted to check out the prospects in the banking world, so be it. Yet, unexpectedly, two things changed the course.

A few months into the banking industry, the stint wasn't going exactly as Rituraj had imagined. For starters, much of the young executive's time was spent being a spectator in meetings, sitting at the back of rooms and taking notes. He was away from the real action. 'It was going to take a lot of time before I worked up the ladder and managed to get a place right at the main table,' he realized. Often, his mind would go back to India and his father's security business.

Things were opening up in India. It was nearly a decade after the Liberalization reforms of the early 1990s. The country had emerged as one of the fastest growing emerging economies. There was a boom among IT companies like Tata Consultancy Services and Infosys. The auto sector, which till then mostly consisted of cars from Fiat Padmini and Ambassador and later Maruti Suzuki, now had Hyundai.

The South Korean carmaker's Santro was a big success. Overall, consumption—driven by a growing and increasingly affluent middle-class—was changing in nature and volume. Globally, the talk was of India becoming one of the biggest drivers of the world economy in the twenty-first century.

Then, out of nowhere, a catastrophic event changed how the world perceived the concept of security. On 11 September 2001, Osama Bin Laden's men crashed two commercial airplanes into the Twin Towers of the World Trade Center in New York, two more into the Pentagon and one into a field in Pennsylvania. The terrorist attack sent shockwaves around the world. Fearing an immediate US retaliation and its cascading impact globally, a sense of fear pervaded globally. Governments, companies, hotels, manufacturing units and even residential colonies scampered to increase their security. The concept of security suddenly changed, and it became a necessity.

Given the changes, Rituraj suddenly saw the opportunities in scaling a business that wasn't big but was built on sound foundations. He was a youngster brimming with ideas, willing to take risks and with a hunger to learn. In fact, his dissertation at the Leeds University Business School was on diversifying the security business and setting up a cash logistics vertical through a foreign partner. A growing India—financial services were taking off—looked like the right place to be for an ambitious young man. And then a conversation with his father was the final pull. 'You can come and join the company. I'm taking a back seat,' R.K. said. He explained the role of Uday Singh, his own ambitions beyond the family business and how, eventually, he hoped Rituraj would take over the reins completely.

There was something more. 'I realized that both of us had different perspectives. I studied in a municipal school; he is an alumnus of Doon. I don't have an MBA like him. So, it was best that father and son don't have a direct reporting relationship,' says R.K.

This was radical. Not only was R.K. stepping away by handing over the operational responsibilities to Uday Singh, he also didn't want a professional relationship with his son. 'Uday had come in as an executive vice president. When Rituraj joined in 2002, I asked Uday to become his mentor, because if I mentor, father–son relations will not go well. That relationship is different. It is not good for business. And mentoring and training are different. So, Uday did the mentoring,' says R.K.

In taking these two key decisions—giving way to Uday Singh and also giving him the responsibility of mentoring Rituraj—R.K. had managed to do something first-generation entrepreneurs rarely can. It needs loads of maturity to accept the company that you founded is now best served by a leader who can equip it well to grow in changing times. Yes, R.K. could have done this himself by staying on and hiring consultants to guide him. Or, even after bringing in Uday Singh, he could have continued to stay on in an operationally active capacity, which would have given him the authority to keep an eye on what was happening. But he chose not to.

Maybe he would have done that if he hadn't got someone like Uday Singh whom he could trust. If Uday Singh had turned down the offer to join SIS, R.K. would have had to find another person, and perhaps then the arrangement would have been different. The possibilities are many. Yet, this was a rare instance of a founder giving up control that comes from handling operations on a day-to-day basis. And by giving Uday Singh a free hand, R.K. had reposed his trust and confidence on the senior professional. It was a decisive change to shift gears from promoter owned and operated to promoter owned and professionally run enterprise.

It was similar with Rituraj. R.K. knew his son. Rituraj was bright, hard-working and willing to learn. But he was not ready to run a company. He didn't have the experience. And while Rituraj had grown up seeing SIS develop, he wasn't yet ready to lead the company. R.K., rightly so, didn't indulge his son. Rituraj didn't join the company as a director on the board or as a chief executive. In such a scenario, Uday Singh would have been reporting to Rituraj. Instead, R.K. ensured the hierarchy by tasking Uday Singh with the job of mentoring the youngster. Rituraj joined in a managerial capacity.

Identifying and understanding the nuances of this arrangement shows why this was a masterstroke, at least to begin with. It was equally important that this plan was successful. Historically, this is a delicate moment for any family-run business. A paper by *Harvard Business Review* says that a quarter of generational transitions fail due to the lack of a prepared heir. Transitions also fail when the father continues to retain control even after 'handing over' the business to the son. That's possible because most of the rank and file at the company—including the senior most leadership—is loyal to the founder and not the son or a new professional chief executive. Eventually, differences of opinion crop up and later manifest in bad blood spilling over into lawsuits. That's the worst outcome for the family and the business.

R.K. had made a decision. He hadn't read any Harvard research or taken advice from any management guru. Could this decision—led by his entrepreneurial instinct—prove to be wrong? Will the generational gap between Uday Singh and Rituraj be too much for them to strike a rapport and form a sound working relationship? Unsurprisingly, there was scepticism within the corridors of SIS. 'The plan with The Laptop [as Uday Singh was called in the initial days after he joined] won't last more than six months' was a prevailing view.

But there was no going back. R.K. had made the call.

10

THE MAKING OF THE DREAM TEAM

This was a crucial time for SIS. R.K. was gradually withdrawing from an operational role. Uday Singh, and then Rituraj, took their places but needed some time before they could meaningfully start making a difference at the company. It was here that the role of Arvind Prasad, someone who had been with the chairman since 1986, came to the fore.

Though Prasad first came in as a finance executive, he had quickly shown interest and aptitude for matters outside the financial realm. Right from accompanying R.K. on his long trips to meeting potential clients and then expanding the core security business, Prasad had played a pivotal role. His imprint, as mentioned earlier, was also seen in the training institute in Garhwa. Prasad was instrumental in introducing martial arts in the training program.

Over time, he had become a close aide and trusted confidant of R.K. Prasad was sharp and among the sharpest minds in the security industry. He understood the nuts and the bolts of a security business. An IT expert, Prasad was also instrumental in SIS creating its tech backbone. It was often to Prasad, that Uday Singh would turn to understand the security business and also get financial information.

"I worked initially with these two gentlemen, Arvind Prasad and Uday Singh. One (Prasad) was super high IQ, razor sharp, and the other had super high EQ (Singh). So it was amazing," says Rituraj.

Uday Singh's high emotional quotient was visible right from his initial days at SIS. What Uday Singh achieved in the first six to twelve months of his stint in SIS could well become a template for any new chief executive replacing a promoter at the top and having to navigate amidst long-time employees as a newcomer.

Uday Singh joined SIS in 2002. Immediately, he was on a sticky wicket. The company was small with a revenue of a little over Rs 20 crore. There was still never enough cash to pay for salaries, which were delayed by up to three months. If Singh was worried about his own pay, he didn't show it. Operationally the company had grown but it was still concentrated in the east and the north. Its sole presence in the south was in Bengaluru, and it was nearly absent in the west. The competition, on the other hand, was growing faster. Clearly, SIS needed to be more aggressive and grow faster than its peers to protect its market share. Growing the market share would be the next step.

Part of the reason for SIS's present state was the way it had operated till then. It was twenty-five years old. Over the years, SIS had become a centralised organization. Nearly every decision was taken at the head office. There would be constant communication between the units and branches on one side, and the head office in Patna. Every question, every report was mailed to the head office. Not the e-mail, but the physical mail. Taking decisions and giving instructions were the retired army men, bureaucrats and policemen. This was almost like SIS's own red tapism that was choking its growth.

There was also a lack of information or data. SIS didn't have an ERP to generate data. ERP, or enterprise resource planning, is a software that companies use to manage critical functions like the supply chain, sales and human resources. While branch managers were well-trained, having passed out from the Garhwa training centre, they didn't know enough about business concepts and financial ratios. They were trained for security operations and could manage and operate a team of guards but didn't understand revenue generation, pushing for sales or the importance of margins. They didn't have a measure of their manpower's efficiency. Without these metrics, the organization was operating blindly.

Despite these shortcomings, Singh was careful as he navigated the first few months in the new company. He didn't want to rub his colleagues the wrong way by being too critical. In fact, the first thing Singh did was to assure his new colleagues that he was not here in place of R.K. There was immense respect for the chairman; employees would often greet R.K. by touching his feet. Uday Singh wasn't there to challenge that loyalty. Secondly, he admitted, he didn't know the security industry and instead he wanted to learn from the employees. He was humble in his questions and listened to every answer to his many questions patiently and respectfully. Thirdly, and most importantly, he needed to show the organization results. Because nothing works like success.

In the first six months, Singh travelled across the country, visiting SIS's sites and branches and holding meetings with guards, branch managers and senior executives. 'I'm new to the industry. I need to learn and understand from you' was his refrain to his colleagues. He was attentive, listened to what they had to say and made notes. People, both senior and junior, appreciated the warmth in these conversations. 'There's something amazing about Mr Singh, something similar to Mr Sinha. When they meet a person for the first time, their first instinct is to trust you. The person in front of them was the most important person at that moment, and nothing else was. It was actually up to the other person to prove they are unworthy of Mr Singh's trust,' says Arvind Prasad. For a finance person like Prasad, this instinct to trust someone first up was an eye-opener. 'A finance person is just the opposite,' says Prasad, who would go on to work very closely with

Singh in the following years. That trust was critical for Singh. It put many of his colleagues at ease.

Yet there were challenges as it is with every organisation that is going through a reset. There is a tussle between the old-timers and the new entrants. Those who had spent years in SIS were used to a working culture, their appetite for growth varied differently with the new, fresh blood who were in a hurry to expand the business. There was also the visible change in the power centre. Patna was the head office. But now with Rituraj in Delhi and Uday Singh in Bengaluru, these became new centres of power and decision making. Original SIS was in Patna. But now these were the new SIS. All these factors led to a chasm. SIS's culture was tested.

'The onus was on me to prove my credibility and my intentions. This was critical for the integration. And also to bring about changes,' says Singh, who realized that as much as he was testing the organization, the people were also testing him. The effort made a difference. After six months, the same people who thought the new executive vice president won't be able to last realized the guy was here to stay. '*Yeh lambi race ka ghoda hain* (he is here for the long run)' was now the common refrain.

Review meetings with branch managers brought open the need for further training of the officers in the organization. Singh would ask about a branch's topline and the branch manager would think Singh was asking how many guards worked under him. '150 people' would be the answer. What is your plan for next month? 'I will add at least twenty-five more people' would be the response. Was the branch profitable, what were the costs, margins, how much was the attrition? These numbers were not known.

Singh was willing to train them. But were the people willing to learn? Here, Singh came across two sets of people. The first set were people who didn't know the basics but also didn't know that they do not know. Instead, they were of the belief that they knew enough.

Singh was clear he couldn't teach this set of people. Fortunately, 80 per cent were from the second set. They realized what they lacked and were willing to learn.

Singh now understood what needed to be done. But then, just as he got a footing in the business and was beginning to understand the steps needed to turn it around, a significant development occurred. That was the time, in early 2003, when R.K. gave him an additional responsibility. 'You will mentor Rituraj. A father cannot mentor a son. Rituraj will report to you.'

Rituraj returned from the UK, leaving the banking industry behind, and joined SIS as Vice President of business development. Singh was elevated to the post of Chief Executive Officer of SIS.

Rituraj, then twenty-three years old, was nearly as old as Singh's own son. Rituraj himself could see the difference in age and experience between them. But he had known Singh since childhood when the latter would visit his father, and the close relationship between the two families was there for all to see. Singh was like an extended family member. In return, Singh trusted his family. This was a big assurance for a youngster who was eager to learn and get on with the family business.

Rituraj found himself in a similar situation with nearly everyone in the senior team. Many of them had indulged him when he was small. '*Godimein khilaaen hain, ham tumko school le jaate th*e (We played with you when you were a baby and have dropped you to school)' is a line that he heard a lot in the initial days. Like Singh, Rituraj had to earn his place on his merit and not just because he was the founder's son. The respect and acceptance among the ranks would only come after that.

Early on, Singh and Rituraj agreed on a few basic tenets of their relationship. Singh knew that having heard and seen the operations grow since his childhood, SIS was in Rituraj's blood. He wasn't absolutely new to the business. He was young, had a lot of ideas and wasn't hesitant to take risks. He was inexperienced but Singh never treated him as a kid. The younger colleague, on the other hand, had respect for Singh's experience, wisdom and high emotional quotient. Singh was process and HR oriented. Rituraj absorbed and drew a lot of professional capabilities from Uday Singh.

The two agreed to disagree. If they had disagreed on a topic, the two would come back the next day and arrive at a logical conclusion. There was no ego at play. Their common interest was the development of SIS.

Rituraj wanted to try new things. Rather than being put off by the enthusiastic youngster, Singh encouraged him. Rituraj had the vision of a promoter, and his ability to take risks was akin to a first-generation entrepreneur. That was markedly different from the professional in Singh, who would hear Rituraj out and give his feedback, always leaving the final decision to Rituraj if he should take the idea ahead or not. A lot of business decisions that SIS took, including many of its eyebrow-raising acquisitions, followed this model.

'Looking back, I'm amazed how much space he gave me, a twenty-three-year-old. He was magnanimous. For all the experimentation I did, he was like a shield, a friend, philosopher, guide, shield around me, to help me every step of the way,' says Rituraj. 'Mr Singh never said his idea was better than my idea. He's like, "Okay, okay." You know, he was very clear that I'm the entrepreneur, he the professional. "So it's your idea, but it's my job to ensure that it's done right." I couldn't have been luckier.'

As Uday Singh and Rituraj eased into their roles, it quickly became apparent that the two, along with Arvind Prasad, formed a kind of a dream team. Prasad managed the operations of the east. He was the go-to man for anything on the security business and was instrumental in setting up systems, including ERP, in the company. Singh was based in Bengaluru and Rituraj in Delhi. While Singh took charge of the operations in the south and the west, Rituraj was responsible for the north. Rituraj was passionate about branding and marketing and had a penchant for sales. He would also network with banking professionals and took a keen interest in public relations. Singh, on the other hand, was a natural in training, setting up systems, taking care of capex and also coordinating with labour officers, critical to manage the security force.

The trust and understanding between thee three was critical to send a message down the ranks—they were a team and one couldn't be instigated against the other. 'It's okay if there is one person running the business. But here, we were more than one. So, it was important that we remained one,' says Singh.

R.K.'s role in making this team successful was critical. Though Rituraj was his son and part of the promoter family, he didn't feature on the board of SIS. Not yet. Singh was on it. It was a message for everyone in the company that even the founder's son would need to earn his spurs to get to the board. The chairman also didn't come in between the reporting relationship that Singh and Rituraj had.

Unknown to many and behind the scenes, there was one more person who helped seal this team: Rita Sinha. It was she who reassured Singh of his own part in the whole arrangement.

In the initial days, even though it was Singh and Rituraj who were handling operations, many old-time clients would still go to R.K. to sort things. It was almost habitual for them to approach the founder as it was R.K. who had been leading the organization for over two decades. It would come to R.K.'s notice that Rituraj had changed a client or the terms of the contract. Now the message would go from R.K. to Rituraj, but via Singh. That was so because, professionally, Rituraj was reporting to Singh and R.K. didn't want to disturb that structure by directly sending a note regarding work to Rituraj. In return, Rituraj would send a reply, but via Singh. At one point in time, Singh wondered if he had become a stumbling block for a father to have a direct communication with his son.

This disturbed Singh. He was a professional and now there was a seed of doubt and uncertainty around his role. If he was out of the equation, there would be direct communication between the two and this could also possibly take away any chance of miscommunication. In his career of over thirty years, Singh had come across and read about many father–son disagreements that had turned ugly. He didn't want to be a part of one or cause one. Unsure what to make of the situation, when the opportunity came, Singh confided in Rita. 'What do you think? Am I leading to confusion? Do you think it will be better if I move out?' he asked Rita.

'Don't even think about it,' was the swift response from Rita. 'You are the bridge between the father and the son. You are contributing to the cause,' she added firmly. That was a relief for Singh and put to rest his misgivings. Singh was assuredly now the go-to man for the Sinha family. He had no vested interest, but the interest of the company.

So, this was the dream team of SIS. Like the Test cricket team of India that once had Sachin Tendulkar, Virender Sehwag, Sourav Ganguly, Rahul Dravid and V.V.S. Laxman. Or the dream team of English football club Arsenal under manager Arsène Wenger. The cricket team with those premier batsmen recorded some of the most memorable wins in Indian cricket, the top being the comeback win over Australia at Kolkata's Eden Gardens. The Arsenal team under Wenger took the English Premier League crown for the 2004 season, undefeated.

In later years, two more crucial members would join this team—Devesh Desai and Dhiraj Singh. Together, they braved the resistance that they faced initially in bringing about the changes within the organization. There was a natural transition too, when many of the old-timers retired. The Group Management Committee was formed with Arvind Prasad, Uday Singh and Rituraj Desai and Dhiraj Singh would join it later. Now it was up to SIS's dream team to make things work.

11

THE BOOM YEARS

Right from the start, Uday Singh brought a sense of urgency into the organization. The goal was to fast track SIS to a growth phase. The key to that was to speed up each part of the operation, the most critical being decision-making. And what's the best way to do it? Through prompt response and clear communication.

As previously mentioned, in 2002 when he joined the company, Singh was a rare sight in the corridors carrying around a laptop. There were questions, probably some ridicule too. 'Manpower business computer/email par chalega ya ground par (the manpower business runs on the ground or in computer/email)?' was one of the questions. But within a year, nearly everyone in leadership positions were also working with laptops. Not everyone was amused. Many of these leaders weren't tech savvy. They hadn't used a laptop before this. In fact, many of them were just about getting used to handling a mobile phone. A laptop was intimidating. They weren't alone. At that time, India was just about adopting computers and similar gadgets as a way of life. Smartphones were not ubiquitous as they are now. Internet was still via dial-up connection.

The apprehensions made way for appreciation when they understood the ease that a laptop brought to communication. Singh himself showed the way by being prompt in replying to emails. That cut through a lot of layers of communication and saved time. 'It was a revelation,' says Narayan Lenka, Chief Operating Officer, Security Solutions, who would work closely with Uday Singh.

The change in thinking also came to travel. SIS employees were used to traveling constantly through the month, year in and year out. The senior executives and functional heads were constantly on the move. Much of the travel happened by train. 'But Mr Singh was the kind of person who used to take a decision after assessing the situation. For instance, how much time would it take to travel by train? How many productive hours would be wasted because of that? What would a flight ticket cost and how many hours of work would it save? What was the eventual cost or benefit to the company? If the answer was that the company benefited overall if the executive took the flight, he would ask them to do that,' says S.S. Ojha, President, Security Solutions. 'People started taking flights more often than the train. I would say that SIS employees started flying after 2003. This brought in another layer of enthusiasm in the team. It was a great motivator,' adds Ojha. The focus had shifted to productivity and saving time.

It also helped that Singh turned nearly every meeting into a training session, where he would teach his colleagues the basics of important financial metrics and management. They needed to go beyond only looking at the number of guards as a measure of business. To enable this, Singh and Rituraj mounted two specific initiatives that brought financial reporting systems and processes within SIS.

First was ERP, or enterprise resource planning. The software integrates data across functions such as finance, HR, manufacturing and the supply chain. This generates data that gives insight into the business—what's working and, most importantly, what's not. These are important tools to have when one needs efficient and assertive decision-making. Singh had been a long advocate of ERP, and now SIS was among the first Indian security companies to get it. Interestingly, incorporating the software led to another big milestone.

SIS engaged a software company to implement the ERP. The first step was to understand the requirements, study the system and make the software that would suit SIS's interests best. It so happened that the software company was taking much more time than had initially been agreed upon. They had a small team that sat in SIS offices to understand operations.

Arvind Prasad was instrumental in designing the ERP. There was no ready product that understood security business operations. Prasad explained the step-by-step process and in the process, SIS created the first 'custom made' ERP for the industry.

This exercise took over a year. Ironically, by exchanging information in meetings and conversations with the software company's team, SIS employees improved their own skills. When the software was finally ready, the company itself went bust. This was a big setback. Work, time and resources expended over an almost three-year period was at risk of going down the drain. Singh and Rituraj made the best of the situation. They convinced the software professionals who had spent considerable time in SIS offices and had developed the software to join the company. They agreed. And the ERP software was eventually launched as a SIS property.

'We didn't have an IT team before,' says Brajesh, the Chief Financial Officer at SIS. 'After this, however, we got an IT team.' This development, though it came after a setback, became an unlikely reason for SIS to develop self-reliance in its IT needs. Over the years, as we will see later, this IT team was instrumental in setting up more systems and processes. 'Today, if we need any software, our first preference is that we do it in-house because our requirements are very peculiar.'

With the ERP in place, it made things easier for Singh and Rituraj to implement the next big reform within SIS. They called it the Seven Finger Model.

In their zeal to accelerate SIS's growth, the biggest handicap the two senior executives faced was the lack of clarity on a branch's performance. Even as they were training their men, they still didn't know enough about their performance and if they were improving or not. They needed a scorecard that would measure the key performance indicators of a branch. And this scorecard would be checked every month as it was critical in tracking performance and making interventions when needed. The two hit upon the Seven Finger Model on a flight back to India after an international trip. And the model itself was charted out on a piece of napkin that Rituraj borrowed from the cabin crew!

They were flying back home after meeting top officials of Securitas AB, a major Swedish multinational security company. Rituraj and Singh met Thomas Berglund, the chief executive officer, and Hakan Winberg, the chief financial officer, to explore a possible deal with the Swedish company. This was the first of many conversations the four would have, which later led to important milestones for SIS. That is for later. For now, Singh and Rituraj were impressed by the way the multinational company functioned. Specifically, they were hooked by the Securitas Toolbox that was used by the company to measure the performance of its people.

It was exactly what SIS needed, something that can be used to measure what was working and what wasn't and could help them plan better—critical to increase their growth rate. Setting up a data-based management was now important. 'What to measure?' is an important question for any organization to answer. In fact, this defines how a business is set up and how it is run.

At the time, the Securitas Toolbox used a Six Finger Model. On that flight, brainstorming even as they cruised 30,000 feet above the ground, Singh and Rituraj came up with their own version—a Seven Finger Model. Hakan himself lists down the constituents of the Seven Finger Model in his book *Approximately Right: Aligning Your Numbers with Your Business*, which dedicates one chapter to the rise of SIS. The seven fingers are:

1. Revenue net change
2. Cost (direct and indirect)
3. Margin
4. Collections
5. New sales
6. Operations management. These were factors impacting customer satisfaction and retention
7. Manpower management, which reflected manpower quality and retention

The seven factors helped in multiple ways. First, it set a benchmark for measuring each aspect of the business. Each factor got a weightage as per the company's system, eventually allowing a comparative scoring out of 100. This meant that each branch's performance could be measured and compared to the other, and then ranked. Eventually, this helped SIS to benchmark itself against the competition, an important exercise if a company wanted to protect its market share and also increase it.

Over the years, Rituraj has passionately explained this model in his novel way. He takes a piece of paper and draws a sketch with four fingers on the top and three fingers on the bottom. The four on top represent new sales, costs, margins and collections. These are the result drivers. The bottom three are the input fingers that measure revenue management, operational performance and manpower management. These help measure performance. If the company does well on the drivers—generating new sales, delivering quality service that helps in client retention, taking care of its employees, reducing attrition and getting receivables on time—then the performance—growing the topline, reducing costs and thereby improving margins and generating more cash—will be better.

Effectively, each branch manager was now measured against these parameters. 'Am I selling better contracts? Am I losing fewer guards than I lost last month? Am I hiring the best people? Am I training them well enough? Am I keeping my customers happy? If you drive these input factors, the output, which is higher revenue, better margins and better collection rate, will follow,' Rituraj explained to Hakan.

It was in 2005 that the Seven Finger Model was first introduced to branch managers. Initially, it led to confusion and frustration. It was the first time they were coming across these concepts. But the ERP came to their aid. They learnt how to use the system to get their numbers. The impact was the most telling in that year's annual conference. While earlier, the managers often didn't have enough data on their performance and their plans for the next year to cite in their presentations, now they could. The numbers gave credence to their presentation and brought transparency to the whole discussion. Decisions taken for the next year were more realistic.

Most importantly, the model gave business managers a mirror to assess themselves rather than wait for a senior to visit them and show their gaps. This led to self-initiated performance improvement and a healthy competitive culture.

'Believe me, all the officers who had passed out of SIS's GTO programme, be it branch managers, operation managers, assistant managers, they all took to this new system and software like a fish takes to the pond,' says Uday Singh.

'All of them had great respect for the knowledge that was being shared with them. Now they had something to correlate it with, they could show their performance in numbers. This resulted in a transformation in them. The same ordinary people started giving extraordinary results. Just imagine, there is no wonder or amazement when an IIT graduate or an IIM degree holder does well. They are expected to. Here, we had ordinary people having the hunger to understand financial and performance parameters and using such tools to succeed in their work,' Singh explains the transformation unleashed by the systems and processes that were introduced.

Changes were seen and felt by all. 'Earlier, we would talk about plans. But we really didn't know what that actually meant. We had heard of the annual business plan and even thought we understood it correctly. But it was not so. We knew the words but not what they actually meant,' says Narayan Lenka. Encouraged by Singh, Lenka started making daily, weekly and monthly plans. Which client was he supposed to meet? Had he followed up on the collection from last week's visit? Where was he supposed to go for his next sales pitch?

'Till then, we would be reactive. If something happened, we would respond to it. But now, we were proactive. Now I knew what I needed to do every day, and what was the work for tomorrow,' says Lenka. 'We became systematic. Everyone now works with a plan,' adds Dinesh Gupta.

The Seven Finger Model became a sort of holy book for SIS. It changed the business culture of the company. Now, every month, there was a branch review meeting. In the next branch review meeting, the manager could check how many of the targets were met and, if some weren't, where things could be improved. Similarly, it became a norm to do the branch's sales review on the first Saturday of the month. Another day was fixed for operational review. 'Just like we had a family culture, now we had a business culture. This was SIS's way of doing things', says Lenka. Minutes of the meetings were taken and a plan of action, or POA, was decided upon till the next meeting.

The company also got better in crucial functions like compliance. 'Earlier, we weren't able to resolve all compliance issues on time as we didn't have the means to do it. That changed,' says Brajesh. The biggest measure of change in the company was when employees began getting their salaries on time, every month. 'I felt we have finally become an organization like any other big name, or like a multinational,' exclaims Brajesh.

If earlier Singh's question to the branch managers about their topline was answered with the number of guards they managed, things were different now. From being purely operational managers, they now were business managers. 'Everybody began to understand revenue, costs and margins. Now if you asked them how business was doing, they would say, my gross margin is fine but my collections need to improve. For a business plan, they would give a sales target, and not just about adding guards. From man management, they started doing business management,' says Singh.

Prakash Binjola explains the impact as a mindset change. Uday Singh taught him the basics of operating a laptop, how to use Excel and, eventually, how to create an ABP. "'If today you are at Rs 1 crore, then how will you reach Rs 5 crore? How will you make it every month?" Singh would ask us. The beauty of this training was that he himself never set the targets. Instead, he would ask us. That gave us a sense of ownership.' After this, Binjola would tell Uday Singh what kind of resources—an area office, a sales manager—that he needed to meet the Rs 5 crore target. 'It was us who actually owned the business, that's what he inculcated in our brains. We became a different kind of leader for SIS.' To further train these senior officers, Uday Singh and Rituraj sent them for formal MBA courses. 'We were ordinary people but he got an extraordinary result from us at that time. Then there was not one Uday Singh working. It was like thirty, forty Uday Singhs were working in different branches. As branch heads got empowered and educated and ambitious targets were set, there was a sense of healthy competition between them. There was a huge change in the mindset,' says Binjola.

The western market was another focus area for Singh. SIS had a presence in Pune, where Narayan Lenka was heading a unit in a paper mill. Singh and Rituraj were keen to start off in Mumbai but it wasn't easy. Lenka, who was given the responsibility to build the business in the commercial capital, brought in candidates to be interviewed by Singh. But none were selected. 'We finally got a retired senior army officer, and slowly we built the team,' says Lenka. The first office came up in Santa Cruz. The big moment came when two iconic buildings of the city, the Oberoi and Trident hotels on Marine Drive, overhauled their security arrangements after the 2008 terrorist attacks. The brazenness of the attack had left the country shocked. Many died, including in the two hotels. When the two hotels went for a change in their security agency, SIS bagged the contracts. They replaced a multinational security company. 'We had slept on the benches of Marine Drive in the nights as we prepared for deployment in the two hotels,' recalls Lenka.

The contract proved to be a game-changer and SIS swiftly expanded in the city and its suburbs, including Thane. From Mumbai, SIS expanded to Nagpur and other cities in Maharashtra. The next big stop was Gujarat.

To cater to changing needs with expanding operations, Singh made another important intervention. Instead of depending solely on the Garhwa centre, he pushed for training to be more localized and customized to the requirements of the local client. This reduced the overall training period and, over time, some trainees earned their spurs after a month's training. In turn, the time taken for a trainee's deployment at a customer's site was also cut short, making SIS nimbler to meet customers' needs.

The standardization of service was accompanied by 'locationlisation' of SIS's presence and its operations. The company was not just making its presence felt in the four parts of the country, but going deeper. It expanded across regions, states and cities, and further into industrial pockets.

SIS's scale spectacularly grew. The focus on performance and its measurement set off a chain reaction. Perhaps this change is better termed the McDonaldization of SIS. The word 'McDonaldization' was coined by sociologist George Ritzer, who used it to describe the process wherein a society—here, a company—took on the features of a fast-food chain like McDonald's. These fast-food chains are known for standardizing practices and services, controlling costs, making operations efficient and, most importantly, bringing predictability to service. A person who loves a McDonald's burger and its French fries is assured of the same product—with its buns, patties and veggies in the same shape, colour and taste!—whenever he enters a McDonald's outlet, be it in the lanes of New York or the malls of Noida.

These features helped the organization to scale up its operations. The retail chain, founded in 1940 by the McDonald brothers, Richard and Maurice, grew to become the biggest restaurant chain in the world. It is today present in more than 100 countries, where it has over 36,000 outlets and serves around 63 million customers daily. Those are mind-boggling numbers.

In the security industry, surely, G4S could well have boasted of a system and process that were superior to SIS's. Sure enough, it grew to be the biggest security provider in India. And, for a while, SIS remained the second largest. But it had already grown at a pace unheard of so far in the industry. The mix of software, training, empowerment and an enabling atmosphere unleashed 'animal spirits' with the organization. From just fourteen branches in 2003, when Rituraj joined Uday Singh at the company, SIS breached the thirty mark by 2007. In other words, the company had added as many branches in four years as it had done in the previous twenty-five years! The Indian security industry had never seen an expansion this rapid. The topline too changed. From Rs 28 crore in 2003, the revenue hit Rs 100 crore in 2007. The employee count, which was 8,400 in 2003, jumped to 14,500 in 2007. By 2010, SIS would have a topline of Rs 1,449 crore and 37,759 employees working across 73 branches. Uday Singh points out SIS grew at a compound annual growth rate (CAGR) of 45 per cent in the ten years since 2002.

'It was by sheer ambition and the opportunity because we were an east India, north India type company and we realized that the right way to grow this business is to do it profit centre by profit centre,' says Rituraj. 'With standardization and software intervention, we designed an extremely replicable model which answers the questions: how will you recruit, how will you train, how will you sell, how will you operate? So, a very flat organization, no hierarchy. We tried to design a branch like a company. So, the branch should have a CEO equivalent, empowered fully. Then, for him to do accounts, instead of a CFO, he has a branch accountant. You also have a recruitment officer, you have a training officer, you have one sales manager. In our heads we were saying that, okay, in every city we are competing with the local colonel sahib, who is the owner cum CEO. So, we create small companies or profit centres and you embed them across the country and you truly become a national operator.'

With the company showing some speed in scaling up and with Uday Singh's stable hand driving the operations, it was time for Rituraj to unleash the kind of entrepreneurial energy that sometimes pivots a company to a completely different level. Sometimes, it may not work out. And that's the reason why every senior in SIS management wasn't exactly amused to hear what the young second-generation entrepreneur had in mind. For sure, some of his ideas seemed like a natural extension of SIS's operations. Others were unheard of at SIS. Few in the Indian or global security industry had dared to attempt something similar. Nearly everyone at SIS were apprehensive. For Rituraj himself, failure came before success. After all, in that moment, SIS had too little money to think big.

12

A FAILURE AND A WIN

A basic requirement for any business looking to grow is capital. It's probably not as acute a need felt by a security business, which is inherently asset-light. It doesn't need huge amounts of investment to start off. But this is also a problem. It generates very little cash, not enough to expand operations. This problem is especially bigger when the promoter of such a company wants to grow fast.

A security business—just like any other service business—is working capital intensive. Every contract needs two to three months of working capital support. In other words, the more you grow, the higher is the need for working capital.

It didn't take much time for Rituraj to understand this. Lack of capital was beginning to be a major block in his endeavour to scale the business. Taking SIS to new cities, opening up branches, investing in technology and fleet and, finally, employees' salaries all required capital. The company was running dry on capital.

But that didn't deter the enterprising young man in his mid-20s. Nearly every second week, he would take a flight from Delhi to Mumbai and go knocking on the doors of bankers and investors like private equity players and high net-worth individuals. It wasn't easy.

Many meetings got cancelled before he reached the location, some right at the door. If a meeting was scheduled for thirty minutes, it would get over in fifteen. Others ended before tea arrived.

The problem? If SIS reached out to banks to raise debt, the lenders wanted assets as collateral that SIS, being an asset-light company, and its promoters didn't have. Private equity players were willing to invest, but demanded higher equity in SIS. These were the days before the startup ecosystem gained strength in India and young entrepreneurs didn't have to sweat much to raise growth capital. Today, an entrepreneur with a bright idea or a good product is spoilt for choices. That was not the case then.

It was around this time in 2005 that Rituraj accompanied Uday to the US for an ASIS conference where they sought out Thomas Berglund and Hakan Winberg of Securitas, as previously mentioned. In their meeting, Rituraj laid down the history of SIS, their previous accomplishments and his grand plans for the business. Would Securitas be interested in partnering with SIS?

Partnership? Here was a company from India that hadn't touched Rs 100 crore in revenues was asking Securitas, a $12 billion global market leader, to partner with it in a market the Swedish company had yet to make its presence felt. Berglund and Winberg weren't sure but they were intrigued. 'What kind of partnership do you have in mind?' Berglund asked. Rituraj promised to get back with a proper plan.

It wasn't that Berglund hadn't thought about the Indian market. Securitas had a dense presence in Europe. Later, it expanded to the US. Asia was the next emerging market and, given India's size, there seemed to be potential. In subsequent meetings with R.K, Uday Singh and Rituraj, he got to know more about the company. He especially liked the family culture that R.K. had instilled in SIS. 'I shared the same core values. R.K. had started a company with the objective to give employment. He showed foresight in starting the training school. And the business itself stood on sound principles ... I may be a Christian, R.K. Sinha a Hindu. But we shared the same values,' says Berglund.

As their interest grew, Winberg flew to India and even visited the training centre in Garhwa. It was something that he hadn't seen anywhere else. The two senior Securitas professionals were also impressed with the mix of management at SIS. R.K. had set the foundation. In Uday Singh there was a sound professional who was a family confidant, and the company had made some concrete progress under him. And there was Rituraj, the young, energetic second-generation entrepreneur with an ambitious vision and hundreds of ideas. 'It was like the Holy Trinity. The Father, the Son and the Holy Spirit!' says Winberg.

A presence in India also made business sense. The security business had matured in Europe and the US. But it was set to explode in India. They also saw promise in Rituraj and Uday Singh's plans. 'We will bring Securitas to India and, along with it, we will get into several businesses including security, cash management and electronic security. We will build the Securitas portfolio to India,' Rituraj promised.

The two sides agreed. In August 2005, R.K., Uday Singh and Rituraj travelled to Stockholm to sign the papers. Also accompanying them was Randhir Kochhar, a consultant from Ernst & Young who was advising them on the deal. The offer was this—Securitas would acquire a 51 per cent stake in SIS, with an option to increase it to a full ownership within ten years. It was a big moment for R.K. and Rituraj. They were going to divest their equity and control. R.K. was finally getting a value for twenty five years of work in the form of liquidity. It's unusual for promoters to get an opportunity like this. Here, he, Rituraj and the rest of the family had the opportunity to cash out and build financial security. One never knew how the security industry was going to pan out and here they had an offer from the world's largest company in the sector. After the two sides signed the term sheet, Berglund hosted his new partners on a river cruise. The lunch was quintessentially European, the landscape of Stockholm as beautiful as it could get.

But something was amiss. Rituraj noticed his father, a self-confessed foodie, had barely touched his food. Back in the hotel, he went to his father's room. R.K. was getting his sugar levels checked. 'It was very high. He didn't utter a word. He was smiling as always but the pain of the very thought of selling SIS was evident,' says Rituraj. That troubled him. On the way back to India, and in his office in Delhi, Rituraj thought over the deal. R.K. hadn't said a word even though they were almost selling the company. Maybe because the whole thing—the deal to sell to Securitas—was Rituraj's idea and now his father didn't want to stop him.

Rituraj changed his mind. He was not going to sell SIS. Not 51 per cent of it, not 49 per cent. He shared this with Uday Singh, and Kochhar of EY. 'Have you gone out of your mind?' 'You will never get this opportunity again.' 'The commercial terms are very attractive, you won't get a similar offer.' 'You will realize it's a mistake after you have missed the deal.' All around him, people pushed him to reconsider. Rituraj didn't care. 'Something inside me told me not to sell.' But then after having pursued them for more than a year, met them several times and having signed along the dotted lines, how could he tell Berglund and Winberg that he had changed his mind? They could even sue him! Fortunately for him, an unexpected development in Sweden opened a door for him.

Securitas underwent a leadership change in March 2006. Berglund stepped down and gave way to his successor, Alf Goransson. Not much later, Winberg also stepped down. In the very first week of assuming office, Goransson flew down to Delhi to review the deal that his predecessor had signed with SIS. He met R.K., Rituraj and Uday Singh in SIS's Delhi office. 'I don't agree to this deal that Berglund has offered you,' the new Securitas CEO declared. 'We can't give you ten years to sell the remaining 49 per cent. We can give only three years.' That was music to Rituraj's ears. He got up, put his hand out and said, 'Thank you, Alf, but that is not happening.' And that was the end of the Securitas deal. If that had gone ahead, the SIS we see today wouldn't have existed.

Rituraj may have got Securitas off his back but he still had the problem of capital to solve. SIS needed financing. As it turned out, that was not the end of the whole episode. Alf Goransson may have thought that the offer to SIS had been too high. But Berglund and Winberg were sure about their assessment of SIS and its leadership. 'It's tough to negotiate with Indians!' Berglund exclaims jokingly. On a more serious note, adds, 'Maybe we extended by a bit. But that is okay. It really doesn't matter that it is a little bit too expensive right now. Because by next year, if the company has grown by 40 per cent, then it will be cheap, isn't that so? So, why should you argue instead of just going ahead with a company that is slated to grow exponentially?'

Berglund and Winberg put their money where their mouth was. The two former colleagues and friends decided to buy 5 per cent of SIS with their own money. R.K., Rituraj and Uday Singh were delighted. Another European trip beckoned, this time to London, where Berglund and Winberg were based. The two sides signed the deal. This time, no one had a second thought. 'That was the first non-promoter investment in SIS. The ex-chief executive officer and ex-chief financial officer of the world's largest security company had invested in us and backed us. More than the money, this was great validation for us,' says Rituraj.

To Rituraj's surprise, this was not the end of the whole episode either. After advising SIS in the deal, Kochhar had moved on from EY and joined D.E. Shaw, one the world's largest hedge funds. A few months after Berglund and Winberg's investment, Rituraj got a call from Kochhar. 'Where are you?' Kochhar asked. 'In office at Nehru

Place,' came Rituraj's reply. 'I'm coming towards Nehru Place and thought of catching up with you. If you could arrange a sandwich, we could have lunch together.' Rituraj asked Kochhar to come over.

In the office, the two exchanged pleasantries. Kochhar informed Rituraj he had moved on from EY and had joined D.E. Shaw. He went on to describe the New York-based global investment company that has over $65 billion in assets. Rituraj was happy for Kochhar. And then, as Kochhar took one bite of the sandwich, he took a sheet out of his bag. 'I have a term sheet for you. I want D.E. Shaw to invest in you,' he said. Rituraj was taken aback but also elated. This was to be SIS's first investment from a private equity firm. There were good reasons to be surprised by the offer too.

D.E. Shaw typically invested a few hundreds of million dollars in a company. In fact, it had just put in about $400 million in DLF, India's largest real estate company. SIS's size itself wasn't more than Rs 100 crore. But Kochhar, having worked with R.K., Rituraj and Uday Singh closely on the Securitas deal, liked what he saw. 'Uday Singh was the bridge between the management, the professional side and the promoter side because I think he shared a relationship with the promoter family which was beyond what a typical professional had. At the same time, he ran the company like a professional. So, I think his being there also was a very strong influence behind why the company was run in a very good, structured, professional manner right from the get-go because, you know, there was someone who came in with a fairly professional background into a company of this size,' says Kochhar. The D.E. Shaw senior executive also appreciated the maturity that Singh brought to the table and as an able advisor and supporter of Rituraj.

'And then there was Rituraj who was, you know, very strong in terms of vision, in terms of looking at what the growth opportunity could be, of thinking really big.'

While it was Kocchhar's conviction that convinced the D.E. Shaw team to go ahead with the investment, the firm did study the industry thoroughly. They studied the market and even met a few of SIS rivals to understand the opportunity and also to explore if there was a better bet than SIS. In fact, along with SIS, D.E. Shaw explored the possibility of a deal with another unnamed security company. It was probably Kochhar's experience and time spent with SIS and its top leadership that swayed the deal SIS's way and convinced D.E. Shaw, even though it was not in the business to write small cheques. 'The amount was not large. Yet, the investment committee in the US supported us. And said, "What's the worst. We would lose $4 million? That's not the end of the world."' It surely wasn't the end of the world for a fund that had the comfort of $70 billion backing it. Once the deal was done, Kochhar got a seat on the board of SIS as the D.E. Shaw representative. For Rituraj and Uday Singh, however, that $5 million, coming soon after the investment from Berglund and Winberg, was the fuel that they had been desperately seeking to power their expansion plans.

This was the second deal in quick succession for Rituraj. And he had made a mark as a dealmaker and negotiator. The comment Berglund had made—'Indians are tough to negotiate with'—was probably meant for Rituraj. Kochhar would agree. Even though it was a small investment in a small company, Rituraj managed to negotiate and include a very interesting clause in the agreement. A structure was built into the deal. As per the clause, the investor had to share a part of the upside beyond a threshold return. In other words, if D.E. Shaw was making, say, more than seven times a return on its investment at the time of its exit, that upside would be shared with SIS. Rituraj insisted on the clause, and D.E. Shaw relented. It was not as if the fund was expecting to make ten times its investment in SIS. There was no harm in keeping a threshold. 'I'd say, hats off to the foresight and acumen which Rituraj showed here,' says Kochhar.

Four years later, when D.E. Shaw did exit SIS, it shared the spoils with SIS.

Having D.E. Shaw by his side was a big boost for Rituraj. Because, as far as he was concerned, he wasn't done with deal-making. This was just the start. With capital in hand and a world-renowned hedge fund as an investor and member of the SIS board, Rituraj was encouraged to broaden his horizons.

13

A STUDY IN DEAL-MAKING

2007 was a significant year for Indian business. They had never been busier buying and selling assets. As per a report in *The Economic Times*, Indian companies announced deals worth $70 billion in 2007, up 150% from 2006! It was also the first time the number of deals crossed the 1,000-mark in a calendar year. Some of the biggest deals included Tata Steel buying Corus, Hindalco's acquisition of Novelis and Vodafone's takeover of Hutch Essar. In each of these, the buyer either got access to a new market or added a new product.

A little over $19 billion of the total deal value of $70 billion came in the form of investments from private equity firms. That was a new high. In 2006, such investments stood at $7.8 billion.

The year held a similar importance for SIS. It became the first company from the security service industry to raise fund from a private equity firm. D.E. Shaw, the American investment major. Six years later, there would be a second such fund raise with C.X. Partners—again a first for the industry.

Apart from these PE deals, SIS formed three joint ventures and made 14 acquisitions in India and overseas. All in a fifteen-year span. That's a remarkable number for any company, even more for an entity from the security industry. It was under Uday Singh and Rituraj that the company identified M&A as a strategy to grow and expand its business. The two PE investments helped raise funds for these deals. There were two big motives:

1. Grow market share
2. Diversify & specialize in new verticals

While Rituraj and Uday Singh drove the M&A strategy in the initial years, they were joined by SIS's legal counsel Mahesh Deviah and chief financial officer Devesh Desai. This was the group that brought in SIS's first wins in M&A. Later, after 2015, Rituraj would be joined by Dhiraj, Vamshidhar Guthikonda, President, M&A and R.S. Murali Krishna, President, SIS International.

SIS also had a high success rate in its M&A. Thirteen of its fourteen deals were successful. That's a success percentage of 92%, a remarkable performance when globally up to 90% of M&A fail to deliver along their objectives, as per a study by Harvard Business Review. What was behind this success? It is down to how SIS approached a M&A before and post a deal. In the process, SIS developed its own model, or strategy, for doing a deal.

First off, how did Rituraj himself go about looking for deals? Guthikonda, who joined SIS as Head of M&A and Investor Relations, explains this well. 'The question to ask was "What were we looking for?" Once we identified that it was growth that we wanted, the next question was "What is our strategy?" For instance, if it was to grow in facility management, the task was to identify the geography. Next, did Rituraj want to do this on his own? If not, then you probably need to look out to buy someone or get into a joint venture. Once you identify these, then we send the feelers to banks. Sometimes, the bankers themselves came to us with leads.'

To get that clarity, Rituraj would often bring in SIS's legal counsel Mahesh Deviah. He is a partner at the Bengaluru-based law firm MD&T Partners. 'There is this process that Rituraj and I have followed all these years. Before deciding on each transaction, we would spend an hour discussing the things we are looking for in a deal.' Rituraj would further point out the two or three things bothering him that he wanted Deviah's help to protect SIS. 'That's a big difference he brings to the table. He knows exactly what he wants from which acquisition. The clarity of thought of what he wants to achieve from the investment, and the understanding of what can go wrong and thus building safeguards into the agreement, is what sets him apart,' says Deviah.

Rituraj also built a reputation of being a tough negotiator. The clauses he sought to be put in deals, ring-fencing SIS's interests were priorities that he didn't budge from. At the same time, Rituraj ensured it was a fair affair. 'He was always respectful. The intent was to engage meaningfully,' says Vivek Chhachhi, Partner, C.X. Partners. That's why Rituraj was tough but not an aggressive negotiator. It was his conviction to also protect the family's equity. He explains: 'What I inherited is shareholding, 100 per cent ownership. There was no capital to be found outside SIS because there wasn't another larger group company. So, who is going to fund you? There was no capital, and the only way to get capital was to dilute equity. I always believe that equity is your heirloom or your family silver. I have always felt that I should pass down as much as I can without compromising the growth objectives of the business. So, with all my private equity deals, I had to basically defend dilution. My intent was only to protect.'

It was thus also important to understand the nature of the promoter he was dealing with. 'You buy from two types of owners. One is a classic multinational or private equity owner. And the second is the promoter. When you buy from a multinational or from private equity, that business is already being run by a set of professionals.

The impact of one individual or few individuals on the business is not there. There's a CEO or a country manager, but there's no one "owner-owner". So we felt that buying 100 per cent is easy because, you know, you buy a business, it's already professionally managed. It's all audited by one of the big auditors. The customers work with the business and not with individuals. Employees work for the company and not for, you know, any one person who they are loyal to,' he says.

That's not the case with a promoter-driven company. A promoter is a big influence in the business. Clients share a personal relationship with them. Employees are loyal to them. Not to forget the risk. Indian promoters often use companies as their personal piggy banks. There is little control on financials.

So, if you were buying a promoter-driven company, you need to get the promoter on your side instead of pushing him out, as is often the case. There is an example in the facility management industry itself, that of an American multinational taking over an Indian regional heavyweight. The previous Indian promoter was edged out. Rituraj, on the other hand, wanted to retain the promoter to ensure the growth of the acquired company didn't suffer after the acquisition. By retaining the promoter, Rituraj was making sure he was indeed making a good buy. That's because promoters tend to always oversell their companies to improve valuation, giving a very optimistic growth outlook. A higher valuation would make their exit all the more profitable. But how does the new owner make sure this was not just hot air?

To cover that, Rituraj made 'staggered acquisition' an important plank of SIS's M&A strategy. This ensured that the interests of the existing as well as the incoming promoter was secure. It also took care of the most contentious issue in a deal, the company valuation. The existing promoter will oversell, while the incoming one will want to pay as little as possible. 'Then came the idea, okay. We want a significant majority stake but the money I'm paying, you treat it as an advance to grow the company. You are the best man to run the business. All the customers are loyal to you, all the employees are loyal to you. Why don't you grow the business? Use our technology, use our money, use whatever we can give, use that, you grow the business for the next three, five years. Then SIS buys the remaining stake basis latest results allowing existing promoters to make money in the final tranche based on hopefully a significantly larger business,' explains Rituraj.

In other words, if the promoter stays back and leads the company to better numbers than the set target, he gets a share of the upside. If the company doesn't deliver as per his claims and expectations, the buyer gets a higher equity stake for the same amount of money he earlier paid. 'The idea was to align the promoter to us rather than to make him a competitor the next day. Plus, it gives a lot of comfort to the employees and customers of the business,' explains Rituraj.

Rituraj also made it a habit not to buy a company outright. This was another way to minimize risk. 'We never bought out companies fully. There's always 30–40 per cent of the stake which we bought out two or three years later. This gave us the time with the existing promoter to discover something about the company that we missed earlier. That would help us in negotiating better when the time came to buy the rest of the stake,' says Guthikonda. Over the years, what stood out for Guthikonda was 'Rituraj's ability to see through what is important in a deal, what is not, what we should focus on and how much we can negotiate.'

This (M&A) structure served Rituraj well. It helped SIS negotiate hard and protect its interests, and money, in the many deals that were made. Second, SIS also got precious talent in the form of promoters. There are at least two major acquisitions where the promoters agreed to stay back and continue to run the very same businesses that they founded, now under the SIS umbrella. This was a rare occurrence for any M&A deal irrespective of the sector or market.

In all, the model that Rituraj developed over the years helped SIS grow from one deal to the other. In all, the company would go on to make fourteen deals in fifteen years. For each deal, there were numerous others that didn't see the light of the day. That's the nature of deal-making. The ones that materialized had a high degree of success. But there was one acquisition that didn't pan out as Rituraj had hoped. This is despite the high degree of protection that he brought in every deal. Even then, getting thirteen out of fourteen is not a bad report card by any means. Even the one that initially fell flat has now been rescued. We will get into it in the upcoming pages.

Apart from the many acquisitions that Rituraj has done under SIS, equally astonishing is the number of multinational companies that he has managed to convince to partner with SIS and set up shop in India. Both of the new verticals—cash logistics and facility management—had partners who were Fortune 500 companies, had a global presence and came with high brand equity. What did these companies see in Rituraj or SIS? They saw the pluck and vision in him, the solid foundation laid by R.K. in SIS's formative years and the stupendous growth of the guarding business that had given the company an immense geographical presence. This convinced them of SIS's understanding of the Indian market.

Cash logistics and facility management seemed like a natural extension of the guarding business. Just like in guarding and security, cash logistics and facility management also needed a lot of manpower. It was also possible that a security client may need a vendor for keepings its offices and industrial premises clean and organized. Similarly, the same client may also need help moving its cash to the bank.

The reasoning is logical. But some of the biggest security companies in the world had resisted the temptation to do something similar. That included Securitas. Hakan Winberg, who took a stake in SIS along with colleague Thomas Berglund, says each of these businesses—guarding, cash management and facility management—is a specialized one. Despite the seemingly similar attributes, they are different from each other. For this reason, they also need separate sets of skills and expertise to be managed. 'Cash logistics is different because the requirements of a guard are not the same as it is in a guarding business. A cash logistics business—because it's handling a highly sensitive and valued product—also needs more controls,' he says.

Even in India, few such companies have dared to flirt with the other businesses. A cash logistics company hasn't set up a guarding business or a facility management provider hasn't branched out to cash logistics. Given this context, some may have assumed Rituraj and the SIS leadership were taking an undue risk in diversifying beyond their core security business. After all, the Australia deal itself was a reset for the organisation. There was a lot of debt too—up to nearly six times SIS's EBITDA. And then the diversification put SIS at risk of spreading itself too thin, capital and management bandwidth-wise.

It's a fundamental question that many companies and entrepreneurs face even as they strive to expand their operations and grow their companies. Did the Sajjan Jindal-led JSW Group need to get into electric vehicles (it has a joint venture with China's SAIC to sell MG Motor vehicles in India) which is inherently a different business from its core steel-making operations? Some diversifications have been spectacular failures. The biggest and most high profile of them probably was that of the United Breweries Group—led by Vijay Mallya—venturing into aviation. Despite its popularity, Kingfisher Airlines lasted for only seven years. It went bankrupt, also taking down Mallya's otherwise hugely successful liquor business. Mallya himself is now in the UK, juggling multiple legal cases which have kept him away from his home country.

Wasn't Rituraj taking an undue risk?

The SIS scion has a different take. 'I have diversified but I also have specialized. Each business is run separately. They have an independent team, a clear mandate, are a separate legal entity and cashflow. Just that they are under the SIS umbrella. At SIS, we have always been aspirational. It's in our DNA. Like they say, *chaadar ke hisaab se payr nahin phailaana hain, payr chaadar ke bahar nikle toh chaadar ko bada karna hain* (It was not about keeping our legs within the sheet, but to make that sheet bigger when the feet outgrow it),' says Rituraj. Adds Dhiraj Singh, SIS's current CEO: 'Our approach is that each business is independent. We bring the right leaders.'

The first joint venture was in cash management. But this didn't take place before some unforgiving years. For that matter, even after a joint venture partner came in, it was not smooth sailing for SIS's first diversification.

14

THE AUDACIOUS DEAL

Entrepreneurs are tuned to take risks. The risk could be anything, a new product or a new market. And then there are entrepreneurs who risk it all, sometimes to survive or to grow. Frederick Wallace Smith, the founder of the world's largest transportation company FedEx, headed to Las Vegas with the last $5,000 he had to raise cash after a business loan got turned down. He won nearly $30,000 gambling and this was enough to cover a gas bill and keep FedEx going for a while longer. When Elon Musk bet his whole fortune from PayPal on Tesla and SpaceX, he nearly went broke but eventually emerged as the world's richest man.

In India, Harsh Mariwala took the risk of convincing his relatives to divide the family business so that he could venture out and create Marico, which later became one of the biggest fast-moving consumer goods companies in India. In 2006, Lakshmi Mittal staked it all and risked making many enemies when his Mittal Steel mounted a takeover attempt of the bigger Arcelor. A year later, Tata Sons chairman Ratan Tata led Tata Steel to buy Corus, a company five times its size, for $13 billion. It remains the biggest acquisition ever done by an Indian company.

These deals made big headlines. These didn't escape Rituraj's eyes. SIS was growing, had become 'slightly successful', as he himself says, after outpacing its peers. There was a positive sentiment around the company. He wanted to do more, something that would pivot SIS's journey. With this thought in the back of his mind, a news development caught his eye. United Technologies Corporation (UTC), an American conglomerate that was present in several sectors including aviation, engineering and industrial products, was selling Chubb, a security provider. UTC had bought Chubb Fire & Security in 2003 for about $1 billion. As a tech company, it was keeping the security product and tech business and selling the security service-related business globally. This included the Australia arm.

Rituraj's interest was piqued. An Australian business will bring scale, cash and a lot of know-how. More importantly, it was the answer to a question that had been bothering him, Arvind Prasad and Uday Singh.

At that point of time, SIS was facing a lot of heat from G4S. The multinational had finally taken note of SIS's rapid rise from 2003. It responded by using its capital power to woo SIS clients promising better payment terms and service, citing their experience as a larger, multinational business. This was beginning to trouble SIS, as the company didn't have a pocket as deep as G4S's and couldn't match the generous payment terms the rival was offering to clients. Between Rituraj, Arvind Prasad and Uday Singh, there would be constant discussions on how to match G4S's might. They couldn't. G4S was generating surplus money in international operations and their cost of capital was cheaper.

"If a MNC can use surplus cash from mature market to invest in an emerging market like India, why can't then an Indian company buy a company in a mature market that grows slow but generates a lot of free cash and use that to fuel its growth in the domestic market? That's how when we saw the large balance sheet of Chubb and the potential if it could be turned around. That became the compelling idea," says Rituraj.

Yet, it was radical. Yes, SIS was beginning to do well and the days of severe cash crunches were over. Still, it didn't have the financial muscle or a management capability to pull off a deal like this. Chubb Australia was up to eight times the size of SIS. Not just that. It was a market that the SIS leadership had little idea of, let alone its regulations or culture.

The moment Mahesh Devaiah, SIS's legal counsel heard about the proposal, he got worried. 'I was frankly terrified that they were going to pick this large company up with the limited resources they had at that point,' he says. After one particular meeting where the deal was being discussed, Devaiah sought out Rituraj to share his fears. 'I know I'm going way above my brief. But given the relationship we have, I wanted to share my sincere feeling,' the senior lawyer said. Devaiah went on to share why he thought Rituraj shouldn't go ahead with the Chubb deal. 'It's too much of a risk,' he said. Rituraj heard Devaiah out and promised to think it over. Devaiah though had an uneasy feeling that Rituraj had already made up his mind. That was true. Rituraj just couldn't push the idea away. He went to R.K. and Uday Singh with the proposal. Both heard him out. It was a risk. If it failed, it could take the whole company down. Still, the two veterans agreed to give it a try.

The three, along with Randhir Kochhar, EY representatives who were SIS advisors and Devesh Desai, who later went on to become the group's chief financial officer, and Dhiraj Singh visited Australia. UTC officials were surprised to see interest from an unknown and small security company from India. But what assured them that there was genuine interest was the presence of D.E. Shaw, in SIS. The UTC executives were still unsure but understood that SIS had a financial backer. Citigroup, which was managing the deal for UTC, had initially refused to entertain SIS but now agreed to give SIS access to Chubb's data for due diligence.

But who could lead the due diligence for SIS? While the company had experienced people on their side, this called for someone who understood the Australian market. Uday Singh and Rituraj decided to engage George Chin, the former managing director, APAC for UTC who had now retired and was based in Sydney.

A few years back, after the disappointment of the failed deal in Securicor (we will come to it later), Rituraj had looked eastwards and approached George Chin, who was then based in Hong Kong and was heading the Asia territory for Chubb. Rituraj and Uday Singh had asked for an appointment. SIS wanted to grow and had ambitious plans. Would Chin be interested in joining hands and bring Chubb to India? Chin was intrigued and impressed by the young man. He liked Rituraj's confidence and articulation. He was young but showed maturity beyond his years. Unfortunately, for the billion-dollar company, JVs were not the preferred growth route. 'The sad story,' as Chin himself calls it, 'is that I actually asked Rituraj to work for me and lead the India business for me.' Rituraj was flattered but politely turned down the offer.

Now, with plans having dramatically changed and with a new fresh proposal on behalf of the SIS promoters, Uday Singh again sought a meeting with Chin, who was more than willing to see them. By now, Chin had moved on from Chubb and had turned to consulting. Given Chin's experience as MD of Chubb in Australia for several years before being elevated to MD, APAC, the senior professional knew the business inside out. He also knew the people, the management and the overall industry. Uday Singh and Rituraj's request was simple. SIS was interested in buying out Chubb Australia. But to make good of it, due diligence needed to be done and there was none better than Chin to lead it. Would he do it?

Chin saw SIS's interest in Chubb as a wild bet. 'Normally, you acquire a company that is of equal size, smaller or marginally bigger. But this was seven times bigger,' says Chin. At the same time, he was excited by the SIS leadership's courage and tenacity. He agreed to fly to Delhi for a meeting. And he liked the three people sitting in front of him. R.K. was stately, Uday Singh was dynamic with sound management experience and Rituraj came with his exuberance. Chin noted that the team also had smart finance executives, and SIS itself had built systems and processes that were unusual for a small company. SIS may have been a small company by topline but it was managing nearly 50,000 people. It showed it had a bandwidth and understanding of the industry. Chin agreed to take up the assignment. This was a big victory for SIS, given Chubb's history and Chin's role.

Under Chin's leadership, Chubb Australia had grown to a revenue of $480 million a year, with profits of $38 million by 2003. He had started new businesses, including nursing services, which were big hits. He had acquired smaller businesses too. The combination of the two made Chubb the second largest security company in Australia, just behind Wilson Security. He had left the company in the safe and capable hands of Mike McKinnon. Chin had brought him into the company and given him several responsibilities before handing over the CEO role in 2003.

But the moment UTC came in as the new owner, trouble started for the Australia business. 'They didn't know how to manage a manpower-intensive service business,' says Chin. It didn't help matters that UTC ran an Australian business in an American way. 'So, all decisions, key decisions, were being made from America. Their lawyer was based in Australia but the decisions were made in the US. This sort of management didn't work with the clients,' says Don Burnett, who joined Chubb in late 2005, when the operations were going downhill. Mike McKinnon had left the company within a year of UTC taking over. 'They put lawyers in charge and, when they got into trouble, they sold bits of the business to keep the company afloat. They sold nursing and a number of other businesses,' says Chin. 'It's like a tree. If the tree grows well, there might be one branch here and one branch there that's a little bit off shape. But if you keep cutting all of the branches, the tree will not survive, and that's what happened. You should know that each branch supports the other.'

The company started losing business, including two of its biggest aviation clients. Later, Chubb announced it was getting out of aviation, which suited its competition. Top leadership was in a flux. The company was now operating on very thin margins of 1 per cent and below. Cash flow was struggling as well. UTC had outsourced back-office functions, which made things worse as processes and systems went out of hand and errors started creeping in. Clients began to lose patience. Collecting payments became a headache. Clients had no problem in making the payments but the error-filled invoices delayed the whole process.

Given the state of the business, it wasn't surprising that, in 2007, UTC announced it was selling Chubb. 'When the sale was announced, we really became the black sheep of the family and they moved us off into a building in the back of the premises. We called it the tin shed. It kind of made us look like the unwanted orphan of the family,' says Burnett. As unfortunate as that was, the unit started working on its own. A recruitment drive was conducted and important functions were filled. 'When the chips are down, that's when people really band together,' says Burnett.

So, even as the business was looking down, culturally the organization was beginning to spread some positivity through its ranks. But that was the only silver lining in otherwise challenging times. The sale announcement had spooked Chubb clients and many started renegotiating contracts. The sale process itself was long drawn out, adding to the uncertainty. This had additional repercussions. Initially, the announcement had attracted scores of private equity players who were hoping to pick up a business in distress, turn it around and make a profitable exit. For the likes of Burnett and other employees in the system, this was positive news. Private equity players came with deep pockets, and cash was what was needed most urgently. SIS, on the other hand, was an unknown Indian company. 'How could a small company buy a much bigger company? How is it going to work? Is their intent to siphon off money from Australia?' Doubts and questions swirled in the air.

Things were just about to get worse. Both for Chubb employees and for Uday Singh and Rituraj. A global economic crisis was cropping up its ugly head. From early 2007, the US real estate market was beginning to feel the pressures of subprime mortgages amid increasing interest rates. Consequently, demand for housing fell. Investment trusts, including New Century Financial, began collapsing. Markets in the US smelled terror, and as the world's biggest and most powerful economy went down the graphs, the rest of the global economy followed. Credit markets collapsed and, in early 2008, the unthinkable happened. Bear Stearns, the fifth largest US investment bank, was sold to JP Morgan Chase & Co. in a fire sale. A few months later, Fannie Mae and Freddie Mac, the firms who owned or guaranteed half of the US real estate market, needed the federal government's intervention.

In short, the year was turning out to be the worst possible time for anyone looking to sell assets and get a good valuation for it. Not surprisingly, many of the private equity suitors who had lined up in front of Citibank, which was managing the Chubb sale for UTC, disappeared overnight. The only serious contender remaining was the unknown, little company from India.

While that wasn't a bad outcome for Rituraj, he had his own fire to tackle. It came from an unlikely place. Randhir Kochhar and D.E.

Shaw were with Rituraj and SIS right through the bidding process and later for due diligence. It was seen as a vote of confidence and the expectation was that, when the time comes, the American hedge fund would also participate in the acquisition. But in the final analysis D.E. Shaw said it couldn't put any money on the table. Though Kochhar himself saw Chubb as an opportunity and backed the deal, the thinking was different in D.E. Shaw's investment committee in the US. They were keener to invest in Indian companies operating in the Indian market. After all, that was the reason why they had put in the money in SIS too. The Indian market was on a high growth path and that's where they wanted to grow. If D.E. Shaw wanted to grow in Australia and invest in the market, it wouldn't do it through an Indian company, but directly.

The reasoning was legit but it could derail SIS's bid. This was a touchy period in the relationship between SIS and D.E. Shaw. SIS was looking at this as a very attractive opportunity and they were banking on their investor. And when it came to the crunch, D.E. Shaw stepped back and said, sorry, we can't do this. But that's when, as Kochhar himself puts it, Rituraj's tenacity came through. 'It's okay. You guys are out. But we'll find a way to make it happen without an external investor,' Rituraj said. And this is where R.K. played a pivotal role in making the deal happen.

Even as Rituraj and Uday Singh were in Australia, R.K. paid a visit to the general manager of State Bank of India's (SBI) international business, T.C.A. Ranganathan. R.K. had called up the deputy general manager of SBI's Delhi circle, where SIS was a client. 'Can you help set up a meeting with Ranganathan? This is about our plan to acquire Chubb,' R.K. said. The deputy then called Ranganathan. The SBI veteran, who by then had already spent over thirty years at the state-owned lender, agreed to meet R.K. He also asked his team to dig up more information on R.K. and SIS.

'He was an old SBI client in the Patna circle and when he came to Delhi he had an account with us. He had grown over time. SIS was already over twenty years old and it had shown steady progress,' says Ranganathan. 'The important thing about him which distinguished his company from a number of other similar ones was that they were very conscious and very focused on providing proper systems and procedures in conducting their business, in conducting their accounting systems, in conducting everything,' recounts the veteran banker. It also impressed Ranganathan that SIS had been doing audits from the branch level even before this was made mandatory. R.K. had created a training infrastructure for the guards, which was again unusual. The structured training system and the overall focus on doing business in an organized way was rare for a small business. But then, SIS now wanted to acquire a company that had a much larger balance sheet. 'I was intrigued. And I wanted to meet him,' says Ranganathan.

That was one of the many meetings that Ranganathan had with R.K. In subsequent meetings, the SIS founder was accompanied by Rituraj and Uday Singh. Ranganathan wanted to check if the SIS top leadership had it in them to acquire a much larger international company. 'I had been in the international division of SBI and was posted in China. I had seen Indian companies coming there, I had assisted them in coming there, I noticed some of them had succeeded, some of them had failed. And the learnings I had acquired taught me that if you want to succeed in a foreign environment, you need to be able to handle different cultures, different people, different attitudes, different styles of working.'

The banker found that most Indian companies were not proficient in this. They somehow didn't understand that running a commercial operation in a foreign market needed a local system, not remote decision-making. 'The quality for decision-making, the empathy you bring into decision-making, has a bearing on how long your staff stays, how well the staff stays, how well the staff is groomed. These are important soft parameters.' Indian companies were not very successful with their international acquisitions because they had not handled this culture shift aspect well enough. 'In fact, even now, I don't think many Indian companies have really succeeded abroad in a major way,' he says. And these were important aspects for the banker to consider before he decided on funding a company.

To his surprise, R.K., Rituraj and Uday Singh were well-versed with the challenges. SIS was the first company in his memory which planned to have local management in the company they planned to acquire. They didn't want to drop an Indian into the position. 'I grilled them quite a bit on this aspect. And they answered all my questions. They were prepared. They were confident, and the way the three handled themselves was remarkable.'

Ranganathan was convinced of SIS's plan and the ability of its top team to execute it. Internally in SBI, however, not everyone shared the same feeling. How could such a small company do an acquisition of this size? But with multiple meetings with SIS's top three, SBI officials came around and finally gave the go ahead. SBI sanctioned SIS the loan to acquire Chubb.

The acquisition was back on track. Chin, with Uday Singh and the EY team, had already made significant progress with due diligence. He had appointed lawyers and HR directors to help SIS understand the industrial relations in Australia. 'We have six states, each one has a state award, then there is a federal rule and then all the major locations like airports or ports or reserve banks, they all have different agreements. You have to understand that,' says Chin.

The due diligence was important because, in Chin's experience, Asian companies had erred by overestimating companies in Australia, overpaying and ending in failure. 'It's a very, very difficult thing. Sixty-eight per cent of Asian companies coming into Australia fail. Sixty-eight per cent fail. They pay too much, they buy lemons and rush,' he says. He points out the example of Japan Post, which acquired Australian logistics company Toll Holdings Ltd for A$6.5 billion in 2005. 'The company was really worth maybe two billion. After they bought it, they realized that the company's liability was more than a billion. Up to today, Japan Post is still paying for their mistakes.' With Chin heading due diligence, SIS wasn't making that mistake.

After getting the green light from the due diligence team and having received the necessary finance from SBI, the SIS top team signed on the dotted line on 5 August 2008, marking an incredible moment in its journey. A company that had just crossed Rs 200 crore in revenue was acquiring a company which had a topline of Rs 1,600 crore. As far as taking a bet goes, this was even bigger than what Ratan Tata had done with Tata Steel's acquisition of Corus. 'This acquisition will help us expand our footprint in Asia, where demand for private security is growing fast,' R.K. had told *Hindustan Times* after the announcement. 'We want to be the market leader in Asia.'

By now, Burnett and employees of Chubb had warmed up to the Indians. That hadn't been easy. From 2007, there have been several instances of racial clashes between Indians and locals in Australia. This coincided with Indian fans being booked for passing racial slurs against Australian cricketer Andrew Symonds during a one-day international match. Attacks against Indian students, whose numbers had been increasing steadily in Australia, had also gone up. There were 1,083 incidents in 2007 and 1,447 a year later.

Fortunately, the Chubb employees' initial apprehensions had given way to relief. 'We met Ravindra Kishore, Uday Singh and Rituraj. Also, the finance team that included Devesh. There was a collective sigh of relief that wow, these people really understand the guarding business,' says Burnett. This was a refreshing change because UTC had little understanding of the guarding business, and little interest.

'It was good that Rituraj and Uday were coming from the industry and we thought they really get it.' That's why even though the sale process had laboured on, most of the deep-pocketed suitors had backed out because of the global financial crisis and, worst of all, many Chubb clients were leaving because of the uncertainty, the employees were happy that there was something to look forward to.

Having signed the deal, it was time for some critical decisions.

15

GETTING THE DEAL RIGHT

As they had promised in their interactions with SBI's T.C.A. Ranganathan, Rituraj and Uday Singh first big decision post the Chubb acquisition was to get a local man to lead the Australian operations.

They needed someone who knew the business, understood the culture and could instil confidence among the local employees. There was only one person who fit the bill—Chin. But the veteran had made it clear he was no longer interested in a managerial role. 'I've retired, I'm not interested,' Chin told Uday Singh and Rituraj in one of their meetings. Uday Singh and Rituraj offered him the chairman's role and requested him to shepherd the company in its initial few years under the new promoter as it tried to turn around operations. Chin wouldn't need to run the business, the two promised, but would have the final word in selecting key people and on all important business decisions.

Chin agreed. He knew just the right person for the role of managing director, which was the most important decision of all. 'All I had to do was find the managing director. All the rest will fall in place, because it's always the head that counts,' says Chin. He arranged a meeting between Mike McKinnon, who had succeeded Chin at Chubb but had left after UTC came in, and Uday Singh and Rituraj. McKinnon had joined Qantas, the Australian airline which was also once Chubb's biggest customer. It was a breakfast meeting. They hardly touched the food but the conversation ran deep on Chubb, its operations, the vision of the new promoters and their willingness to delegate operational controls to McKinnon and Chin. McKinnon accepted the offer, and that was the beginning of Chubb's new journey under its new owner.

There were a few immediate concerns at Chubb. First was getting a new identity and branding. The company was renamed MSS Security, its original name before it was acquired and rebranded as Chubb. Next was to arrest the fall in revenue and assure clients and government establishments that the company was here to stay. Chin did the groundwork of reaching out to important stakeholders. He went to the federal government office in Canberra. He met the top management of the biggest clients, including the airlines. He had breakfast meetings with bank heads. 'I took Uday to go and meet customers, I took him everywhere. Whenever he visited Australia, I would take him out to visit customers,' says Chin.

To instil confidence on both sides, Chin called for a meeting of all state managers at a hotel near the airport in Sydney. Rituraj did a presentation and R.K. spoke about SIS and the employee-centric ethos of the company. When his turn came, Chin assured the continuity of operations at MSS under the new owners. 'I'm here as the chairman. We have worked together before and have shown what we can do,' he told them. That was true. Nearly half of the people assembled there had worked with Chin and an opportunity to get back to those days was a positive outcome for them. He told them that he would be the bridge with the new owners so that the two sides could begin to understand each other. Seeing the comfort the veteran himself had with SIS's top leadership, the state managers left Sydney more hopeful than they had been in the last four years. Comfort also came after the announcement of McKinnon as the new MD.

The initial months—all part of a 100-day plan that was drawn up by the SIS leadership with McKinnon and the MSS top team—saw several such meetings and interactions, not just with employees. 'There's a lot of things you do when you have an acquisition. There are customers, vendors, employees, managers, banks. Everyone has to be given that confidence, especially when it's the first time and when the company is unknown to them. So, we have to give everyone else confidence also. In fact, I used to frequently meet the auditors and the tax advisors there, and that gave them the confidence that we knew what we were doing, we knew what we're talking about and we could establish a direct line of communication with them,' says Devesh Desai.

Desai had joined SIS just after the deal was announced. His was a crucial role, though done behind the scenes. He had a stint in Air Deccan and had worked with Uday Singh in Praxair. Desai's profile was to guide SIS through the acquisition and then take the lead in the post-acquisition period. Few in SIS had M&A experience, whereas he came with a track record of having worked in fundraising, IPOs and M&As. Through the Chubb deal he led the copious amount of work needed in completing the paperwork and closing the deal. He would constantly fly to Sydney. 'Once a deal is finalized, there is a lot of paperwork, agreements and due diligence or make sure everything is fine. If something is not fine, how do you bake this into the terms and then, after the agreements are signed, you work with both sides, work together to complete all the other documents to achieve what you call closing.'

And once that is done, it is again the finance department that leads the integration exercise. Care has to be taken not to put off the new people coming into the system. Or make them feel scared. It was awkward too. The parent company was significantly smaller than the subsidiary. 'We have to work with them and ensure transition into the systems and the processes, and the culture, and all the policies, which this current group practises and implements. So it's a step-by-step process. The finance team is critically involved in these things,' says Desai.

This was also important because the erstwhile Chubb Australia unit was part of a bigger organization. Much of the important functions, including finance and HR, were centralized and it borrowed the systems and processes from the parent. But now it had been spun off and was suddenly a standalone company. It needed support and hand-holding with its financial requirements, reporting systems, engagement with clients and proper controls within the organization.

Uday Singh, Rituraj and Desai worked collectively. Rituraj and Uday Singh worked with McKinnon and the leadership team on strategy, on how to connect with customers, set up feedback mechanisms and retain customers after acquisition. This was important to get the cash stuck with customers back in the system. The independent feedback mechanism now came from customers to the managing director, who would travel across states meeting the former.

Desai worked on the Australian unit's accounting and financial reporting which, surprisingly, was nearly absent. The unit did not have a monthly reporting system. Desai worked closely with Burnett's team to set the whole system and the processes and the methodology for the exercise. The predictability of this was important so that everyone knew which day of the month the information was coming to them, and they could make important business decisions based on the numbers. A system was built to send a monthly report to the Governing Board consisting of Chin, Uday Singh and Rituraj, and this included all the financial metrics that showed how the acquisition was doing. Later, Desai himself started getting a short report every month. 'I used to go around every state in Australia, like twice a year, and meet the local teams,' says Desai. This was an exercise that Rituraj and Uday Singh would also undertake. 'The three of us were doing this almost day in and day out with them, till MSS was ready to operate in sync with SIS parent.'

The critical aspect of this exercise was to instil confidence in each other. Both parties had to believe that the sole focus was on getting the business back on track. As soon as both sides realized this, they were more confident about each other. It was hard work, and the first eighteen months needed intense involvement from both sides. The team in Australia also instantly saw that SIS was bringing a lot of its learning in creating systems and processes to the table. 'If you can bring something to the table which they don't have, then it's not very difficult to get across to them,' says Desai. One of the biggest changes was the new rostering system that Uday Singh helped build in MSS. The software was tailored for different sites, agreements and regulations. 'In Australia,' Chin explains, 'there are different rates for wages. For example, if you start work early in the morning you attract a certain percentage increase, late evening you attract another percentage. On Saturdays, the rate is one and a half times the usual. Sundays, it's double; on public holidays, you pay two and a half times the morning wage. So every roster has to meet the criteria of the legal structure it is framing. So your registering system must be able to calculate every pay of this. Calculate the roster, calculate the pay. Don't break the rules. Every state is different. Every major site has a different agreement. It's very complex.'

Unlike the earlier system that didn't factor in these complexities of the work, the new software suggested by Uday Singh and put in place with help of SIS suited the Australian operations. 'MSS suddenly came back at the top of the market because the rostering system began to work. The system also synced in the HR requirements of the organization. It helps in onboarding people, so that quality personnel get the right job, and then it completes the pay and does the invoicing.

The earlier system had a separate invoicing package, which often led to errors,' explains Chin.

MSS employees started seeing the value in SIS's involvement. Slowly but surely, after a year of intense work, the improvements were beginning to show. Encouraged by Uday Singh and Rituraj to cut costs, the business in Australia moved out of expensive real estate. The new rostering system drastically reduced complaints among employees of being paid the wrong amount, which was a common grouse earlier. This improved productivity.

'Our ledger system was pretty basic whereas in India, SIS really had quite a comprehensive ERP system that was built specifically for the business. Even though they were much smaller than the Australian business, SIS was more advanced than MSS in that area,' says Burnett. The Indian parent was also a services business-oriented and it focused on ease of doing business for its customers. Taking cue, the Australia business too tweaked its processes keeping customer comfort in mind. The key thing was to speed up decision making so that the company could respond to customers faster.

As things began to improve, advised by Chin, Rituraj and Uday Singh visited Sydney less often. McKinnon was taking over and leading from the front. If earlier, they were at MSS office every month, slowly the visits were reduced to once in two months and then once a quarter. Devesh Desai, who was closely working with Burnett's team, also began spacing out his visits. And each visit started becoming shorter. This was an important indication for the Australian team that things were getting better and there wouldn't be any intervention unless they required it. If earlier the MSS team had just about enough time to dig up the numbers and data that Desai was asking for, the improvement in systems and processes made financial reporting faster and more reliable. This left them time to manage and grow the local business. 'I think the owners should know how to ask questions, when to ask questions and when to just let things fly.

I think that's very important, and that probably is wisdom, and also experience,' says Chin.

'This was in the early days and so we were trying to do all sorts of things to keep the business afloat and sometimes we felt that there were demands being placed on us from India for information that was just so hard to get because it was never available we were part of Chubb. At the same time, those were the things that probably helped us set up the processes and systems,' says Burnett.

In later years, it became a custom for MSS's top team to travel to India for the annual conference. The event was an eye-opener for the MSS team. It was rare for a company to hold such large events where each team was reviewed and its report card discussed publicly. The transparency and honesty shown by both the top leadership and the ranks lower down the order got the MSS team to appreciate what SIS had created in India.

Back in Australia, McKinnon's leadership was central to the turnaround, and then growth of the local business. Under UTC, once he had moved on, leadership at Chubb was unstable. There were frequent exits. Decision-making suffered. But now with McKinnon firmly at the top and with the backing of Chin and SIS, the stability of leadership sent a positive message down the ranks. Focus was on making bids for better and stronger contracts. Questions were raised and addressed on controlling costs. Successes were shared. 'We got better and better at doing our work. If one particular state got a big cash payment, the commercial manager would call and share the news. It was similar when a branch managed to retain a client—collective enjoyment and celebration,' says Burnett. And where needed, McKinnon let people go. Under the previous owner, discipline had suffered and, as Burnett puts it, 'Mike doesn't suffer fools lightly.' Those who were not delivering were given a change or moved to different locations. If things still didn't improve, they were let go.

Invoicing errors reduced, the debt profile improved, payroll errors came down. 'We could sleep a little better. Now we didn't miss a payroll cycle or paying a vendor … we stopped bleeding after nine months. The wins started exceeding the losses,' says Burnett. Taking a cue from SIS, MSS set up a training organization. It restructured some parts of its business. Aviation became a standalone business as it was a 'national' client and managing it state-wise would have led to inconsistencies.

MSS was now back as Australia's leading security company. It was now time to expand and get into the mobile patrol and alarm response business. MSS acquired a 10 per cent stake in Southern Cross Protection in 2012. It was Australia's largest provider of security patrols. Interestingly, the company was part of Chubb under UTC's. Now, it was back with MSS, as a partner company. Eventually, SIS bought another 41 per cent stake in the mobile patrol company, making it the majority shareholder. Later, as the businesses consolidated, Southern Cross Protection became a 100 percent subsidiary of SIS group.

MSS also built a specialized medical and emergency services vertical. Later, the acquisition of Safety Direct Solutions brought the company clients in heavy construction and mining. This acquisition also included operations in New Zealand. There was more action in the southern neighbour's market. SIS bought Auckland-based Platform 4 Group, which had customers in manufacturing, construction and hospitality. It was a big moment for MSS because the company had been scouting for acquisitions in New Zealand but was unable to find a suitable one or, if they did find one, they wouldn't agree to a deal. Two years later, in 2019, SIS acquired Triton through Platform 4. Triton added the alarm monitoring business to SIS's New Zealand acquisitions.

Overall, MSS in Australia and New Zealand progressed handsomely since the 2008 acquisition. These units were consolidated under

SIS International. From A$ 300 million in 2008, SIS International's consolidated topline stood at A$1 billion in 2024. The business is profitable and, equally important, MSS has regained its presence in Australian business. It's the biggest security solutions provider in Australia. It handles most marquee events, including the Melbourne Cup, an annual thoroughbred horse race. MSS is in also in charge of the security at the iconic Melbourne Cricket Ground. Another high-profile event is the Australian Grand Prix, where MSS provides security and event day services.

Notably, MSS, despite its Indian ownership, retains its Australian identity. Its top leadership—even after McKinnon and Chin moved on—consists entirely of Australian professionals. R.K, Uday Singh and Rituraj had certainly kept the promise they had given to Ranganathan.

As the SIS top leadership helped turn around the business in Australia, the acquisition of Chubb had a huge impact on its operations in India.

'It helped SIS to break out of a small league into the big league and get counted seriously. And when you get counted seriously, opportunities start coming to you,' says Desai.

Funding opened up. Capital and fundraising is otherwise difficult in India for a small company, especially from the security industry. Banks ask for collateral before they agree to lend money. Security companies, on the other hand, have few assets as they are service focused unlike a manufacturing company. That's probably one reason why the security industry in India has never seen much of M&As. 'Whoever is able to get finance is going to take this market,' says Rituraj.

This is where the Australian business came to help. After MSS repaid the loan that was raised to finance the 2008 acquisition, the finance team from SIS raised A$80 million in revolving finance. The revolving credit line meant that SIS could repeatedly access this amount. In other words, Rituraj could use this to further look for acquisitions and mergers in his pursuit for growth. From SIS's point of view, it mattered that the loan was raised against MSS's cash flows. 'I converted the international business to a cash cow to fund growth here in India,' says Rituraj. It completed the cycle, cash from a mature market was now helping grow business in an emerging market.

By 2009-10, the Chubb acquisition had already made SIS a Rs 2,000-crore company. The additional firepower was just the kind of ammunition Rituraj needed.

A sidenote. In hindsight, it may now look like D.E. Shaw made a mistake by staying out of SIS's Chubb acquisition. Randhir Kochhar accepts it in as many words. 'It was a huge mistake made by D.E. Shaw not to fund it. And it was a blessing in disguise for the promoters,' he says. That's right. Had D.E. Shaw funded that acquisition, it would have increased its stake in SIS. Its investment would have been between $5 to $10 million. 'The $10 million would have brought us another 20 to 30 per cent of the company and we would have owned half of SIS, which would have been a fantastic outcome for the investor,' says Kochhar. On the other hand, R.K. and Rituraj had saved the day by convincing SBI to lend the money, and within a year it was clear they had a winner in their hands.

D.E. Shaw still made good of its investment. It had invested less than Rs 50 crore in SIS in 2008. By the time it exited the security company in 2013, it had made seven times that in returns, an outcome that will please any investor. Taking the American hedge fund's place was C.X. Partners, an India-focused private equity fund that invests across healthcare, financial services and outsourced service industries. It invested Rs 300 crore in SIS, with an option of adding another Rs 200 crore. In all, it took a 20 per cent stake. 'As the private security industry becomes more compliant with government regulations, we will see more deals in the space,' Ajay Relan, Managing Partner of C.X. Partners, told the *The Economic Times*. A portion of the money, he added, would be used by SIS to make acquisitions.

Both the points that Relan made were important. The first was about the security industry becoming more compliant. It reveals the worry investors have always had about the sector. Because of low or no regulation, barriers to entry are practically non-existent. This meant every security vendor was offering a lower rate than the other, eating into the already thin margin. C.X. Partners had bet on SIS to fare differently from the rest of the industry. Despite being in a business with low margins, SIS had grown. Its workforce and managers were motivated; there was a comprehensive training programme in place.

'What struck us was the quality of culture and leadership and the vision. SIS was head and shoulders above rest. Not only other players in the sector, but comparable to the best. It was a family-owned business that had turned professional,' says Vivek Chhachhi, Partner at C.X. Partners. Chhachhi was particularly impressed with the transition in leadership from R.K. to Uday Singh and Rituraj. 'The transition is incredibly hard for most family businesses, not just in India but globally,' he says. The biggest hurdle is the promoter's mindset. There is an expectation that the professional CEO will be a sort of a magician, able to deliver what's not been done till then. But when things don't necessarily work out as hoped for, disillusionment creeps in.

In SIS, however, the boundaries had been seamless, says Chhachhi. 'The sculpture was already superbly set by the time we came in. When Mr Uday Singh spoke during annual conferences—and I was invited by Rituraj to attend one—he spoke with authority and with the belief that he wouldn't be undercut by Mr Sinha or by Rituraj. Similarly, Rituraj was immensely balanced in his head. He was decisive with the Australian acquisition. In our deal too, he negotiated hard. He is a tough negotiator. But also fair and respectful through the process. The intent was to develop a relationship based on trust.'

And that brings us to the second point that Relan made, of SIS going in for more deals. That's what Rituraj did. And of course, Relan, Chhachhi and the rest of the team at C.X. Partners were hoping their bet on SIS would lead them to a profitable exit, possibly through an IPO. But before that, SIS had to grow.

16

BRINGING A COLLEGE PROJECT TO REALITY

At Leeds University Business School, all students had to present a project in their final year. Rituraj's project was on setting up a cash logistics business in India. SIS, his project had proposed, could team up with Securicor, the British cash management major. The joint venture would be among the earliest entrants into the cash management space in India.

'Securicor had a big cash logistics business in Europe and I felt there was a great opportunity in India, especially with the growth of the Indian banking sector. Moreover, cash management is a little more evolved compared to the security business and delivers substantially higher margins,' says Rituraj.

That was true. Back in the early 2000s, the Indian banking sector was beginning to take off after the turn of the century. This was mostly led by private banks, including ICICI Bank and HDFC Bank, who were relentless in expanding their retail network. These banks needed to move cash from one branch to the other. This was accompanied by the installation of automatic telling machines, or ATMs, which revolutionized the way consumers interacted with their banks. Gone was the long wait at the cashier's counter to withdraw money. Later, even other banking functions like submitting a cheque could be done inside an ATM.

The ease of an ATM made it an immediate favourite among customers. Imagine this. In 1999, India had 1,521 ATMs. This increased to 3,000 in 2001 and over 12,000 by 2004. Now, handling cash in a branch or in the ATMs was not a core operation of a bank. There were two requirements here. One was moving the cash. Second was managing the cash logistics of an ATM, securing it and the small box like room that hosted it. A security company like SIS could deploy its personnel to guard the ATM. And it could also handle cash in the ATM and also transport it by training its personnel and adding a fleet of armoured vehicles.

Rituraj's project reflected foresight and understanding of a business that was set to boom. The panel of three professors who examined his work were impressed. Rituraj says, 'One of the professors wrote this on the project sheet: "This is so good that you should actually consider doing it."' The project was on the top of the list for Rituraj when he finally moved from the UK and joined his father's business in India.

Arguably, Rituraj wasn't exactly the first person to think about a cash management business in India. Group 4 had already added the cash management business to its guarding vertical. 'People at that time were primarily into moving cash only. And then there was the movement of bullion, which gradually began as part of this same vertical. But, in the initial years, it was the cash management that dominated,' says Swaranjit Duggal, who handled the cash business as managing director for Group 4 in India. There was also Brink's Retail Cash Management, probably the first cash management company to operate in the country. Group 4, given its European legacy and global presence, also made inroads with multinational banks like Citi that were also expanding their retail presence. This was akin to the natural advantage that Group 4 had in its security business too.

This was a good business to be in. As Rituraj had understood about the business while preparing his project, Group 4 enjoyed high margins, up to 25 per cent in the cash management. The demand for its cash and bullion services soared as retail banking took roots across the country. By 2006, the multinational had eighty-seven vaults in different states, says Duggal. It went on to servicing about 25,000 ATMs in the country. These were impressive numbers.

Rituraj was carefully tracking Group 4's progress. In 2003, while SIS was being fixed, Uday Singh and Rituraj approached Securicor for a joint venture in India. They were not present in India and seemed liked a perfect partner to have and taken on Group 4 and Brink's in India.

The young SIS Vice President's first call was Hong Kong, the Asia headquarters of Securicor. Would the company be open to exploring a joint venture with SIS for a cash management business in India? The British multinational could see the potential and reciprocated. They visited India and the terms for the joint venture were drafted. This was then put forward to Securicor's parent board in the UK. It looked like their first big venture out of the SIS was beginning to take shape. Bringing Securicor to India would be a big win.

Even as Rituraj was firming up plans for the rollout of the operations in India, he got a call. 'Have you seen the news?' the caller asked. Intrigued, Rituraj switched on the business news. And he immediately found out what the call was about. Group 4 and Securicor had announced a merger in February 2004. Both were listed on the London Stock Exchange. The merger created G4S, a security behemoth with operations in ninety countries with over 5 lakh employees. The merged entity would need to relook its operations in every country. Group 4 had already made its presence felt in India's nascent but fast-growing cash management business.

Securicor no longer needed to piggyback on SIS to enter the Indian market. The deal between Securicor and SIS never got discussed by the multinational's board. Rituraj's ambitious project had come a cropper.

It was an unexpected setback for the twenty-four-year-old youngster. It was to be his big break. 'He was emotionally invested in this. He spent two days shut up in his room,' says Pallavi Sinha, Rituraj's girlfriend and then wife, recounts. Rituraj himself termed it a 'good lesson to get early in life'. He bounced back fast and did the next best thing. While he also approached Securitas and Chubb with the joint venture idea, but in parallel he decided SIS will set up its own cash management business. And whom did Rituraj convince to set this up? Duggal himself.

As it happened, the Group 4 and Securicor merger also led to a restructuring of the India team and the local unit's organization. Duggal was moved to head the company's business in Sri Lanka. There was a change in G4S's local partner in the country, and approval for a new setup got caught in a bureaucratic web. Duggal was constantly flying to and from Colombo. Around this time, he got a call from R.K. The SIS founder had got wind of Duggal's change in profile. 'You know we are looking to start a cash management business. Rituraj is closely involved in that. Can we meet?' R.K. asked.

Duggal was pleased. He had often met R.K. in industry events and respected what the latter had created in SIS. Duggal had also seen SIS make its presence felt during exhibitions and had observed its growth in recent years. The industry was beginning to take notice, though SIS remained smaller than G4S. In fact, it was 1/10th the size of G4S. 'It was like a poor man's G4S,' says Duggal. At the same time, 'I was very impressed with what Uday Singh and Rituraj had done in the few years they had been in SIS.'

Duggal met R.K. and Rituraj. They were courteous, and the meeting went very well. Interestingly, what Duggal remembers the most about the meeting is not the business part. 'Both were very down to earth. After the meeting was over, I stepped out to leave. Rituraj came all the way to my car to drop me. The respect he showed proved he was a thorough gentleman and he remained so in all my years at SIS,' says Duggal. He joined SIS in 2007.

By then SIS's cash management business had onboarded its first client. Bank of Baroda was already using SIS as its security provider, and Rituraj managed to bag the contract for cash management too. As part of the contract, SIS deployed over 100 vehicles as cash vans. This was the biggest order for the company's overall fleet. From about 35 vehicles, now it had nearly 150 vehicles.

'Rituraj wanted the deployment to be on time,' says Sanjay Pandey, Vice President, Fleet, SIS. But the issue was that in many of the cities that SIS was to serve Bank of Baroda, in regions of Uttar Pradesh, Gujarat and Karnataka, it had no presence. Which meant that the company didn't have address proof to register the cash vans. Once that was sorted, each vehicle needed to be fabricated to fit safety features, including grills. As a newly constituted team, the fleet vertical had few people, and it took a mammoth effort from Pandey and his small team to pull off the project in the mandated three months. 'We didn't see our families in those three months. My bag was packed all the time because I had to travel at any time,' says Pandey. This first big order set the template and process for growing the fleet as the cash vertical began adding clients.

Meanwhile, Uday Singh put Dinesh Gupta, as vice president in the cash management vertical, to create the manual for ISO certification of the cash business. 'Mr Singh was a mentor. I had the opportunity to work with him when we were working on the ISO certification of SIS's core guarding business,' says Gupta.

Duggal's presence at the top helped add to the customer base. He brought into play his network in the banking sector. 'I had worked for over a decade with banks. The general managers I knew in my initial years were now chief executives. That helped,' he says. The cash business vertical broadened its clientele. The business grew and, by 2010, SIS had 400 vehicles that could move cash for its banking clients. But there was a hitch. Even as the competition from the likes of G4S and Brink's grew, pricing came under pressure. All the more because the nationalized banks, says Duggal, weren't ready to increase the rates.

Until 2010, cash in transit (CIT) was the biggest business for the cash management vertical. There were about 100 ATMs that SIS operated. But as the young company expanded its market both in CIT and ATMs, it came across its biggest challenge yet. It was not about the competition or the fast-changing business environment. It was about pilferage. In simpler terms, many of its employees, by themselves or in connivance with bank employees, resorted to fraud. There were many instances of cash disappearing. Some of these are worth mentioning here, because it also led to the cash management vertical learning from these setbacks and setting up stronger checks and balances.

The cash management team was handling Delhi Metro's cash logistics. The Delhi government had launched the urban transport network amidst much fanfare. The project was headed by E. Sreedharan, who came to be known as India's metro man. Delhi Metro changed the way people travelled. Its network was big and getting denser, and it was a high-profile client for SIS. Prime Minister Atal Bihari Vajpayee had flagged it off. The unfortunate incident happened when the network had just six stations.

It was like any other day. After collecting the money from the stations, the SIS cash van had to reach Union Bank of India. But the cash—Rs 52 lakh—never reached the bank's vaults. The guy responsible for handling the cash was nowhere to be found. He had run off the with money. 'We went back to his documents and checked every detail,' says J.K. Akash, a senior vice president at SIS. He and his team were taken aback by what they found. Each and every detail, including his address, the address proof document and education certificates were fake. For Akash, who had recently joined SIS cash services from Group 4, this was the first lesson in his new job.

'I suggested to Rituraj to add a process called field verification. This included verification from the police, third-party verification, physical house inspection of the candidate, feedback from neighbours and other people who have been referenced by him,' says Akash. Sometimes, even SIS employees, apart from the third-party vendors, got involved in these field inspections to ensure they had the right person for the job. And did the company finally get the guy who scooted away with Rs 52 lakh? Yes, after a chase in full coordination with the Delhi Police.

A few years later, in a similar but much bigger incident, a cash van was transporting Rs 20 crore. On the way to the bank, a guard asked the vehicle to be stopped to answer nature's call. Thinking he had the opportunity of a lifetime to ensure a luxurious life, the van's driver scooted away with the money. And this was a big amount that wasn't even completely covered by insurance. Fortunately, again with the help of Delhi Police and coordination among several SIS offices, the driver was caught inside a mill in the outskirts of Delhi. He hadn't spent a rupee and had been waiting it out.

The third incident is of a lower amount but the fraud here was much more complicated, similar to a script from a bank heist movie. This happened in a bank's branch in Muzaffarpur in Bihar. While the indent (the formal request) from SIS's client was for Rs 1 crore and the money was being withdrawn from the branch, on the ground only Rs 80 lakh was being shown. The remaining Rs 20 lakh was being equally split between SIS's employee and the bank employee. '*Dono ki milli bhagat thi* (the two had schemed the whole thing),' says Akash. This meant that only Rs 80 lakh was being loaded on the ATMs. 'The counters, the reports, everything was manipulated. They had forged all the documents,' he adds. Only later, when the physical inspection was done, did everyone realize that cash up to Rs 7 crore had gone missing.

These incidents from 2010 and later were a sign that while Rituraj had spotted the opportunity correctly in the cash management business, SIS had little know-how in running it. Unlike the guarding business, this was more sophisticated, involved more technology and needed even more robust processes and systems. Technology was not alien to SIS. R.K. had prioritized it in the security business. The difference in cash management was that there was competition that already had access to these technologies, and Rituraj and the cash business didn't have the time to acquire this know-how and create a system by trial and error or organically. Instead, it needed a partner who knew all of this. That was the reason Rituraj was hoping to get Securicor. But now it was time to get another partner on board.

It was around the same time that Prosegur, a Spanish security services major, was looking to expand its market. It had a presence in over 30 countries and was a global leader in cash logistics. Its promoter and CEO Christian Gut was especially keen to enter Asia. The region had some of the fastest growing emerging economies and research done by Prosegur's internal team had shown that growth rates in these economies would outpace those in mature markets like Europe by a mile.

Gut asked senior executives Jose Antonio and Oscar Esteban to explore the Asian market. Esteban had deftly led the company through a challenging period recently when Europe changed its currency to the euro. Esteban was in charge of the operations in Spain and Portugal. It was a challenging and ambitious exercise. Unimaginable amounts of old currency notes had to be replaced with the new euro notes. 'It was a mess because consider something, 1 euro was equivalent to 166.36 pesetas. So, it's not like 1 euro is 100 pesetas or 1 euro is 200 pesetas. It was 166 points, and I don't know how many decimals. When people were making the conversion, there were a lot of mistakes, and mistakes in our industry cost a lot of money. Normally, if you give more money to someone, they won't complain but when you give less, they will.'

Yet, Esteban, who was in logistics major DHL when Gut brought him to Prosegur for this very exercise, had managed to lead through the tricky situation. And now, he was on his way to Asia. It was 2010. The search for a new market in Asia led Esteben to China, Singapore and later to Mumbai and Delhi. In Mumbai, the Spaniard landed in the city when it was having one of its infamous monsoon downpours. 'I will never live in this country,' was Esteban's first thought. But he went through the grind, doing road shows with potential partners. He met with executives from Tops, one of the most well-known security agencies led by second-generation entrepreneur Rahul Nanda. Esteban also met CMS and Writer Corporation, which were dominant in the cash management business. There was also a meeting with AGS, which wanted to get into cash management. None of the talks made much headway.

At the end of the year, Antonio and Gut were attending an international conference on cash management in Istanbul. During the conference they met Rituraj. While SIS had appeared in their internal research on the Indian market, they hadn't bothered to contact it. After all, it was just the sixth largest cash management company in the country. At the time, SIS was mostly present in the cash-in-transit business and had a nascent presence in ATMs. The chance meeting in Istanbul went well, and Antonio, who was then head of M&A asked Esteban to look into the company a little closer. Its security business has been growing fast in recent years. The mix of promoter and professional management was interesting. There were a few similarities between Prosegur and SIS. Both were family-led.

And both were now being handled by the second generation. Esteban met R.K. and Rituraj and instantly took a liking to the father-son duo.

Gut invited the SIS top leadership to Madrid. There, over two days, the two sides explored the possibility of a joint venture (JV). 'We arrived at an initial agreement. And then, in consequent meetings, we decided on the details,' says Esteban.

The two sides signed along the dotted line in May 2011. Prosegur, the world's second largest cash handling company, would take 40 per cent in the JV, and the majority would be with SIS. This was a big milestone for SIS. The company had got its first joint venture and its partner was a multinational and that with well-established technological know-how. Thus an idea, which was conceived in 2001, saw realisation 10 years later, and post failed discussions with Securicor, Chubb and Securitas.

Interestingly, even though SIS was the bigger partner in the JV, Rituraj agreed that a Prosegur employee should lead the new entity. It was an important decision. Cash management as a business was still taking form in India. Europe was at a higher learning curve. A person from Prosegur would have a better understanding of the business. Not only that, given the inherent risks of a cash business, Rituraj wanted someone who was a stickler for process. And that is how both sides agreed, given Prosegur's experience in the business, Esteban would lead the JV.

The reality of the business was not rosy. The cash vertical had low volumes, small network and rudimentary operational technology in place. Over the next years, Esteban worked closely with Rituraj, Uday Singh and Devesh Desai. Among the first things the JV did was build a cash processing centre in Delhi. IT was a critical infrastructure to have. But there was a problem. The company didn't really deal with enough cash to use the centre meaningfully. That's when a big opportunity came by.

In June 2012, the government, as part of its financial inclusion mission, announced plans to open 60,000 ATMs in rural areas over the next two years. All of these ATMs would be owned by public sector banks, led by State Bank of India, the country's largest bank. This was a big opportunity for SIS, and Rituraj wanted to make the most of it. He put Akash and Neerja Goswami, Vice President, SIS Prosegur, in charge of executing the project.

SIS bagged contracts for over 9,000 ATMs. Within a couple of years, the JV hit the mark of 10,000 ATMs, a 10x jump in two years. While this was a big accomplishment, the challenge was implementation. The ATMs were spread across the hinterlands of the country—Bihar, Madhya Pradesh, Jharkhand (which had been carved out of Bihar), Chhattisgarh and the North East. 'One needs to follow a protocol while taking over an ATM. At a time, you could probably take over about six to seven ATMs a day. But here we were talking about thousands of ATMs over a limited period of time,' says Akash. Not just that. In many of these markets, the bank executives hadn't heard about SIS. 'I remember meeting the regional head of a bank in Hyderabad. He didn't have a clue about SIS or what I was trying to say about setting up ATMs. Only after I showed him a copy of the contract did he realize I was serious,' says Akash.

The biggest challenge was to back this expansion with the latest technology, systems and processes. The requirement was accentuated by several incidents of fraud and pilferage. 'Over the years, with the help of Prosegur and with the involvement of SIS's own IT team, we developed over ten systems that manage each and every part of the operation,' says Akash. It's important to list a few, especially the ones that helped prevent frauds.

The nucleus of the cash management company's tech platform is the National Operations Centre, or the NOC. It keeps an eye through a network of cameras and GPS-enabled devices. Even locks of vaults are centrally managed from the NOC located in Delhi. The centre itself looks like a scene straight out of a sci-fi film set with cameras covering walls and employees manning scores of screens. The screens on the walls and desks track the movement of each cash van with the SIS Prosegur stamp.

Regular cash vans transformed into high-risk cash vans if they were transporting big amounts of cash. Their routes are geofenced and, if at any time a route was altered—like when the driver went away with Rs 20 crore—it triggered an alarm. In addition, these vehicles were fit with online cameras in crew and cargo areas, panic alarm switches that triggered an alarm at the NOC and also SMS alerts followed by IVR calls to crew. Most interestingly, these vehicles could also be immobilized from the NOC.

The JV uses a proprietary cash management system owned by Prosegur, which tracks each and every movement of the cash, from the moment clients make indents to movement on routes and at points where the crew handle the notes. It also allows for cash traceability, a key security feature, and supervises cassette swap operations at ATMs. Cassettes are the containers inside an ATM that hold the currency notes. Prosegur also brought in tech for cash processing systems and phone applications that record data and help in real-time execution. These apps support the JV's businesses in cash in transit, ATMs and doorstep banking.

One of the biggest tech interventions to prevent fraud of the kind that happened in that Muzaffarpur bank branch has been developed jointly by SIS and Prosegur. It's called Cyclo, which is an ATM reconciliation tool for tracking cash differences and allowing traceability. The tool enables process monitoring, immediate identification of differences, quick infestation and automatic resolution of exception and transaction disputes. Similarly, another tech jointly developed by the two partners is RMS, which again prevents mismatches and mistakes.

Getting these technologies on board helped SIS Prosegur to scale up faster. But there was a problem. The business was still loss making. 'Right through the expansion phase, we didn't make profits,' says

Esteban. The company by now had 15,000 ATMs and a growing CIT business, but no profits to show. The issue, the leadership realized, was SIS's absence in the growing sector of doorstep banking. One of the newer innovations in banking service, a customer doesn't need to visit a bank branch. Instead, some banking needs, like picking up and delivering documents or financial/digital services can be provided at the customer's doorstep.

One way to get into this growing segment was to start from scratch. The second and easier way to immediately get a foothold was to acquire. That's what Rituraj did when Danish major ISS decided to sell its cash management business in India. SIS bought the business in 2014. Given ISS's presence in the south—it operated out of Chennai—and in western markets, it immediately brought scale to the joint venture. SIS jumped to fourth place in the pecking order of the country's largest cash management companies.

The deal helped plug a big hole in ISS. 'The company didn't have technology of its own but was dependent on a vendor that managed everything for the company. The problem is when differences crop up with the vendor, like even a minor delay in payments, they can put your systems on hold. That's a very big risk to have in a business where continuity is very crucial,' says Akash. SIS Prosegur's tech strength helped manage the scale that ISS's business brought in, especially in the southern and western markets, where the JV didn't have a large presence. Today, the unit is known as SISCO. Two years later, in 2016, SIS made another acquisition, of the Delhi-based SSMS. The company specialized in ATM operations.

After these acquisitions, things were finally looking up for SIS Prosegur. But before the JV could begin integrating the new companies, an unexpected event disrupted the whole industry. It was set off by an address by Prime Minister Narendra Modi on the night of 8 September.

17

LEADING THE WAY DURING DEMONETIZATION

The evening of 8 November 2016 went as per plan. Rituraj, along with Uday Singh and a few other senior executives of SIS, had just landed in Mumbai after completing a roadshow in the US. The SIS top brass had been meeting investors for a planned initial public offering of the security company.

Rituraj checked into a hotel in Worli, in Mumbai. He was meeting a friend for dinner at 8 p.m. He switched on the TV for his favourite news channel and went for a shower. When he got out, with about half an hour to go before his dinner appointment, he saw Prime Minister Narendra Modi was addressing the nation. The country, Modi said, was about to witness a shudhikaran drive. To counter black money and tax evasion, the government was about to ban currency notes of Rs 500 and Rs 1,000 from midnight. Instead, a new series of Rs 500 and Rs 2,000 notes would be introduced.

Rituraj's jaw dropped, he could scarcely believe his ears. As he sat down for dinner with his friend, his phone didn't stop ringing. He cut short his appointment and, back in his room, attended to the calls from his customers, senior colleagues and family. 'What was going on?' 'What will we do?' Rituraj didn't have the answers but he reassured them. He also got another call, this time from a senior government official. 'Is this Rituraj Sinha?' Rituraj confirmed he was. 'Are you the president of the Cash Logistics Association?' the caller asked. Rituraj again answered in the affirmative. 'When can you come to Mumbai?' Rituraj answered that he was in Mumbai and said, 'Let's meet tomorrow morning.'

The association was formed in 2012, after a few of the industry players—with Rituraj playing a pivotal role—came together with a realization that they needed recognition from the government. The cash logistics industry was unregulated. It was always the underdog when it came to negotiating with banks and other clients. Rituraj, like R.K. had in the security industry, took a keen interest in taking forward the industry's concerns with the government. He had held meetings with officials at the Reserve Bank of India (RBI), Ministry of Finance and Indian Banks' Association.

Now, Demonetization had pushed the industry and the association into the limelight. Suddenly, everyone right from the Ministry of Finance to the RBI wanted to know more about the industry. The reason was simple—without the industry, the Demonetization drive wasn't going to happen.

Soon after he got done with the call with the senior government official, Rituraj called for a meeting of the leadership at SIS Prosegur. 'The first priority was to understand what was happening. Over the next few days, people would be depositing Rs 500 and Rs 1,000 currency notes. These had to be taken back to the banks,' explains Esteban. Also, the new Rs 2,000 notes had to be deposited in the ATM cassettes.

Rituraj prepared a note to present at the meeting. It was on the role the industry could play in taking back the old notes. And how fast the whole exercise could be done with the new notes. He later presented the note to the Ministry of Finance, with Finance

Minister Arun Jaitley in attendance. The government and the central bank acknowledged the suggestions made by Rituraj. And soon the directive came.

A war room was set up in Mumbai. It included representatives from the cash logistics industry, banking, original equipment manufacturers of ATMs and companies who managed ATMs. Rituraj, Esteban and Akash were among those from SIS. As the second largest cash logistics player in the country, SIS had to play a critical role. Rituraj was the president of the industry association. This meant that both Rituraj and SIS were right at the forefront of this monumental exercise.

There was no mistaking its magnitude. SIS managed about 15,000 ATMs at that moment. It also had a fleet of about 3,000 cash vans. This was one-third of the whole industry's capacity. 'As the industry president, if I had to lead this, I also had to prepare my own team,' says Rituraj. He called a town hall of his team in Delhi. 'We all are worried. I am, too. We are facing a shortage of money to buy necessary things for our family. As the country's second largest cash logistics company, we can play a big role in solving this. You, as a driver, a guard or a custodian, can do things to make this possible. The thing is, either we can worry about our own problems or worry about our country. We have one-third of the industry's vans and people. You tell me what we should do,' Rituraj asked.

The response was unanimous. Be it a junior level crew member, manager or the vault team, or custodian. 'Sir, don't worry. We will do this. Just tell us what we need to do,' was the common response. Others suggested travelling to and from home would take time, so if the management could arrange a makeshift kitchen and mattresses to rest and sleep, the employees could stay in the offices itself and attend to work as much as possible.

'Not one of them asked what will I gain from it, or why should I do it or why I should be concerned. Nothing,' says Rituraj. After the town hall, calls went to all regional branches of SIS Prosegur. The template was the same. Arrange for a temporary kitchen and places to rest and sleep. 'In no time, SIS was up and running.'

Demonetization was complicated. As the days passed, it became even more so. Many of the Rs 500 and Rs 1,000 notes were soiled and damaged. Not all banks were ready to accept these. But the RBI came down upon the banks to accept them. Second, all the notes had to be 'evacuated' from the ATMs. For this, the machines had to be disconnected so that nobody from the public could operate them. 'By the fourth day, we were able to evacuate 70 per cent of the cash from the 15,000 ATMs we were managing. No company was able to manage this,' says Esteban. But then, another problem cropped up. The banks which were supposed to accept these notes refused to do so. They didn't have the space to keep the thousands of bundles that came in. Instead, SIS decided to park these notes in its own vaults across the nation. 'At one point of time, we had thousands of crores of notes lying in our vaults,' says Avinash Kumar, the chief operating officer of the cash business.

Now the only currency notes that were in circulation were of smaller denominations. If you withdrew Rs 500 or of Rs 1,000, instead of a single note, now you got five and ten notes respectively of Rs 100. This meant that the ATM cassettes, which could hold only so many notes at a time, were getting emptied in no time. That's when the government put a limit for daily withdrawal at Rs 2,000. 'There were instances where the public standing at the ATMs got angry when the cassettes became empty and attacked our men,' says Akash.

Now, to the other big challenge that the Demonetization drive threw up. While it was novel of having thought about a new Rs 2,000 currency, its dimensions were different from the notes that were presently in circulation. Even the new Rs 500 note was of a different size. That mattered a lot in the logistics of managing an

ATM as the cassettes are designed as per the size of the notes. 'The whole mechanics of a cassette didn't work with the new dimensions,' says Estaben. This meant that cassettes in all the ATMs needed to be reconfigured and recalibrated. And this couldn't be done by the guards and custodians that companies like SIS usually deployed. It needed engineers. At the same time, given the safety and security aspect of an ATM, an engineer alone couldn't have been given access but needed to be accompanied by security. This added to the complexity. Despite these challenges, SIS Prosegur managed to reconfigure and recalibrate 96 per cent of the ATMs in its contract within ten days. This was ahead of the rest of the industry—another indication that the company's resources and workforce were in sync to execute the exercise.

Interestingly, Demonetization, for the first time, brought some bargaining power for the cash logistics industry in its negotiations with banks.

On the whole, Demonetization was a coming-of-age moment for the cash logistics industry. SIS in particular, thanks to its own position in the industry and because of Rituraj's leadership, shone bright. 'Rituraj was instrumental in this as he took the lead. The Demonetization exercise wouldn't have been successful but for him,' says Esteban. There was a lot of interest from the media. International channels like the British Broadcasting Corporation, or BBC, and scores of Indian channels visited the cash processing centres where SIS was handling the cash. 'For all the money we handled, not one rupee was lost from SIS Prosegur. The employees put in much more effort than we could imagine. Despite the challenges, we came through. We are fortunate to work with a wonderful team,' says Rituraj.

Rituraj's leadership had turned a crisis into an opportunity with Demonetization. SIS itself shone through in its swiftness in sorting out challenges, and the industry finally got its long-due recognition. But a basic problem remained. SIS was still making losses. It was high time for the business to be turned around. Under the initiative, the committee intervened in three broad areas: relook every contract, reduce losses and plug leakages even further.

To plug leakage, there was strict monitoring using the tech interventions that were listed in the earlier chapter. 'We looked at data every day,' says Avinash Kumar. The custodian was changed every three months. As the person is responsible for an ATM's overall operation, the move was to ensure that there was no overfamiliarity with one region or route. Reconciliation of the cash was now done the same night or the next day. This used to take about ten to fifteen days earlier. 'So, we know if something is missing immediately because we have data from the bank and the custodians,' Kumar explains.

Also, people handling cash were more closely monitored. If a particular custodian was particularly leaky when it came to handling cash, he was let go. 'We set a tougher limit. Earlier, the limit was Rs 20,000 per custodian. We halved it,' says Kumar.

Next in line was reviewing each contract. These included contracts where the clients had refused to revise rates in five years. 'There was zero increase, even though our costs were going up, including the fuel rates—a big cost for the fleet. Instead, some even asked for a lower revision in rates,' says Kumar. The management decided to put a stop to this. Clients who refused to reconsider were let go. To reduce operational costs, employees were incentivized. For instance, if the drivers showed mileage better than the set limit, they were rewarded.

The sales team got a renewed push to change their thinking. 'If they had been happy so far adding four clients in the CIT business a month, the numbers went up. It went to seventeen to eighteen wins (new contracts), up to forty,' says Akash. 'Today, the same team thinks even forty is not enough.' What changed the approach towards business? The sales team focused on individual clients to get a higher share of their wallets. Earlier, it was about volume. Now, it was about margins. And about cash. For instance, days sales outstanding—the measure for collecting payment, which is critical to ensure cash flow—became a focus area. Earlier, the acceptable time limit was about 140 days. Now, it was halved. To fix targets, and responsibility, each branch and regional head was given the task. Where they used to approach the business purely from an operational point of view, now—just like the change in the security business—they were responsible for the branch's P&L. Review of operations, again taking a leaf from the security business, became an integral part of keeping operations tight and profitable.

'We have our own server, we have our own software team, we have our own development team, so we are not dependent,' says Akash. This capability has strengthened the cash operations to a point where it doesn't suffer leakages like it used to earlier.

An added impetus came in the form of government regulation in 2018. In April, the RBI announced guidelines that changed the way banks engaged with their cash management vendors. There were two critical changes—banks could engage with only those cash management companies who had a net worth of at least Rs 100 crore. Also, they needed to have a fleet of 300 cash vans. Through these measures, and given the experience of Demonetization, the central bank was ensuring that only those cash management companies who were financially stable were involved in this critical function.

In October of the same year, a big move was taken to ensure that the cash logistics industry itself was geared up for setting up better standards. Nine leading cash logistics companies, which made up for 90 per cent of the market share, got together to form the Currency Cycle Association (CCA), a self-regulatory body that would supervise the industry. 'One of the aspects that this brought in was compliance. We had an industry, and we had a set of compliance [from RBI]. We then needed somebody who was making sure that these compliances were being followed,' Esteban explains the role of the CCA.

This was a big win for Rituraj. Like his father, Rituraj was a firm believer in the regulations to bring in minimum standards and fair practices in the industry. He had taken the lead in engaging the RBI and the finance ministry, laying down the importance of and need for a self-regulatory body. The industry's work with Demonetization had underlined the role it played in availability of money for the general public. It was SIS Prosegur that brought in the lawyer to prepare the draft, taking a cue from similar organizations worldwide.

One of the most pathbreaking initiatives from the CCA was the introduction of the one-time code (OTC) to operate an ATM. Till then, the custodian had the key to operate an ATM. The challenge here was that the system was dependent on one individual with a confidential piece of information. That changed with the OTC. Instead of the key that was with the custodian, the code comes from a call centre. 'This is the safest and most secure way to operate an ATM. The code is random, consists of about eight to 10 digits and that opens the electronic lock. This provides better security to the ATM and avoids the misappropriation of cash by an individual,' says Esteban. Like all regulations, this one also took time before it got running on the ground. But when it did in 2019, SIS was among the first to implement it. 'We were the first company to operate all our ATMs using an OTC,' Esteban points out.

These steps, within the organization and in the industry, helped SIS Prosegur improve its numbers. In the aftermath of Demonetization, it hit the breakeven mark for the first time.

But just as things were improving, the coronavirus pandemic hit every business in March 2020. People were locked in. Business plummeted. As people stopped going to ATMs, or their visits became much less frequent, there wasn't much work for SIS Prosegur's large fleet. 'Our fleet and our men will only go around and work if there is business. There was none,' says Esteban. There was no cash to be collected or deposited. 'We have a problem,' Esteban told Rituraj. 'Unlike other cash management companies, our fleet is on our books. These are our assets. We have to find a way to use them.'

And this is where the nimbleness of an entrepreneur came through. Some could call it jugaad or even accuse the businessperson of being opportunistic. 'If our vehicles can move around, why don't we use them? We had a competitive advantage. Let's transport things that the public needs at the moment,' said Rituraj. And that's how the joint venture company began its Value Cargo vertical.

The new vertical started off with hand sanitizers, computers and laptops, some of the things that were hot in demand as cleanliness became a necessity and people started working from home. 'We moved anything and everything, from high-end sarees to passports. We worked for government departments and moved important documents. Every quarter, we carried question papers to examination centres and the answer sheet back. Once, there was a customer who said he wanted to transport cars. Each was around Rs 5 crore. We deployed men and escort vehicles when these cars were transported,' adds Kumar.

Value cargo is today a standalone business within SIS. Not a big amount, but it does its bit in utilizing an asset efficiently and adds to the topline. 'Since then, our company has continued to grow, has become profitable after COVID. We were among the few who kept looking for avenues to keep growing even though the larger business was shut,' says Esteban.

Since the 2021 financial year, SIS Prosegur has grown 97 per cent, even as the larger industry grew in the 48 per cent to 64 per cent range. The company's margins have jumped 744 per cent! The competition has grown in the range of 15 to 300 per cent, says Esteban. 'This is the bright period of the company. I think we committed many mistakes, strategic mistakes to be honest, but we were smart enough to rectify and to learn from them, to create the company that we have today. That is incontestably the second largest in the industry. Though we are not the largest, we are leaders in a number of things and, if I may, we are the leaders on innovation. Some of the business lines that we have, nobody has, and this is something recognized by the market.'

That is true. Unlike in the early years, SIS Prosegur is not overly dependent on one line of business. Instead, it now has nine business lines. The highest contribution of one single business is 47 per cent. On the other hand, among peers, their one business contributes to 80–90 per cent of revenue. In other words, the joint venture company has diversified its risks. A product portfolio as this one has now enabled the JV to offer its services under the umbrella of Bank Outsourcing Solutions. For instance, while earlier SIS Prosegur was providing only CIT services to HDFC, one of the biggest banks in the country, it now provides nine different services. This is in line with the stated objective of having a higher share of a client's wallet.

The cash management business also has many feathers in its cap. It is the only company that has an environmental certification according to ISO14000. 'No other cash management company has this sort of certification,' says Esteban. SIS Prosegur has added electric vehicles to its fleet. Moreover, the company has the lowest number of losses in the industry, in absolute terms and also as percentage of revenue. This is despite it being the second largest in the industry. In an audit conducted by the CCA, the self-regulatory organization, SIS Prosegur was the only one to get satisfactory certificates for all thirty cities the audit was conducted in.

The turnaround in the operations is a happy moment for the joint venture that is now over a decade old. It hasn't been easy. Esteban himself admits Prosegur has been more impatient than SIS itself. 'Prosegur, at a given moment in time, was a bit tired of the continuous poor results of the company. There was a bit of tension. But Rituraj always had a complete faith in the industry. The main supporter of our business in India has been Rituraj,' says the Spanish national. 'He has been a firm believer, even in the tough times, in the bad times. I cannot tell the same from Prosegur, to be honest, because Prosegur is not in this country. They don't understand this country.' Rituraj, in his communication and in every meeting with his partner, had reiterated his belief in the industry, the market and in the joint venture itself.

The worry has now turned into satisfaction. SIS Prosegur is considering an initial public offering, which will see it list on the National Stock Exchange.

It's not that there are no challenges. There are two that have gradually come up. One, banks themselves are getting into the cash-in-transit business, one of the biggest topline generators for a company like SIS. Two, intense competition within the industry has seen rates coming down, making business a tough proposition. 'Both are big problems. Banks have bigger and deeper pockets. Also, once the rate goes down, sometimes it takes a decade to get back to the previous levels,' says Esteban. The joint venture is clear it doesn't want to get into a price war. Instead, it is looking to further create niches for itself, introduce more products and get into more markets. One of them is to move beyond markets in the metros and big cities to smaller towns and even rural areas.

The focus is clear. Rituraj would want to be the biggest player in every industry he operates in. But right now, there is a significant gap between SIS Prosegur and CMS, the largest player.

Things have turned around significantly for Esteban himself. The job that he had initially set out to do is nearly accomplished. SIS Prosegur is profitable, it's about to list on the exchanges. Given that he 'never wanted to live in this country' when he first landed in India, does he now want to go back home? 'I did dislike it initially. My wife didn't. You know, I'm the only foreign national in a company of 11,600 people. But I have adjusted. And now I don't want to be in any other place. Where should I go? Europe? No. India is growing. I see the promise in the eyes of the people here. Things are beginning to happen in India,' he says. 'And, when I was in Spain, I didn't have a son. But I have a son now.'

What probably sealed it was when the teacher at his son's school asked his son to talk about his country. And he spoke about India, not Spain.

18

THE SECOND DIVERSIFICATION

In 2009, Rituraj doubled down on his diversification drive. He added facility management to SIS's overall product portfolio. In doing so, he was going against the advice those close to him had given him. "You are spreading SIS too thin, especially because the diversification was coming close at the heels of the Australian acquisition," he was told.

Rituraj could see the risk. But he was convinced. For one, he could see that there was a boom in demand for facility management backed by the IT industry's growth, and with multinationals setting up shop in the Indian market. This was the opportune time to get into the segment, otherwise it would be too late. Rituraj was young, but his entrepreneurial instinct told him 'it was now or never.'

What helped him convincing those around him was the backing of ServiceMaster Clean, which was part of ServiceMaster, an American Fortune 500 company. It was over fifty years old and was present in over 4,500 locations around the world. SIS took a franchise of SMC in India.

Getting ServiceMaster on board was a masterstroke. The company had developed its own patented processes and services that could be introduced in India. Its patent footprint extended to cleaning and for technology products that helped customize services as per customer needs. Combining this with SIS's expanding footprint across India and its own infrastructure of training and IT processes put new venture on a strong footing.

Adding heft to the venture was the involvement of Dhiraj Singh, who first came on board in 2009 as an advisor for all emerging businesses. While he didn't have an official role, Singh was deeply involved in setting up the facility management business, right from drafting letters to the bank to taking colleagues out for a dinner and meeting clients. It seemed all the basic requirements of setting up a successful operation were in place. But, to the dismay of everyone involved, including Rituraj and Uday Singh, the facility management business didn't take off as planned.

The joint venture started off from Bengaluru under the watchful eyes of Uday Singh. He and Rituraj had asked Prakash Binjola to move from the security business to the newly opened vertical and help set it up. For training, Binjola went to the US where he visited ServiceMaster Clean's local facilities to understand their practices and standardization processes. Binjola was part of Singh's team that had formed the ISO manual for SIS. Now, he did the same for the facility management business. 'I made the quality manual, starting the process from the US, understanding and tweaking it based on what India needs and then putting it in our normal simplified language,' says Binjola, who throughout the process stayed in touch with his counterparts in the US to ensure adherence to the franchisee agreement. The senior executive went on a recruitment drive to create a team for the new business, getting help from his colleagues in the security operations to spot talent.

The most generous helping hand was Uday Singh's. 'Though ServiceMaster Clean was licensed, it was with Mr Singh's help that I sorted much of the things to set up an operation, right from the rental agreement of the office, setting up the basic office infrastructure to the kind of people we needed to hire. We used to talk almost daily. So, during that phase, I mean a period of around a year—I won't call it a formal classroom training—but Mr Singh did give me a lifetime's worth of coaching,' says Binjola.

Setting up the processes, office and hiring a team took time and it was only after this was completed that the new company pushed for its first sales. That's when Bijnola faced his first big test. 'We couldn't generate sales. On a daily basis, I was on the verge of despair. For one or the other reason, sales were not happening.'

As it turned out, the facility management industry was intensely competitive. There were three layers of players in the industry. On top were the IPCs, the international property consultants. These were the likes of CBRE and JLL. Both were formidable. CBRE was, like ServiceMaster, a Fortune 500 company, but bigger. It was the world's largest real estate services firm that also managed properties. JLL was the UK counterpart. These companies had been in India for a while and their clients came with global mandates. Meaning, anywhere in the world, their clients would do business only with them. Nearly all the big brands and multinationals were already in their kitty. They were aggregators and would subcontract to local Indian players. It was near impossible to break into this layer.

Next came the multinational specialists in facility management, the likes of Compass and ISS. Again, these companies, given their pedigree, had big companies as clients. The ones CBRE and JLL didn't have on their lists.

The third layer consisted of India companies like DTSS and UDS. These were regional heavyweights. DTSS was centred in Bengaluru, UDS in Chennai. Among the three layers of companies, they had very well covered the business. How could SIS ServiceMaster Clean, despite the ServiceMaster brand, break through this wall?

As one month after another passed by without a breakthrough, Binjola was at his wit's end. That's when chairman came to visit SIS's Bengaluru business. Binjola received him at the airport. 'How is everything going on?' the chairman asked Binjola about the new vertical. He confided in the chairman. It wasn't good. He hadn't cracked a single contract. After discussing the issues involved, R.K. said, 'Meeting customers alone may not be enough. Because if you go to them, they will ask for reference. And as a new company you won't have a reference. Instead, use the appointment to pitch a contract that would bring a difference to the company and will help it cut costs.'

And it's by following the same process that Binjola finally got a break. 'I followed the process. Meeting the client, making a survey and putting our best proposal forward. And that's the process we continued. Even the second contract came through like that. Not with a reference,' says Binjola. The first sale had taken six months. It wasn't a big one but it was a breakthrough nonetheless. Rituraj shared the news with the whole organization through an email.

It helped that the first client, Tata Motors, already had SIS's security arm as its vendor. In fact, the facility management business 'piggybacked on the SIS network a lot,' as Dhiraj Singh points out. 'That was a key strategy, and for the first four years, it was more secondary to SIS, which was leading it in a way, supporting it,' says Singh.

Yet, it was not as if the business took off. The joint venture grew in the southern and northern markets. But it didn't disrupt the industry as much as Rituraj would have wanted it to. The facility management company remained a marginal player for a while. It was not a coincidence that it was around 2011 that R.K. fell ill and had to be taken to Singapore for an extensive surgical intervention. Rituraj stayed with his father through this time, managing his work commitments from the Southeast Asian country. Attention was also given to the cash logistics JV with Prosegur. In all this, the facilities management business grew but not at the searing pace that SIS's core guarding business was moving at. For a minute, it seemed like the setbacks of diversifying quickly and spreading themselves too thin were proving to be true for SIS.

Rituraj wasn't oblivious to what was happening. Just that he needed a break with his attempts until then to bring in talent to the facility management operations. Or if only he could get that one deal that would pivot the venture to the big leagues. He was relentless. And finally, there was a glimmer of hope.

The first break came in the form of a joint venture with American pest management major Terminix. The multinational had a presence in seventy countries, and this was its maiden entry into the Indian market. This was a landmark deal for the domestic market. It's not that big names hadn't come in before this. Godrej Consumer Products had ventured into the segment in 2004 through Godrej HiCare. But it later exited the business and sold its stake to a Danish company, ISS, in 2009. By bringing in Terminix, SIS was differentiating its offering in a space which was otherwise dispersed and unorganized. The JV was called Terminix SIS India. The agreement was signed between the two sides in Bali, where Rituraj and Dhiraj Singh met officials from Terminix. With the new pest management vertical, Rituraj's goal was to differentiate the business by expanding the FM service portfolio. To lead the JV, Rituraj brought in Anil Dias, who was heading Godrej ISS HiCare. Dias had continued with the company after Godrej's exit. It was a great hire for Rituraj and a testament to SIS's growth—especially fuelled by the Chubb acquisition. It was now big enough to attract the best of talent in the industry. Dias himself was convinced after meeting Rituraj and Dhiraj Singh. They had flown him in from Mumbai and opened the SIS office in Delhi for Dias even though it was a Sunday.

Having Terminix as a partner, says Dias, brought in domain expertise that was appreciated by customers. 'SIS had already built a wide offering that was centred around security. There was guarding, cash logistics and facility management. And now for pest control, we added Terminix.'

The joint venture started off serving clients both in the B2B and B2C (business to business and business to customer) segments. The second aspect, which was retail in approach and interacted directly with individual customers as opposed to institutions, was new. 'It took some time to get the B2B side of business, and I think in the first three, four years after this, we graduated to about 50:50, 50 per cent of B2C and 50 per cent to B2B,' says Dias. In the following years, that number kept changing and eventually the pest management JV went completely B2B. 'The reason that happened is because the core competency of the group is more around that of B2B. Secondly, we realized that despite all the investment in time and effort and money which is happening, the stickiness is not there with many of the B2C customers. So, you get the customer, you serve them well but, at the end of it, they may still go somewhere else,' says Dias.

The pest management business was a critical addition to SIS's offering. It was time to make a similar, decisive move in the core facility management business. A prominent facility management company was in the market to dilute its equity even as one of its existing investors was looking to exit it. This is where Rituraj made his move. What happened next was a rare case of M&A in India. SIS not just acquired DTSS, the Bengaluru-based facility management that had made a name for itself, but also convinced its founder Shamsher Puri to stay back.

In many ways, Shamsher Puri is similar to Rituraj. His ambitions for his company Dusters Total Solutions Services, or DTSS, were akin to what Rituraj had for SIS. Focus on a specialized product, scale it up, raise funds by bringing in investors and bank on M&A to grow rapidly.

Shamsher Puri founded DTSS in 1994 after brushes with the hospitality industry and an adventurous entrepreneurial stint of making caravans and recreational vans from scratch. With DTSS, he found himself at the right place at the right time. Bengaluru was undergoing an IT boom and real estate began to develop in various forms—residential and commercial. Healthcare and education followed. Nearly all of these outsourced many of their housekeeping requirements. DTSS started off small. A friend had asked Puri to take care of a housekeeping need of an acquaintance's commercial establishment. More business came in, mainly because Puri made a mark in the regional market for customer engagement and service quality.

'There is a very low barrier of entry in the facility management industry. Anyone with a 10 by 10 square foot office and a couple of people can begin operations. But the moment you scale up to about Rs 50 crore in topline, you need systems. You need to have a training structure, IT systems and good people. Now it has become a serious business. Cash flow management becomes important and one bad customer could send your business into a tailspin,' says Puri. But not many entrepreneurs understand the importance of having these proper systems in place and their growth goes out of control. Many fold up and others get bought by bigger players.

Shamsher Puri instead raised capital to grow better. In 2009, TVS Shriram Growth Fund, managed by TVS Capital Funds, invested $2.25 million in DTSS. A year later, it invested $5.38 million more. Puri used the money to expand DTSS to more sectors, and then for a M&A deal. In 2011, DTSS invested a 50 per cent stake in Sinar Jernih, a Chennai-based unit of the Malaysian company by the same name. Two years later, DTSS bought out the Malaysian company. By the time DTSS digested the acquisition, it was time for Puri to give exit to TVS Capital, and he went into the market looking for suitors. Puri was also beginning to rethink his own vision for DTSS.

'The vision was to become the largest. My vision was to become the largest in Bangalore to begin with. Then I thought, okay, once I have become the biggest in Bangalore then I want to become the biggest in South India,' says Puri. After the Sinar acquisition, DTSS did become one of the biggest players in the southern market. Now what?

The vision didn't end here. 'You need to find good people with whom you can share the vision.' He found what he was looking for when he met Rituraj for the first time, and then engaged with Uday Singh and Dhiraj Singh. 'They had a similar vision to grow the facility management business,' says Puri. And he found comfort in the common ethos that he enjoyed with Rituraj: a family-led business with a similar cultural bent and the importance of processes and systems to support growth. 'I couldn't have asked for a better company to come in as investors. There was a commitment to grow, make the business more digital and keep making it more profitable.' Rituraj and Puri bonded over their common vision to build an institution out of their companies, which would outlast entrepreneurs like themselves. What was needed was to collaborate with each other in building a company that will be hungry to grow, expand and become more important and relevant for its customers.

The two got along well. 'He is a solid entrepreneur. He is literally one of the guys who built the facility management industry in India. He is easy to work with and is absolutely a legend in his industry,' Rituraj says of Puri. Having seen the quality of the business Puri had built in DTSS, Rituraj was elated to have him continue with DTSS. SIS acquired DTSS in August 2016 for an enterprise value of Rs 175 crore. TVS Capital Fund completely exited the company. Most importantly, Rituraj convinced Puri to continue in the company and gave him free rein to keep building the business.

Mahesh Devaiah had advised SIS on the deal. And, as it turned out, the law firm was also well known to Shamsher Puri. Both SIS and DTSS had MD&T Partners as their legal advisors, an almost unheard-of practice as this could possibly lead to a conflict of interest either on the buyer or the seller's part. The same reason made the deal special for Devaiah. 'The transaction gave me a lot of satisfaction that, you know, two clients, both the acquirer and the target company, wanted our work. The most striking was the SIS family. They had trust that we would protect their interest despite us knowing the other target company so well. A large amount of credit for all of this should also go to Mr Uday Singh.'

The deal was finalized and with the founder continuing under the new arrangement. This generated a positive sentiment among DTSS employees and cleared off any uncertainty that usually crops up after such a deal. 'Even now the culture remains the same. We had a family culture; it was structured with a proper review mechanism. The company continued to be built on meritocracy where high performers were respected and given more responsibility so that they can unlock and realize their full potential,' says Puri. Just like guards rose to become chief executives in SIS, similarly in DTSS, over the next years there were instances of employees going up the ranks. 'A housekeeping staff is today a zonal manager. They look after a business that has a topline of Rs 40 crore a year,' says Shamsher. In other words, there was no disruption in the organization. Nobody, reiterates Shamsher Puri, left DTSS because of the change in ownership.

Dhiraj Singh, who had joined SIS in a full-time role in 2013, played an important by engaging with Puri, the team in DTSS and SIS's own FM vertical. "It was a lot of work that went into the promoters, working relationship with me individually, and because we built a very strong rapport between the promoters, myself and then the management team at DTSS. So it was a very cohesive integration and yes, that was a perfect model for bringing the synergies of both sides."

For Puri, it mattered that the SIS leadership continued to give him the space, respect and independence that usually a promoter enjoys in running a business. He continued to take risks. Some worked and some didn't. He even tried out strategies that hadn't worked before. 'They have not been obsessive about that. There have been people who were brought on board but who didn't work out. So, I continue to do things as I have done as an entrepreneur.' The big difference is that the systems and processes are even sturdier to vet out what works and what wouldn't. There are more people whom Puri can reach out to discuss his strategy. At the end of the day, however, it's his decision to make. 'I like it that they let me be that entrepreneur as well. There was a new digital product or a service line I wanted to try. They were never like, no, don't do it. '

That also included the acquisition of a small company called Adis Enterprises in Bengaluru. Rituraj wasn't completely sure about it but didn't say no. Shamsher Puri was keen to buy it because it would have allowed DTSS to enter a new product line. The deal worked in some parts and didn't in many. It was an experiment. But as an entrepreneur himself, Rituraj knew this was part of the process to expand one's business.

The DTSS business grew faster under the new management. "DTSS, before our acquisition was growing at about 8-9%, but post that they grew at about 30% for the next three years," says Dhiraj Singh. Post-COVID, DTSS grew at a CAGR of 16% over the last three years to become a Rs 1,300 crore company by the end of March 31, 2025. In 2016, when it was acquired, DTSS had revenues of Rs 342 crore. Shamsher Puri not just stayed for two more years after SIS's acquisition of DTSS, as Rituraj had asked him to, he continued to stay in the business.

THE SECOND DIVERSIFICATION

There was a clear leadership transition too. Sanjeev Kumar, who had joined DTSS in 2010 and was a key member in Puri's team, took on more leadership role from 2019. It was an important decision. SIS could have appointed someone from the mother organisation for the role, but it saw the advantage in Kumar's experience in the FM business. Kumar was made president, with overall responsibility of DTSS's operations. Under him, the DTSS business has moved from depending on the IPCs for its business, to landing service contracts by itself. 'Today, only 25 percent of the business—against 80 percent earlier—comes from the IPCs. The rest is from direct lines,' says Kumar. 'We have migrated from a manpower supplier and emerged as a FM partner for our clients. We manage the compete space for our clients,' says Kumar who took over as chief operating officer in 2022, and eventually has taken over the chief executive officer in 2025. That was the recognition for playing a pivotal role in scaling DTSS from Rs 342 crore to nearly Rs 1,300 crore. DTSS was a splendidly successful acquisition for Rituraj. In one shot, not only did it add scale and muscle to the facility management business of SIS—which was just chugging along till then—but in Puri he found a leader apt to continue leading the new company. Given that DTSS was on target with its growth rate and the brand had a strong recall among customers in its core markets of Bengaluru and Chennai, the SIS leadership decided to keep it a standalone business. That meant that SIS ServiceMaster Clean still needed an intervention.

It was time for Rituraj to ring someone he had sought out more than ten years ago.

The first time Edward D'Souza interacted with Rituraj, he came back impressed. This was in 2008. D'Souza knew a few SIS executives, who had then recommended his name to Rituraj for a possible leadership position at the facility management business. SIS had just acquired Chubb in Australia, and D'Souza noted that the company had sound reporting systems backed by a strong software infrastructure. D'Souza himself had an impressive resume, having started as a steward in a five-star hotel and worked his way up to senior leadership positions in several organizations. Rituraj asked D'Souza to take the reins of the facility management business and grow it for SIS as the head of the joint venture with ServiceMaster Clean. D'Souza was excited. As a young professional, he shared similar ambitions as Rituraj. But there was a problem. A Mumbaikar, D'Souza couldn't get himself to uproot from his beloved city and move to either Bengaluru or Delhi. He politely declined the offer.

The next time D'Souza got a call from SIS was in 2017. In the nine years since the first call, he had worked in three multinationals in the facility management industry, rising up to be the India head in the last one. A head-hunting agency with a mandate to look for a CEO for the ServiceMaster SBU of SIS contacted him. Was he open to explore a position with the company? With fond memories of his last interaction with Rituraj, and now more open to the idea of moving out of Mumbai, D'Souza said yes.

SIS was quick to send him a flight ticket. It was a Sunday when D'Souza landed in Delhi to meet Rituraj and Dhiraj Singh. They were waiting for him near the airport. The three had a long chat of over four hours. D'Souza had grown in his career. Rituraj and Dhiraj Singh had studied his updated resume and they were as impressed as they had been nine years ago. D'Souza was equally excited to see SIS's march in security and cash management businesses. He accepted the offer.

'We needed more growth oriented leaders. That is when we got Edward, who's a hands-on leader, right, hands-on person in this business, and Edward brought his skills,' says Dhiraj Singh.

In facility management, D'Souza noticed, the joint venture between SIS and ServiceMaster Clean had made some progress. It was yet to break even. The team wasn't big. The operations of the company were mostly limited to the south and some in the northern markets. There was nearly no presence in the west. Much of the client list were from the government and public sector companies. Clearly, the initial challenge of intense competition in the private sector had remained for SIS's facility management vertical. D'Souza could almost see what needed to be done. His experience of having headed the India unit of Aramark, another American multinational in the industry, would come in handy.

First up, there was no point in competing with the biggies in their stronghold. 'There was nothing new to do in that space. We went back to the drawing board and we said, fine, first we will go into those sectors where there are no IPCs. Second, we will go into those spaces that required a certain amount of specialty, a certain amount of expertise to operate those spaces,' says D'Souza. He had considerable experience in catering to the healthcare industry in India and globally. It was a different space. One couldn't manage a hospital like an office. Just keeping the premises clean was not enough in a hospital. Instead, the process was more evolved. It was about hygiene. 'In a hospital, one needed to be more scientific, as how the hospital is maintained also impacts a patient's outcome. We needed solutions for infection prevention and control,' says D'Souza.

With his leadership, SMC developed an operating programme in its concept note for healthcare clients. It was unique and customized according to the needs of the hospital. 'We were not selling manpower or material machinery, which is what technically everybody else sells. Instead, we focused on value proposition. If I come in and maintain a property, how can I improve the patient experience, how can I help reduce your infection issues in the hospital with my scientific method of operating the hospital? We had all the processes and programmes in place,' says D'Souza. The whole concept took time. A team had to be formed. People needed sector specialization, and that required training.

The timing was opportune. Private healthcare chains, the likes of Apollo, Fortis and Max, were taking off in the metros. In other urban markets, there were big standalone hospitals which also gave equal importance to hygiene. From 2017, the healthcare industry was to grow at a compounded rate of nearly 25 per cent. SIS's bet took off. From about two to three clients in the healthcare industry in 2017, SIS ServiceMaster Clean today has over a hundred. 'In the last seven years, we have developed as one of the best professional subject matter experts,' says D'Souza.

A similar concept was created for large-format retail malls. IPCs were not present in this segment and thus the competition was less. Also, given the resources needed to manage spaces that average about 18 lakh square feet, not many local players got into it. 'A large mall has to be like a five-star hotel. We got into mall management but needed to get into branded large malls where we need to improve the shopping experience, right from the washrooms to the food courts. That's where a lot of shoppers spend time. This needed a more sophisticated and mechanized approach, like the hospitality approach from our teams. These were big properties and these are big-ticket sales contracts,' says D'Souza. The approach helped, and SMC got into its fold twenty-five of the largest malls in India.

The third area of operations was large and heavy industrial facility management. These are typical auto, engineering facilities that have a huge manufacturing presence requiring heavy duty machinery and equipment. Their upkeep is highly mechanized. 'What's the solution, what's the approach we can bring there? We thought we need to bring in the concept of employee health safety. We need to bring in the concept of high mechanization and fewer people that will lower the chances of industrial unrest, which is often seen in such units. High mechanization also reduced the safety risk as one accident can bring the entire productivity down, crores of production loss,' says D'Souza. What also worked was that these contracts needed huge investments of up to Rs 3–4 crore each. Not everyone had deep pockets. SMC brought in high-end equipment to manage these facilities. These included high suction machines, sprinkler systems, JCBs and movers. Clearly, this was not an average housekeeping contract. The focus helped. Some of the biggest names in the manufacturing sector have become clients, including Tata Steel and JSW Steel.

Encouraged by these successes, it was time to get into segments that already had competition but where the JV could bring a difference. One such area was the modern, high-rise residential towers. 'People are spending Rs 2–3 crore for houses, and need high-quality services. The traditional help with a jhadu isn't enough to clean the big lobbies and clubhouses,' D'Souza said. Instead, apart from bringing in well-trained housekeeping staff and a high degree of mechanization, solutions like pest control and energy management were introduced.

To execute these contracts successfully, interventions were required at the backend. One was in terms of hiring and training people. D'Souza took a leaf out of SIS's GTO programme for the security business. The facility management company built a junior management training programme. Most of the people picked for this were graduates with hotel management degrees. They were chosen from all over the country, and their training came handy as it covered the basics of managing a facility. Beyond that, they were trained for three months to become subject matter experts in facility management.

The sales team was also trained to specialize in the requirements of facility management customers. 'The idea was to have focus selling and concept selling to ensure that the concept we had created for each consumer segment was implemented,' says D'Souza. Each of these officers, just like their counterparts in the SIS security business, could manage all the functions of a branch. 'We made them into mini-CEOs and they worked with supreme ownership. The biggest problem in the FM industry is a lot of people don't stay for long but here I had a great team that was very stable.' This stability was critical to execute contracts without any disruption. At the senior level, D'Souza began hiring subject experts who could head each vertical. Apart from the training, the company invested in software. For client engagement, a customer relationship management system was set up. 'We needed to have technology intervention. Customers wanted to see tech-oriented activities.'

The result of these initiatives in creating products suited to the needs of the customer, training of people and investment in technology was soon visible in the financials. The company hit a growth rate of 20 to 30 per cent CAGR. By 2019, the company started reporting positive EBITDA numbers.

A significant boost came in the form of another acquisition, that of Rare Hospitality in 2018. The company was a regional player based in Mumbai. In its thirty years, it had developed into a sound, small-sized company with a topline of Rs 70 crore with specialization in the healthcare segment. It had EBITDA margins of 7 per cent. Most of its clients were in Mumbai, Pune and Goa. This was a market where SIS's hadn't yet made its presence felt. D'Souza had taken the proposal to acquire Rare for Dhiraj Singh and Rituraj, who immediately warmed up to the idea.

Rituraj's time-tested acquisition model was executed here too. Rare, like its name, had the distinction of being run by a team that mostly consists of women. Right from the commercial manager to sales to the P&L head, almost 80 per cent of the employees are women. 'A very nice niche company, run by a successful women entrepreneur leadership team,' comments D'Souza.

Again, the owners were convinced to stay back for two years, and the two sides mutually agreed to set a target for the period. It was only after the two years, and once the targets had been reached, that SIS took over 100 per cent of Rare. Again, as in the case of Shamsher Puri at DTSS, the leadership at Rare continued 'When we took over, we worked with the promoter for one year, transitioning, and then we took more direct charge. Now, we've more than doubled that business. It's a brand on its own,' says Dhiraj Singh.

Now, with four successful facility management operations running in parallel, the obvious question to ask was: why keep them separate? Wouldn't merging them together bring in benefits of scale and cut costs? It would also prevent cannibalizing each other's territories and clientele.

Rituraj and Dhiraj Singh decided to go against traditional wisdom and kept the four independent. The reasons were many. Each had their own brand equity. For instance, Rare is a well-known name in Mumbai's healthcare market. Customers come asking for Rare. 'Why kill thirty years of legacy? We thought we should probably keep it separate and continue to build; we may want to build it more as a hospitality company and keep SMC as a high-end engineering facility management company. So, we're trying to differentiate the offerings in both,' says D'Souza. The same rationale kept DTSS also separate. What Rare is in Mumbai, DTSS is in Bengaluru. There is a difference though. While DTSS too has a presence in healthcare, it is also into pharmaceuticals and data centres, making for a different client profile. Nearly 60 per cent of its topline comes from Bengaluru, and another significant chunk from Chennai.

There is also the culture factor. While there is the common thread of SIS ownership that connects all the three parts, each of them has their own specific culture owing to their legacies and histories. 'So, I think there is enough space, enough bandwidth for every company to grow and I think DTSS has its own strength, its own recall value, its own customer base it has developed over the last twenty years and they continue to grow,' says D'Souza. It thus made sense for each company to have its own leadership team, focus on their niche market and go deeper into their specialization. 'It is easy to have multiple companies focusing on different pockets and carving out their niche into sectors and expanding the growth,' says D'Souza.

What mattered was that SIS now had the biggest facility management business in the country. And the parts were growing faster than the industry, at a rate of 15–20 per cent every year. The JV itself was evolving towards more specialized solutions for its clients and was increasingly pitching itself as a company that provided high-end engineering services for facilities upkeep. But there was an issue. With the ServiceMaster Clean link, selling this proposition was proving to be difficult. D'Souza explains by providing a hypothetical example of Odomos, the popular mosquito repellent cream, trying to come up with a toothpaste by the same name. The customer will think twice and probably wouldn't buy a toothpaste called Odomos because of the implications of its name. The customer will continue going for a Colgate.

'Similarly, in our business too, if your name is ServiceMaster Clean and you want to pitch engineering services, the client doesn't take you seriously. "Get lost, you are a cleaning company," is the first response. I can't even start a conversation,' says D'Souza. To get over this challenge, he, with Dhiraj Singh's backing, took a proposal to the board to exit the JV and go all alone in the FM business. The operations had scaled, there was significant volume, so SIS could be independent and also save considerable licensing fee costs. After a long deliberation, the board agreed to the proposal and gave its go-ahead. Singh and D'Souza reached out to their JV partner and, after multiple rounds of talk, the two sides agreed to cut short their partnership. The licensing agreement, which was originally to last till 2029, was shortened to 2023. The company changed its name and took on a new identity as SMC Integrated Facility Management Solutions Limited. 'SMC' stands for 'Smart Maintenance Company'. The team took a year's time to communicate the change and transition from housekeeping company to a much more evolved solutions provider in facility management.

In all, SIS's FM vertical stands on a strong footing, having come a long way after a wobbly start. At present, it has nearly 79,000 employees working through 109 branches that connect 7,700 sites and serve 2,606 customers. Along with the success of cash logistics, Rituraj had now comprehensively answered the diversification question. It was possible to have diversified businesses and specialize in each of them. With the leadership provided by Dhiraj Singh and the heads of four SBUs, SIS's FM business is today India's biggest. That's a remarkable achievement for a business that took off only in 2009. If the FM business was considered a startup, this would be a rare achievement. But then, the vertical benefited immensely from SIS's backing, and the growth impetus that came from acquisitions and tech interventions. A remarkable story in itself.

19

THE TECH EVOLUTION OF SIS

In 2010, Rituraj was just thirty-one years old. Uday Singh was eight years away from his retirement. There was still a lot of time for a transition plan at SIS's executive leadership. Yet, that year, the two of them, through consultation with R.K., set off an exercise that had a definitive and long-term impact on how SIS would be run. The idea was to make decision-making independent of an individual. Create a system—along with accompanying processes—that would enable the organization across levels to monitor and review its operations and accordingly take decisions within a specific time period.

At that time, there were three people who were effectively taking most of the decisions in SIS: Uday Singh, Rituraj and Arvind Prasad. They had worked as a team and had been splendid. Rituraj was mostly in Delhi, Singh in Bengaluru and Prasad in Patna. They didn't agree on everything but were mature and experienced enough to eventually take the right decision for the company. This arrangement may have worked in the SIS of 2003 but it was no longer tenable. SIS had grown rapidly in the last seven years, gained considerably in scale and was now also a multinational. It had revenues of Rs 1,449 crore in 2010 and was spread across 73 branches, with a little over

37,000 employees. There was no way the organization could keep growing at the same pace and at the same time be largely error-free if much of the review and decision-making was being done by three people. Instead, more of performance management had to be built into technology and not depend on human intervention in each step.

Amit Garg, founder of MXV Consulting, was brought in. Garg, a BITS Pilani and IIM Ahmedabad alumnus, was an associate director at Boston Consulting Group before he founded MXV Consulting. Based out of Bengaluru, he had worked with several leading Indian and multinational companies, especially in the IT field. 'We consider some of the IT companies as our role models. And we would like to develop software like they have for our performance management process,' Rituraj told Garg when they met.

The consultant was taken aback. He didn't expect a guarding company's promoter to say that. In fact, it was the last thing for a guarding company to say that it was modelled after a software company. And it's not that SIS had an IT team to match software companies. Its IT team didn't come with fancy degrees; they were a motley crowd who worked out of a basement room in SIS's Delhi office. Yet, Rituraj wanted much of the software needed for the new performance management process to be developed in-house.

Garg was pleasantly surprised. Rituraj and Uday Singh were crystal clear on what they wanted from him. Garg and his team met over 100 people in the organization and travelled across branches to understand the operations, looking at productivity, sales and other operational parameters. Garg and his team got a lot of room and license. Though they were the first external agency that SIS worked with, Garg wasn't interrupted in his work. 'It's something that I've always found really valuable in this organization. I don't think we encountered micromanagement even though we were a brand new external agency. I mean, once you build trust, it's a different thing. But at that stage we were brand new.'

There were disagreements on the way. One particular exchange with a senior executive left Garg with the dreadful thought that he and his team would be sent packing. Instead, the next day, the senior executive agreed to what Garg had suggested. 'It showed that everyone was very protective about SIS interests. They wouldn't yield an inch, but if it helped SIS, they would agree,' says Garg.

Over the next ten years during which time Garg closely worked with SIS, the IT team developed software that changed the way the company operated, right from the recruitment of guards and engagement with clients to sales pitches, monitoring, reviewing and awards. Five critical systems were created. Holding these together was a network of twenty regional quality centres, headed by the National Quality Centre in Gurugram. Five basic software drive the operations, supervised by quality centres:

1. Automated recruitment kiosk (ARK), used for recruitment. This was introduced in 2014.
2. iOPS, a mobile app-based management platform. Introduced from 2016.
3. Sales Maxx: Tech-enabled sales platform. Implemented from 2018.
4. MTrainer: Introduced in 2018, has made training mobile.
5. MySIS: Online since 2021, this allowed facial recognition-based attendance and has become an all-purpose app for frontline employees.

'After a couple of cycles, these new technologies started getting streamlined. Now, a guard sitting at a customer site in Cuttack knows what his KPIs [key performance indicators] are. He knows that these are the five measures. He knows that this is his data. He knows that he can log on to MySIS and see,' says Garg. 'There are few organizations with such a performance management system.' Annual reviews became more accurate, relevant and swift. 'The financial year closes on 31 March, and by 15 May or something, performance management is done for the entire organization, including all managerial and back office staff.' With Sales Maxx, he adds, there was a 50 per cent improvement in sales in the very next financial year. These software applications helped improve productivity at the branch level by taking a closer look at the cost structure and improving profits.

And it looked like the SIS's IT team was out to prove his doubts wrong. 'Yes, they didn't have a fancy degree or pedigree. But they did some exceptional work,' says Garg. There were mistakes to start with. But they decided to launch some of the software, take it out there and perfect it along the way. 'Despite us thinking that they couldn't do it, the IT team proved us wrong. There are times when one is very happy to be proved wrong,' says Garg.

The impact was seen in the financials. By the 2014 financial year, SIS's revenues had crossed the Rs 3,000 crore mark. By 2020, when Garg's contract was over, the topline had hit Rs 8,485 crore. SIS had 16 strategic business units (SBUs), 392 branches and over 2 lakh employees.

Rituraj also drove the team towards tech-enabled solutions. The focus was towards two ends. One, was the technology to drive internal, back of the house requirements that would improve efficiency, effectiveness, productivity and bring in cost optimisation. The second part was the customer facing technology to enable customised solutions.

In a major step towards this, TechSIS was founded in 2010. This is the electronic security arm of SIS and it further developed the technological prowess of the company. Building on the strength of its in-house IT team, the company developed tech-enabled solutions.

These ranged from what the company calls 'conventional solutions,' which included the use of CCTV, fire and intrusion alarm systems and integrated command centres. More sophisticated and specialized offering were in fire suppression and detection services. 'Man tech solutions' reinforced the traditional guarding business with state-of-the-art technology. The product is built on a comprehensive 4D approach: Deter, Delay, Detect and Defend. This includes body-worn cameras, drone and UAV solutions and entry automation solutions which are particularly designed for large industrial areas and facilities. A step higher in the software offering are SAAS-based solutions. These are marketed as aerial navigation, smart guard, smart parking and IoT solutions. 'IoT' stands for 'Internet of Things'. The basic promise driving all of these products is this: as per research, poor maintenance strategies can reduce a company's production capacity by as much as 20 per cent. Use of these products, in other words, improves efficiencies, reduces bottlenecks and saves costs.

Dhiraj calls TechSIS one of the larger 'system integrators' for a security company. 'We have done some very big, complex projects for the government and critical sectors like oil and gas. Now we are bringing those skills into our core business and combining them with man guarding to offer electronic security solutions to the clients. And the other part of this tech story is that we have projects which are largely B2B, then there's a B2G and AMC, or annual maintenance contract, which is a large business.'

The progress SIS made on the technology front became the differential when the business was disrupted by the pandemic in 2019.

One of the after-effects of the pandemic was the increasing preference of customers to have tech-enabled solutions that require minimal human intervention. The concept of security evolved. While it used to be more about preventing theft, burglary or an intrusion that would be physically managed by a guard, now it was about responding to an emergency through technology and third-party intervention. The definition of security became broader and deeper.

While this was fine, the customer wanted to pay even less. The pandemic had made cost minimization a top priority for every organization. They didn't want to compromise security; in fact, they wanted better security for their people, resources and infrastructure. But they also wanted it at lower costs.

The future of security, it became clear, was not about being manpower-less, but rather it was about less use of manpower, for higher effectiveness, lower costs and lesser dependency on human.

This resulted in an immediate course correction in one of the innovative products that SIS launched in recent years—VProtect. It was launched in 2017 as an alarm monitoring and response business focusing on retail customers. To head it, Rituraj brought in Shankar Subramanian, who for twenty-five years had sold consumer goods like air conditioners, laptops, digital cameras and then moved on to paints and industrial products for multinational and Indian companies.

A command centre was set up in Gurugram with state-of-the-art software procured from Israel. 'We were the first one in the country to introduce the entire three parts—alarm, monitoring and response. It's basically a beautiful integration of technology and human resources in an optimal manner. That is how I define VProtect, where technology plays a crucial role in identifying alerts from the premises and the people part manage those alerts at the backend and also provide response in case of emergency. This creates a beautiful synergy between technology and the people associated with that particular technology,' explains Subramanian.

The new product started off targeting residences in Gurugram. A pilot was done, the first of the customers were onboarded and the business was slowly scaling up when the pandemic struck. Demand for retail plummeted but, at the same time, institutional clients began asking for solutions similar to what VProtect was offering. Spotting an opportunity, Rituraj and the team led by Subramanian immediately pivoted VProtect's focus from B2C to B2B.

'We established our credentials, rather our leadership during the COVID, and then it got accelerated post-COVID because people saw a lot of value in using technology which has got a human interface as and when it is required to create a holistic solution. It is flexible and dependable, reliable, easy to install, operate and maintain,' says Subramanian.

The senior executive gave the example of an ATM to drive to the point. The norm used to be to have a guard posted at the ATM. Through the day, there would be two or three of them depending on their shift hours. If one guard was getting Rs 10,000 a month—hypothetically—the bank was spending Rs 30,000 a month just on one ATM. Apart from this, the bank also needed someone to clean the premises, monitor the lights, AC and the battery used as a power backup. Now, what if each of these functions could be given to just one vendor, who would not only provide security but also manage the premises? That's what VProtect does.

Through its command centre in Gurugram, it monitors half a million sites across the country using a software called Mastermind, procured from the Israeli company. Nearly 200 people sit in the command centre, working in three shifts to monitor the sites. Each person has a desk with dual monitors. The software helps make a customized SOP as per a customer's requirement. Depending on the SOP, the alarms and monitoring systems are programmed in each site. Taking the ATM example, the command centre controls each ATM remotely. If an alarm is set off—for example, if more than the prescribed number of people are present inside an ATM and thus causing a security breach—the alarm goes off. A warning goes from the command centre to the people in the ATM. If they don't heed the warning, that sets off the next level—where the command centre contacts the closest police station. The last part is response. 'We immediately inform the police of the incident and share the location of the ATM,' says Subramanian. That's not all. The command centre can even control the lights inside the ATM, switching it off during the night hours when footfall is low, again saving money for the customer. The command centre typically handles 500 'incidents' every quarter.

VProtect has quickly scaled in financial services and banking. Warehousing is another growing area. The next stop would be to take the product to manufacturing companies where it will combine robotics, drones and artificial intelligence to offer customized solutions. 'We are trying to see what kind of solutions we can build for a manufacturing or a large setup scenario,' says Subramanian. At the same time, the residential part of the business is also picking up. After Gurugram and the rest of the market in the National Capital Region, the plan is to take it to residential colonies in ten leading cities in the north and the south.

The design of VProtect ensures it is a high margin business. This is especially so because of the product customization done for customers. For instance, SIS serves State Bank of India across 6,000 locations in the country. The scale opens up the opportunity to customize SIS's offerings as per SBI's needs. This brings in additional margins. 'We were able to build a complete comprehensive solution for them. I think that is now getting replicated with many other banks. It brings a lot of value also. Prior to this, we were designing vanilla solutions that were available for, say, 100 bucks. With a customized solution, the offering has gone to about say 130, 140 bucks. So, there is a substantial increase in what you call the service offering but at the same time there is a substantial increase for the service provider in terms of gross margins, margin structure as well,' explains Subramanian. VProtect has EBITDA margins of 18–20 per cent, making it among the most profitable businesses within the SIS fold.

Is VProtect, because of the way it is designed, cannibalizing the basic core guarding business of SIS? It doesn't, says Subramanian. 'Many of the clients are not customers of our security vertical. In the places where we have replaced physical security, it's not SIS that has lost out. We will not go and cannibalize our own sale unless the customer asks for it but we would replace manpower security in most of the places, either in one shift or two shifts. In all my applications where I've gone for ATM deployment, there's a hundred percent shift from a physical guard to a tech-enabled solution, so that is a 100 per cent shift which has happened.'

In a fast-changing technological landscape with evolving customers' demands, the ground reality of the security business confronts an entrepreneur like Rituraj. SIS has to keep pace. And it has been doing so. VProtect is only one of the many initiatives the company has taken to put technology at the forefront of its engagement with customers. It has also become clear that the three businesses can no longer function in silos but have to work in sync. That caters to customers' tendency or preference to work with a single vendor for all their service needs. 'One has two choices—cannibalize yourself to meet customer expectations or allow customer to find someone else to replace you. You have to work with the principle "what's good for the customer will be good for business in the long term",' says Rituraj.

The same solutioning approach is happening on the facility management side as well. On the facility management side of the business is OneSIS. It's formed along the lines of the JLLs and CBREs of the world. 'We can do all of the services as a partner to the main client and then subcontract, sometimes even to external companies, not just to SIS. So, we adopted that model,' says Dhiraj. 'Like the IPCs function, we work as a partner with the companies and will manage the whole requirement of the client in terms of getting the best vendors and the best terms, subcontracting and managing them, coordinating with them, getting reports, making payments, taking care of certification and audits, as well as other value added services,' explains Dhiraj Singh. In short, under the umbrella of OneSIS, the client gets services related to housekeeping, cash logistics and security. OneSIS offers the convenience of having one person to talk to rather than four. 'So, it's kind of a key account management here,' says Shamsher Puri.

The potential of OneSIS became clearer, ironically, as SIS worked with IPCs, who in effect are the aggregators of several services. Most of their client relationships come from their home markets and get carried over into foreign ones, including in India. More often than not, they don't go looking to expand their clientele beyond this group. So that leaves a market of companies who also have a similar requirement—a single vendor who does multiple jobs. This is the opportunity that Rituraj and Dhiraj are utilizing through OneSIS. 'These customers want security, FM, maybe transport food and also control pests in their premises, all these services routed through one entity,' says Shamsher.

OneSIS is a step forward in the stated objective to have a higher share of a customer's wallet. Like VProtect, OneSIS also means that a customer is retained for longer and is more engaged. This is also because the investment that SIS needs to do for that one customer is high. And there is a tacit understanding that the traditional contract tenure of a year is not enough for the vendor to recover the investment. Instead, the agreement is signed for as long as five years.

The concept was launched in 2023, and both Rituraj and Dhiraj Singh are hoping it drives business down the line for all three verticals. In just about two years, OneSIS has surpassed the pest management business in topline. It's not difficult to see why. It opened up the opportunity of cross-selling.

'If I am offering some service to a client, I am already there inside the premises for a certain period of time. I have that opportunity to bring in FM services or some other services, like pest services, in that particular customer segment to build that whole story,' says Shankar Subramanian. This message has now gone to all the branches in the SIS universe. Each branch has a clear understanding and mandate to work with other businesses in the group to explore the cross-selling opportunity. 'The leaders work together on that. Leaders across levels, so it can be a regional, the zonal head or the national head. They all come together and work towards that particular goal,' says Subramanian.

That is a concept which is built to address multiple things, but firstly to ensure customer concerns are addressed. That is one part. The second is to explore the cross-sell opportunity between various businesses. Third, it is a platform for all businesses to come together. 'Normally, if you look at it, we would either meet during our half yearly or yearly conference or maybe twice a year or once a year, but in this case we get an opportunity to meet at least every two months. That creates a lot of bonding, facilitates the exchange of ideas and also helps to build that business cohesively,' says Subramanian.

Cross-selling is now officially recognized in the books of SIS. Subramanian says it is now documented on a bimonthly basis. 'A report is published that addresses the questions: What is the cross-sale that has happened, between which business? Who is the donor? Who is the beneficiary? What is the value? What is the quantum? What are the terms of the contract? All that is done in a very structured manner. One good thing about SIS is, when they talk about process, there is a structure defined on which it will be mapped, monitored and also shared on a periodic basis for people to know how, where and how much we are progressing. If at all we are not progressing, who are those guys who are not? So, everything is clearly visible for all,' Subramanian says.

Pulling this off is not easy. It calls for a common purpose, where one branch head is competing with the other but there is also a sense of a common goal to push SIS's overall numbers. Executing this requires excellent and continuous communication, meetings and discussions between these branch, zonal and regional heads. That's where the city coordinator comes in.

The position came in vogue within the SIS system during the pandemic. Each branch needed to be in constant touch with the other. A lot of work, including moving of materials and people, was impossible without constant coordination. That's how the position of city coordinator was created. This made the whole organization more agile. But its need didn't go away in the pandemic's aftermath. Instead, the need to be swift on the feet was a necessity to grow faster. The leadership identified around thirty cities that contributed to nearly three-fourth of India's GDP. So, if the country's GDP was growing at 8 per cent, these cities would be growing at least two or three times faster than that. This meant SIS needed to have a deeper presence in these cities, better coordination among its teams within a vertical and also among the three main businesses.

'The cross function heads now meet once every two months. It can be a business development, HR, finance or the operations team,' says Vinod Advani. This engagement is important to avoid confusion and uncertainty. One of the challenges, for instance, is not to oversell the services to a single client, who can't be faulted for being irritated if he is approached by multiple sales teams of SIS. Advani accepts that this may happen sometimes. But as teams are divided geographically, there is an understanding that a branch sales person approaches a client of a certain size and leaves the biggest of the clients to the regional sales executive, who is more experienced.

The launch of products like VProtect and OneSIS have marked the evolution of SIS's businesses. SIS Prosegur, as already discussed in the previous chapters, has also moved from providing basic cash logistics services to clients, to bank outsourcing solutions. These range from cash sorting, tech-enabled secure transport service and doorstep banking. In all, the three businesses—security, cash logistics and facility management—are no longer standalone operations. Instead, all of them constitute the pillars of what is collectively called business service solutions. It helps SIS leverage the strength of the specialization it has developed in each, collectively.

For Rituraj, personally, SIS's strength in technology-led interventions is now a big part of his vision for the company and for his own ambitions. Technology has enabled the evolution of SIS and will keep fuelling it. SIS's engagement with technology is unprecedented in the security services industry. It comes from what Rituraj says is the 'relentless experimentation without fear of failure.' SIS group's businesses have pivoted as customer requirements evolved, and staying ahead of the curve by using technology as the accelerator.

20

GOING PUBLIC

In recent years, an initial public offering and listing on exchange have become a rite of passage for a startup. A host of big-name startups, many of them unicorns, hit the bourse amid an IPO boom in 2023 and 2024. However, once the hype subsided, the aftermath has seen many of these stocks plummeting. This has led to serious questions on these companies' performance as many of them were loss-making at the time of listing. It has been a tough reality check. The most striking is the pace in which the startups move to listing. The food and groceries delivery app Swiggy got listed within ten years of its formation.

In comparison, SIS's listing was a long time coming. But not without reasons. Rituraj, Uday Singh and Dhiraj Singh needed a credible and promising story to sell to investors before they could go for an IPO. This journey began in 2008, at least subconsciously. Rituraj and Uday Singh brought on board Devesh Desai as the chief financial officer of SIS International Holdings Ltd, the overseas arm of the company. Desai, as we have mentioned before, came with 'IPO experience'. His immediate task was the Chubb acquisition and its aftermath, when he spent considerable time with his Australian counterpart Don Burnett in shaping the turnaround of the Australian business.

It was also the year when SIS began restructuring and reinventing itself, an exercise that was crucial for its listing journey. In the 2008–09 financial year, SIS published its first annual report. 'Annual report are not only numbers, they are everything about the company, its customers, its values, its vision and its expansion in each segment, as well as details of each business. We started it in 2009. That's the first step we took towards listing,' says Desai.

That was a start. But the path to listing needed more fuel. The most definite move came after C.X. Partners came on board, taking the place vacated by D.E. Shaw. There was a tacit understanding that once C.X. Partners came in, SIS would explore the IPO route to provide the private equity fund an exit. A private equity fund usually has a window of five years. The clock was thus set off once C.X. Partners came in. That was 2013. It was also the time that Rituraj started looking at acquisition targets to convert SIS from a security business to market leader across the three verticals—security, cash management and facility management. The vision was to build SIS into a platform for outsourced services. This needed money.

An IPO would undoubtedly help towards that goal as it opens up avenues. 'Tomorrow, you want a large amount of funding. You will obviously have one more source of capital which is the equity investors. Otherwise, if you're a private company, unlisted, you can only do that much. So these are things which are used also to open up opportunities and allow you to break out of the league you are in and get into another league,' explains Desai.

Rituraj also looked at IPO as a natural progression in SIS's journey. Apart from giving C.X. Partners an exit, 'We were thinking about the next step for the business. It was a mix of business requirements and I also felt that there's validation for the business in a lot of ways as a listed company, the first listed company in this space,' he says. The senior Sinha, as he has been in the past, was always open to doing new things and was again encouraging in this matter. He listened to what Rituraj had in his mind and said, 'You want to do an IPO, let's go ahead.'

It was nearly 2016 when Rituraj, Uday Singh, Dhiraj and Desai took a formal decision. The time had come to prepare SIS and the organization for a listing. A lot of things needed to be done to reach that end. First up, the mindset had to change to make the transition from a privately held company to a listed one. When you're a private company you can do what you want, but when you're public, you are answerable to the larger investor community to whom you have to explain everything. 'Why did I do this acquisition, for example. Why I decided this year not to grow my revenue and concentrate on my profit. Why I decided to go after revenue and not profit margin. We have to explain all this,' says Desai. A private company has the luxury of avoiding these questions. It doesn't need to explain or defend its decisions. But as soon as a private company accepts public investors' money and its stock is traded on the exchange, the world changes around it. A change in behaviour has to come in. It's not just about the ability to explain, but also to willingly engage with brokerage analysts and investors month after month and explain the business to anyone and everyone.

The mindset change had to come right from the top. Uday Singh and Rituraj made a conscious effort to show the way. The company's senior leadership was professionalized. There was now a clear process to identify talent within and groom them for larger roles. Thanks to the training culture set by R.K., that was a natural progress. More striking was lateral hiring and the increasing instances of Uday Singh and Rituraj identifying talent from outside the company. The outside talent was not just from the security industry but often from other sectors. Desai himself had never worked in a security industry but had worked with Singh in earlier assignments. The list only got longer—Anil Dias in pest management, Edward D'Souza in facility management and Shamsher Puri who came in with the Dusters deal are just a few examples. The biggest consolidation of leadership at the top was of Dhiraj Singh, the IIT Bombay graduate who had established several startups in the infrastructure and services sector. He had joined SIS in 2013 and would quickly move on as the central piece of the leadership transition that Rituraj had planned. We will come to it later.

The other exercise was to change the composition of the Board of Directors. From 2013, SIS onboarded seasoned professionals. These included Arun Kumar Batra, a chartered accountant who had four decades of experience in companies such as Nestle India and Group4 Securicor India, and Ashok Kumar Mattoo, a thirty-year corporate veteran with stints in Tata Steel and BHEL. R.K. and Rita Sinha continued on the board, representing the promoter family, and Uday Singh as the group CEO rounded off the board. Rituraj's absence from the board was striking. Usually, it's the norm to see the second generation get an automatic entry to this exclusive group in any company. By not doing so, SIS sent a clear statement to the markets and investors. While Rituraj was the company's future and one of its two executive leaders managing operations, his elevation to the board needed more time. SIS was not a typical family business that had relatives and friends on its board—the stress was on having a balance. There was the promoter family, a professional CEO and the rest were independent directors.

While making the organization stronger and deeper with trained and experienced professionals was the first step, Rituraj and Uday Singh also brought changes in reporting systems and strengthened the compliance and secretarial teams. 'They allowed us to sort of freely set up the whole backend and reporting systems and helped us strengthen the secretarial team, the compliance team, the financial reporting and the financial accounting teams, and this generally encouraged the mindset change,' says Desai.

The backend was the most important part for a company looking to attract investors. It needed to show banks and institutional investors a compliance and reporting system that would instil confidence in the company's robust internal infrastructure. Key to this was transparency of numbers and data. That came with the formalization of the monthly closing process, accounting systems, quarterly reporting, monthly reporting and the audit. 'During the IPO, you are required to constantly be on top of the data and the numbers and constantly feeding it to the team which is helping you do your IPO. It gives them confidence that, okay, these guys have everything available. Whenever I ask for something, I'll get it, and that's also very important for them to get confidence, and then of course, we have to make sure that you actually deliver what you're saying. If you're going to say I'm going to deliver 'X' crore of EBITDA next year, you better make sure you're going to deliver. Otherwise, everyone's confidence goes down. The bankers would think these guys don't know what they're saying and then they find it difficult to market their IPO,' says Desai.

SIS had brought in big names from the banking industry to manage the IPO. Axis Capital, ICICI Securities, Kotak Investment Banking, SBI Capital Markets, Yes Securities and IDBI Capital were the global coordinators and book running lead managers. It was the responsibility of SIS leadership to deliver the numbers so that these coordinators and lead managers themselves had confidence in the company and thus marketed the IPO accordingly.

Arvind Prasad, Brajesh Kumar, and Desai, the chief financial officer for the international business, played pivotal roles. Their presence was instrumental in bringing in predictability and formality in SIS's finance function. And that's because it had become complex in later years. After the Chubb acquisition, there were joint ventures with Prosegur for cash logistics, ServiceMaster Clean for facility management and Terminix for pest management. In the core security business itself, as the operations expanded under the leadership of Uday Singh and Rituraj, the finance function went deep with branch level accounting coming into practice. New SBUs like TechSIS also came in. Yet, the finance function—like the practice usually is in major companies—wasn't centralized out of the corporate office. While the implementation of ERP under the guidance of Arvind Prasad had made things better, nearly every finance team was functioning separately.

'MSS was a separate team, SIS was a separate team and SMC got formed. There was a separate team formed over there. By that time, ERPs were already in place in early stages and they were evolving over a period of time. Different functional models were added but everyone was working on their own,' says Desai.

To change this, the finance teams across verticals began collaborating more. 'We collaborated on converting the basic information into financial statements through automatic systems,' says Desai. The India team, for instance, worked together with their counterparts in Australia to step up and change and deliver numbers and data much faster than what was the practice. A predictable end-of-month closing of books was the big part. Australia had almost perfected the system of monthly closing. While there was a similar practice in the India business too, it was more like a soft close rather than hard close. The finance teams worked in tandem to bridge the gap, creating common platforms, systems and methods of doing things. 'Over a period of time, from different teams that didn't collaborate much with each other, today it's one unified team. They talk the same language; they meet five different people, then on certain specified questions, you'll get the same answer,' says Desai. This evolution in accounting systems and processes meant that routine things got automated. SIS's finance team moved from being data compilers to being data analysers. Focus now moved from routine things to value-added work that helped the organization take a deeper look into the business and help in better decision-making.

Getting ready for the IPO also meant bringing together forty years of SIS's history. Each and every detail of its operations needed to be typed up to ensure the DRHP met the accuracy and details that the market regulator, Securities and Exchange Board of India, was looking for. One of the toughest exercises here was taking into account each and every ESOP that the company had given to its employees till now. By 2017, SIS had given nearly 300 employees. To comply with SEBI's regulations, the company's promoters now needed to offer to buy back these ESOPs. 'I think it was one of the toughest assignments my team handled,' says Brajesh, Executive Director, Finance.

The next big task, of course, was to market SIS's IPO. There had to be a compelling story that also held promise of future growth. Only such a story could attract quality investors. It wasn't easy. One, not everyone was aware of the security industry. It was commonly seen as an unorganized sector with scores of players and low barriers of entry. From the outside, it didn't look like an industry that enabled its players to make handsome profits or build a large business. Now, while to the credit of the company's leadership, it had pulled off the Chubb acquisition, investors weren't sure how to gauge the Australian business. In 2016 and 2017, Chubb still constituted a large chunk of SIS's overall revenue and bottom line. How should an investor value this business?

The task of answering these questions and instilling confidence among investors fell on the shoulders of Uday Singh, Rituraj, Desai and Vamsi Guthikonda, who had joined the company in 2016 as President, M&A and Investor Relations. It was Guthikonda's responsibility to maintain the lines with the banks and investors. This group of gentlemen hit the road doing shows in India and across the world, selling and marketing the SIS story. 'When you go on roadshows, the investors like to see the promoter, founder, the CEO and the CFO. They don't really want to see anyone else. So that is where the focus was. Rituraj and Uday Singh were working on crafting the presentation stories to investors—what's the message to give them, how to tell the story about the company and its future,' explains Desai.

The team spent considerable time in India meeting senior executives from the mutual funds industry. This was an important group as mutual funds were beginning to expand their presence in the financial markets. Interest in the stock market was increasing among India's upper and middle classes, and the trend of investing in mutual funds through monthly systematic investment plans was catching up. The more challenging part was meeting investors overseas. There were four important markets to tap—US, the UK, Singapore and Hong Kong. The plan was to spend a week each in these markets. It was not possible to do this together. In the US alone, the plan was to meet investors in New York, Boston, Washington, San Francisco, Salt Lake City and Chicago. The team split in two. Rituraj and Desai were one, and Uday Singh and Gothikonda the other. Each day, they would cover one city, with the team flying every day across time zones. The plan was similar in the UK, Singapore and Hong Kong.

'There are a lot of funds from the US and Europe that have offices in Asia. So, we met them in their Singapore or Hong Kong offices. And it made sense because these funds have an Asia, or India, focus. You don't need to go to the US and Europe or anywhere to meet them,' says Desai.

These meetings are never easy. How much can you impress someone in an hour-long meeting? It's difficult to measure an investor's interest in just one meeting. It also mattered that the IPO wasn't big. SIS was proposing to raise Rs 780 crore. Also, it was unusual for these funds to get feelers and meeting requests from a security company, and that too from India. There was just no precedent here. SIS was proposing to be the first security company from India to list on the exchange. Marketing would have been easier if there was already a listed security company. It helps investors value a business, compare the financial ratios and understand if the company is on par with a listed peer and accordingly put a value to its shares. SIS was often compared to TeamLease, which was listed in 2016. But then, it was a staffing company and inherently different from SIS. 'Yes, there was education to be done. Investors had put in money in security companies such as TOPS, which was better known in Mumbai. But it had ended in failure,' points out Chhachhi of C.X. Partners.

At the same time, Uday Singh and Rituraj made for a strong team. As in the case of D.E. Shaw and C.X. Partners, investors were also impressed with the leadership transition from R.K. to Uday Singh and Rituraj, and SIS's growth trajectory in India in the last decade and a half. It was the second largest security services provider in the country. Not to mention the fact that even as SIS was preparing for the IPO and meeting investors, the company had been busy. Just in the last year, it had done an acquisition (Dusters) in India and in Australia (SXP). Its workforce had crossed the 100,000 mark and revenue had topped Rs 4,000 crore for the first time. New products and SBUs like the automated recruitment kiosk and VProtect had also been launched. It had also successfully made the transition to the new GST (goods and services tax) regime in 2017. In short, the company was busy growing, and every investor likes to see an ambitious, thriving company.

But nothing in the world of business is predictable. It was after returning from a roadshow in the US that Rituraj was hit by the Demonetization news. With cash logistics instantly taking a hit, and with all of Rituraj's focus and attention now centred on executing the Demonetization exercise successfully, the IPO was delayed. The markets had also responded sharply, with Sensex falling by over 5 per cent in the days following the note ban. Not an ideal time for any company to list. The SIS IPO was put off and revived only after the Demonetization got over by the end of 2016. Internally, the company was hoping to relaunch the IPO and list by February 2017. But investors wanted to see the full year's financial results for the 2017 fiscal. SIS had weathered the Demonetization storm well. Workforce now was at 150,000, revenue at Rs 4,500 crore and SBUs had increased from six to nine.

'It was important for us not to lose the momentum that we had before Demonetization. During the following months we kept engaging with investors,' says Guthikonda. In July 2017, there was big news. SIS had allotted 42 lakh shares to 18 anchor investors and raised Rs 350 crore. The list of investors included Abu Dhabi Investment Authority, Reliance Capital Trustee Co. Ltd, Aditya Birla Sun Life Trustee Pvt. Ltd, Amundi Funds Equity India and Canara HSBC Oriental Bank of Commerce Life Insurance Co. Ltd. These were among the leading institutional investors.

The big day beckoned.

Finally, the long wait ended. On 10 August 2017, SIS listed on the National Stock Exchange. The benchmark NSE Nifty index opened 36 points lower. The other oft-followed market index, Sensex, was on a similar trend, down 47 points. 'Negative sentiments,' market pundits said, had gripped the market. Yet, SIS was defying the trend. The first trade on its share took place at Rs 855 on the NSE, a 4.9 per cent premium over its issue price of Rs 815 a share. In the pre-opening session, the fifteen-minute stretch before the actual market opens, SIS shares had settled at 8 per cent above the issue price. This was by no means a spectacular debut in the markets but was successful enough. It was in line with the response the company got for its public issue. It was subscribed seven times over. 'We didn't want to leave a lot of money on the table, right? What's the point of having a thirty times over subscription and the company going down 50 per cent on day one?' says Guthikonda, pointing to some of the companies in recent years that flopped on the listing day.

The mood was celebratory. But there was none of the over-the-top celebration and punching in the air and high fives as one has seen in many recent listings of startups. That wasn't needed. Everyone present there very well understood the magnitude of the moment. Accompanying R.K. was his wife Rita, Rituraj, daughter Rivoli, Uday Singh and other senior executives from the company. There was a sense of relief. The listing journey had taken much more time and energy than anyone had thought. A successful listing, even though a moderate one at that, was rewarding.

The bigger emotion was of achievement. For R.K., it was a culmination of a long journey of an unlikely entrepreneur and a business that was founded on doing social good. He was proud to have led a company founded in Bihar that was now listed and its shares could be bought by anyone in the country. He was proud of SIS's origins. A few months before the listing, a banker had suggested that SIS moved its registration from Bihar to Delhi. 'After all, you are based in Delhi. Why not move completely?' It would have been good for optics. But R.K. couldn't be more certain. 'It's not happening in my lifetime. My tax will be paid in Bihar. My GST will be paid in Bihar, my registered address and the registered address of my business shall remain in Bihar,' was his response.

SIS was possibly the only multinational from India that was registered in Bihar. It's also the largest private employer and tax payer in the state. There are other two achievements too. SIS is possibly the only NSE 500 stock with its headquarters in Bihar. And R.K. is amongst the few Biharis who have featured in Forbes list of richest Asians.

Rituraj was proud to have played his role in the listing of the company his father had founded. There was little doubt in his mind, or in the minds of SIS's employees and investors, that it would be him who would lead the company in the coming years. SIS as a listed company, with its ticker now flashing on business news channels, had made a big transition. Rituraj, as he took on the responsibility of engaging with brokerage analysts, answering their questions and appearing on business news channels explaining the company's performance, was the face of SIS.

Yet, it didn't take long for a reality check. It came at the end of 10 August. The SIS stock had erased its early gains and had ended the day at Rs 756 a share, down 7 per cent from its listing price. 'The medium-term outlook will depend on how the company actually performs, otherwise valuations are not comfortable at all,' Alpesh Thacker, an analyst at Centrum Broking, told *Financial Express*.

Clearly, a new rigour had set in immediately. Desai likens it to running on a treadmill. 'Listing, the whole process, is a one-time thing. Post the listing, however, you have to be at it continuously. You're running on a treadmill. There is reporting every quarter, you are talking to investors and analysts. Reporting, talking, reporting, talking. Everyone wants improvement every quarter. But the reality is that every metric can't improve every quarter. The work is constantly trying to understand what the investors want, constantly educating them as to how you should see the business and what you should track and what you should look for,' says Desai.

The challenge remained and acquired more layers after the pandemic struck. Similar to all financial markets, SIS's shares also dived, going down to Rs 345 a share in the market meltdown post outbreak. But, as the months passed, it became clear that SIS had turned the crisis into an opportunity. In 31 March 2020 quarter itself, SIS's profits had jumped 48 per cent. In the second quarter of the 2021 financial year, even as India's GDP contracted by 7.5 per cent, SIS was having an exceptional year. By September, it had reached 94 per cent of its March revenue business. Its international security operations, concentrated in Australia, was at 121 per cent. Sure enough, investor perception of the company seemed to be changing. By February 2022, the company stock had climbed back to Rs 550 a share level. Since then, however, the shares haven't picked up. At present, they hover around the Rs 350 a share level. In other words, SIS's stock has never regained its listing glory. This is despite the obvious growth in its topline, bottom line, addition in verticals and acquisition of new businesses.

What more could the company do to convince investors?

'We did a more aggressive outreach. We constantly met investors. We invited them to our annual conference so that they can themselves see the scale the company has gained. The top team of Rituraj, Dhiraj Singh and Desai made multiple trips to Mumbai, meeting the analysts. But the stock hasn't climbed. It was a sore point for us,' admits Gothikonda.

It hasn't been easy for Rituraj, Singh and Desai. The shares hadn't done as well as they had expected. 'That's something that puzzles us. What else do I need to do? Since the IPO, our revenue has doubled, our profits have doubled, but the share price...' Desai's voice trails off. That is true. SIS revenue has grown three times from Rs 4,500 to over Rs 13,000 crore in the 2025 financial year. The EBITDA was at Rs 220 crore at the time of listing. That's at Rs 600 crore now, again a 3x growth. 'So what else to do? We do not know, but we will figure out,' he says.

There are many views. Some say it's because SIS doesn't have a steady quarter on quarter growth in revenue and profit. Others feel maybe the international business is dragging it down and yet others that they expected better margins. Rituraj has addressed these concerns. But little has changed. 'The problem is that it's not that there's a consistent voice coming through. Different people say different thing. We decided to focus on running the business well; ultimately, only that's in our control. So, focus on delivering revenue growth, increasing profit percentages and generating cash and let's see if it makes a difference or things change at some point,' says Desai.

Rituraj agrees. The stagnant stock has disappointed him. It has been a letdown for employees and investors alike. 'I feel sad about it and I want to fix it,' he says. That's one of the many things that are on his priority list as he looks at the next five years of SIS—Vision 2030. What is he going to do?

21

FIGHTING THE PANDEMIC

It was a real crisis, the ultimate test for business continuity plan. The country went under a lockdown on 21 March 2020. It was inevitable. There was no other way to contain the spread of coronavirus, or COVID. It was devastating for life in general, and for business. For an essential services company like SIS, the lockdown was especially debilitating. Each of its businesses—guarding, cash logistics and facility management—depended on the ability of people—both customers and its own employees—to move around. But now, clients shut shop. There was no need for a guard to stand by a gate or for a janitor to clean the office. Businesses had sent their employees to work from home. Retail spaces were shuttered. Banks had minimal functioning. In short, business, just like life outside, came to a complete standstill.

This was the worst nightmare for a promoter. On the first day of the lockdown, Rituraj visited eight branches to gauge the mood. People were scared but also re-assured. It was not the first time that Rituraj was feeling under pressure. In 2008, the high-risk acquisition of Chubb was done in the midst of a global financial crisis. The deal had made SIS highly leveraged, it paid seven times Chubb's EBITDA levels. Fortunately, the swift turnaround in the Australia business and the sustained growth in SIS's core operations in India carried the company through. This time, however, the crisis appeared even more serious.

For one, the pandemic forced Rituraj to drop an important fundraiser. SIS was just about to launch a follow on public offer. This was to be invested in expanding operations in each of the businesses. But as soon as the pandemic struck, Rituraj was forced to drop the idea. SIS's stock, which was hovering around the Rs 600-mark, plummeted like the rest of the financial market and went down to Rs 300-levels. Not only that, severe cash crunch was beginning to take shape as receivables from customers piled up.

Every month, SIS pays hundreds of crores to its employees and vendors. The monthly wage bill itself was Rs 400 crore. But clients, who were also looking to cut costs, either delayed payments or asked for a reduction in service volume or rates. Frontline employees were uncertain about their jobs. Even if they continued to have one, would they get the infection on the job? And if they flee to their villages, what would happen to their jobs? 'Just imagine having to deal with thousands of customers on the one hand and lack of frontline employees scared for their jobs and lives, on the other,' says Rituraj.

The SIS leadership team was in a flux. There were too many questions in the air—will we go WFH like others? What will happen to frontline employees and customer sites? Will there be a pay cut? Worse, will people lose their jobs like in other security companies? It was the perfect storm. And right in the eye of the storm was Rituraj.

It's in these moments of crisis when leadership shines through to show a path even though all seems lost. Leadership comes from thought and influence. Being the first, solving it first. SIS did both. Rituraj took the lead and made some strategic interventions. In hindsight, some of these may seem obvious but in the moment a lot of it stemmed from his instinctive reaction to protect his company, his people and his industry.

The group managing director needed his people to be safe. On the first day of the lockdown, Rituraj was at his Noida house and was on an online call with his top team. The use of Zoom for calls would become a common practice in SIS, as it did everywhere else. As he was listening to his colleagues, Rituraj saw that an unusually large amount of groceries were being brought in by his staff into the house. 'What's happening?' he asked Pallavi. 'It's a lockdown. We need to stock up,' she replied. Something struck Rituraj. 'Guys,' he went back to the Zoom call with his colleagues, 'my wife has called in for one month's ration at home. Has it happened in your house also?' Most answered in the affirmative. It disturbed Rituraj. He and his senior leadership could afford to buy a month's worth of groceries in advance. How about the guards and janitors on the ground? They didn't have enough money to buy ration and stock it. He immediately told his team. 'We need to transfer an advance salary to everyone on the payroll tomorrow so that everyone can buy ration for their families.' 'But some of these people may still leave us and go back to their native place. Should we spend money, especially in a time like this?' some of his colleagues asked. 'It doesn't matter. We may take a hit but this has to be done,' Rituraj said. In his mind, these were the moments when the leadership had to reinforce the family culture that they often talked about and professed to their colleagues during meetings and conferences. This was the time to put your money where your mouth is. The amount being transferred was significant for employees—lakhs of guards, janitors and cash crew members.

Rituraj was also worried about the welfare of SIS employees who got infected. There was the whole affordability issue, with the cost of testing, and then the loss of pay during quarantine and recovery period. Those who were infected also needed access to oxygen cylinders, one of the most sought after commodity during the pandemic. To address these issues, and as per advice from R.K., SIS set up Humare Heroes

Welfare Fund, which provided Rs 10,000 to every employee who got infected. The fund also provided a life cover.

To make such financial assistance possible, R.K. had set up a Rs 10 crore Hamare Heroes Welfare Fund. 'Medical insurance didn't cover COVID at that time. So, this fund was a big help for employees and their facilities. Without the fund, many would have lost their lives,' says Dinesh Gupta.

The other intervention came in the form of pursuing the government for formal recognition of security services, cash logistics and facility management as 'essential services.' This was important to allow employees to go to customer sites, assist customers and protect client premises that were shut during the lockdown.

'There were passes which we could use. But it was still difficult,' says Akash. He lived in Greater Noida, technically in Uttar Pradesh. The SIS office was in Delhi's Okhla. 'Every day, the police would stop our vehicle. We had a pass but that was also not valid for both the cities. We used to try to convince the policemen. Sometimes it worked, sometimes it didn't.' As more and more employees shared the practical difficulties they faced, and many others from the industry echoed these sentiments, Rituraj understood the need for intervention at the government level.

Rituraj made several rounds of the home ministry, which was responsible for making the essential services list. He met policymakers and bureaucrats. He had two main points to put across to them. One, it was not possible for the police to ensure lockdown and also ensure security of millions of establishments, from factories to malls to hotels that had been non-operational and therefore vulnerable. They needed help. The guarding industry had up to 50 lakh security guards. If all of them were forced to stay inside their houses, what would happen to the general law and order? Also, it was about the livelihood of the very 50 lakh guards and their families. If they didn't work, they wouldn't have any money to feed their families. The visits to the ministry and meetings with senior government officers helped and there was a breakthrough. The final call was taken by the Home Minister Amit Shah himself after Rituraj briefed him as chairman of FICCI's private security committee. The home ministry amended the list of essential services to include guarding and housekeeping. It was a big moment for the whole industry. By getting the essential services tag, Rituraj had saved the industry and brought it back from the brink.

'A lot of lobbying was done and it was down to Rituraj's leadership that made the difference. He was the chair of the private security committee of FICCI. He represented the whole industry,' says Gurbir Singh. It was indeed so. As the restrictions at that time prevented people gathering together, it was mostly Rituraj who would make the rounds of the ministry on his own. After every meeting, he would update his industry colleagues.

This was just the kind of intervention Rituraj needed. First, it emboldened the ranks of SIS. 'How could we sit at home when we saw the GMD coming to the office every day. Everyone was inspired to be proactive,' says Natalie Hansda, who works in Rituraj's office. Second, it made a huge difference to the operations. It became the basic plank on which SIS now offered its services to its clients. Everyone from the branch level called up customers and offered business continuity planning. 'This was an opportunity to show them business continuity planning in action. I said, "Go out and ask all your customers. Do you want to send someone to the hospital? It's not my job but SIS will do it. If your child is stuck in Kota and if you want to bring him back to Calcutta from Kota, SIS will help you get it done." It's not my job but I will do it,' says Rituraj.

Not just did SIS and its employees get people back home but they made available sanitizers, gloves, masks, vaccines and, most importantly, oxygen cylinders to anyone and everyone who reached out to them. These included customers and their friends and relatives, employees, friends, friends of friends and relatives. Rituraj himself fielded calls by the minute, coordinating with colleagues from across the country. 'It was like GMD had ten hands!' says Hansda. With Rituraj showing the way, the rest of the leadership followed suit.

SIS also declared work from office for all employees except for those who were at a high risk of getting infected, for instance those above the age of 55, or with co-morbidities. The top leadership too came to office. "We can't be WFH and expect frontliners to be at sites. This is both morally unfair and clear departure from SIS culture. In crisis, branch level, regional level, SBU level and group level leaders must lead from the front and be seen on the ground," says Rituraj.

As soon as vaccines became available, SIS started the Hamare Heroes Vaccination Drive. SIS was among the first organizations in the country to launch a company-wide, countrywide campaign to vaccinate its employees. In total, nearly 5.5 lakh doses were administered to SIS employees between the two doses that were needed by each person. 'There was shortage of time. But after close to one year of concentrated effort, we were able to do the vaccinations. Within the corporate world, especially in India, I don't think any other company was able to accomplish that,' says Amit Bajaj, General Manager (HRD), SIS.

These three steps galvanized the workforce. 'Initially, we were unsure what to do,' says Natalie Hansda. 'No one was sure if we should take the vaccine or not.' That was because of the many doubts and rumours making the rounds on the efficacy and side-effects of the vaccine. 'But when we saw Chairman Sir and GMD Sir taking the vaccines and showing the way for others. That gave us a boost, and we also went for the vaccination,' she adds.

Remarkably, there were no job cuts or salary cuts in SIS. That was unheard of across corporate India. Nearly every company had asked its employees to accept delayed salaries, a cut in their take-home pay, and lakhs were sent on leave without pay. Not SIS. 'Everyone around us was astonished. My relatives and neighbours would ask which company are you working for which hasn't cut salaries or jobs,' says Hansda. Their bewilderment would increase after hearing that SIS, in fact, had even given salaries in advance to its people.

This was important for Rituraj as the company's leader. 'I was petrified to make a decision which could cost somebody's life. It sounds motivating and inspiring to say everyone went to work. But if somebody gets COVID and dies who would take responsibility?' he admits. The services business was inherently a risky job because guards came in close proximity with people, especially those working in hospitals. While the whole country was keeping a distance from each other, the SIS men and women on the ground couldn't. In the cash logistics business, the regulations said five people were needed inside a cash van to ensure security. If one of them got infected, the other four would have to be quarantined too. ATMs had a constant presence of people coming in and out, making them highly vulnerable spaces.

Rituraj took steps to send the message down the line that everyone had to take care of themselves. The seniors were tasked to supervise this. 'The GMD called a meeting of the executive council, which has representatives from all the verticals. He said this is that one moment where we have to serve our country. At the same time, we have to take care of ourselves and take precautions,' recalls Akash.

An SOP was established for the organization in terms of availability of masks, sanitizers and gloves in each branch across the country. There were separate instructions on following safety guidelines in the workplace—from hospitals to ATMs. In ATMs, for instance, the cash custodian was asked to first ensure the inside of the ATM was sanitized before he went in. 'In the senior leadership, on a weekly basis I used to take the reporting of all the people across branches. We had set up a structure for that. We took very strong preventive steps making sure the salaries were given on time. All the sites were running. We didn't close any of our offices. We all came to the offices almost every day,' says Dhiraj Singh.

Despite precautions, it was inevitable that people got infected. Lives were lost. But the support the organization lent to its employees and their families during these tough times made the difference. When Akash himself needed to be hospitalized, among the first ones to call him was Rituraj. The GMD himself came down with the viral infection twice. The message had gone down the ranks—the organization will be with you through thick and thin.

'If there is any issue, I had the assurance that the leadership will always be standing behind me or he [Rituraj] will always be with me. That's the feeling, that's the connection you get with this organization. I keep telling my team members, this is one organization where you will see people staying on for long,' says Akash.

The business continuity plan started showing how SIS responded to the changing needs of its customers. As mentioned before, the cash logistics team started Value Cargo, a new vertical to move critical items for its customers. This ensured that its large fleet was put to use, helping their customers and in the process also making money for the company. The vertical continued to do well even after the pandemic subsided and is today one of the offerings of the cash logistics operations.

In the post-lockdown period, SIS's ServiceMaster Clean JV launched new concepts that focused on providing better hygiene. One was a smart surface disinfection programme. Another product that was launched was airborne infection prevention control solutions through germicidal UV technology. 'As a group we said we needed to go to the market and give solutions because everybody was grappling with infection. We offered hospital-grade cleaning services to non-healthcare customers because post-COVID everybody was very sensitive. Everybody was wearing gloves and they were washing hands ten times a day. They were saying they need their homes and offices cleaned the way it was done in hospitals,' says D'Souza. 'We were the first ones in the industry to be able to offer this service.'

Healthcare, in fact, became an area of focus for both the facility management and guarding businesses. With customer outreach and customized solutions in hand, SIS added healthcare clients in both verticals. 'Though business in other sectors were impacted, we added in healthcare and that kind of balanced things out,' says D'Souza.

This was also the time when SIS took a tough stance with customers who were reluctant to acknowledge the additional services that SIS was giving them. Shamsher Puri cites the example of a major customer who was worth Rs 40 crore of business in a year. 'But the customer was adamant about a drastic cut in rates, citing the COVID excuse. That would have impacted our margins. We had taken a call to not be in contracts that didn't give healthy margins,' he says. When the customer didn't see reason at the negotiating table, Puri walked out of the room. The customer was taken aback and agreed to reconsider. Puri had called their bluff.

Unsurprisingly, despite all efforts, COVID had an impact. The facility management segment, for instance, saw a 33 per cent drop in business because of the big share of Indian Railways in its topline. Indian Railways, for the first time in its more than 150-year history, had come to a standstill as travel was banned. But then, the healthcare segment took off and initiatives taken by the team worked well. 'The hospital became a big thing and that was the centre of survival of my business because we were in healthcare and we became an essential services provider. So, business in healthcare grew a little bit during those years, and we also got additional work in healthcare that helped us sustain. But because we had so many solutions in place and we had healthcare grade solutions that we could offer to all of our other customers, in a year's time we had an absolute V-shaped recovery. We doubled the turnover. From Rs 460 crore we dropped to Rs 300 crore and from Rs 300 crore we came to Rs 600 crore,' says D'Souza.

It underlined the fact—one often overlooked—that hospitals don't run on doctors and nurses alone. It takes an array of support services to make a hospital run. Most of these services were done by SIS and facility management companies.

Some of the big ticket wins in the time included the jumbo quarantine facilities that cropped up across cities, managed by local governments. SIS was one of the biggest providers of service solutions to these centres. And the results were there to show at the end of the 2021 financial year. Even though the country's GDP shrank by 7 per cent, SIS's numbers grew.

'For the first four to five months, our business went downward but then we recovered very fast,' says Brajesh. 'In the India security business, in the first year of COVID, we got 1 per cent growth and there was no drop during COVID and, in the second year, the growth was 10 per cent. In the first year of COVID, when every company was suffering and there was a complete shutdown of the entire economy, we still got one per cent growth during that time. And, internationally, we got 10–12 per cent growth at that time. The topline margin of international business was really very good. Even in India, we didn't incur any major business loss.' On a consolidated basis, SIS revenues for the 2021 financial year grew by 7 per cent.

SIS, though on the brink in the initial days of the pandemic, had recovered spectacularly and transformed a crisis into an opportunity. Rituraj also used the time to push the company to get better processes. 'We strengthened the reporting system, strengthened the way systems work, put in platforms and generally tried to take things to a new level of automation and efficiency. From that point of view, it was a black period in one sense. But in another sense, we made improvements,' says Devesh Desai. 'Rituraj encouraged us to reengineer all the platforms and processes. We embarked on that particular project and fought these things through, and during COVID also he encouraged us to constantly be at it rather than sit still because nothing was happening, we had to make things happen. In fact, we rolled out the financial accounting platform Oracle Solutions during COVID.'

Customers have shown their appreciation. 'In the wake of outbreak of COVID-19, we would like to admire the efforts put in by SIS for providing cash management services,' Axis Bank said in a testimonial for the SIS-Prosegur's services during the pandemic. Similarly, Accenture said, 'Thanks for the security support received during this unprecedented lockdown situation of managing COVID-19.'

Internationally, while the Australian business held on strong. It was now being led by Geoff Alcock, the managing director of MSS. 'The way the pandemic hit us, quite frankly we didn't know if we could have a business. But the way we responded, working with the clients, it was very challenging and also very rewarding,' says Alcock. Like with SIS in India, MSS in Australia was among the first companies to vaccinate its employees. 'We had 6,000 people. We made a decision to incentivise the staff to get vaccination,' says Alcock.

There was a hit to the business. Aviation was among the biggest sector for the Australian business. But it was also among the sectors that was hit the most by the pandemic. But MSS made up for the loss in aviation by adding contracts from the government. 'We did some work for the government in South Australia and West Australia in the quarantine programme,' says Alcock. The rebound in the Australian business was among the highlights in an otherwise slow year for SIS's consolidated business. It also showed that the local organization had come a long way in its turnaround journey and held on despite the team in India unable to travel across because of travel restrictions.

But there was a setback in Singapore. In January 2019, SIS had acquired Henderson Security Services for Rs 226 crore. The company provided man guarding services and also had an electronic security vertical. It worked in over 200 sites in Singapore and had about 1,500 employees. It looked like a solid, strategic investment that gave SIS a dominant presence in Singapore. Like in other acquisitions, Rituraj had led SIS to acquire 60 per cent in Henderson. The rest of the stake would be acquired over the next four years and there were conditions built in on the targets that the Henderson owners—who had agreed to continue in the company—had to deliver.

But once the pandemic struck, the owner pressed the panic button. He wanted to immediately sell the remaining 40 per cent. Sitting in India and unable to travel to Singapore, Rituraj and his team were helpless and had to give in to the demands. The promoter exited the company and took key executives and even key clients. For the first time in his life, Rituraj onboarded a new chief executive through a video conference call.

The business is now back on track and has even delivered profits.

Personally, it was a trying time for Rituraj. As COVID's severity became obvious, R.K. and the rest of the family along with Rituraj's sister Rivoli, wife Pallavi and the children—Rivoli's son and Rituraj and Pallavi's two daughters and son—moved to Dehradun. R.K. had set up Indian Public School in the Uttarakhand capital. Later, they had converted a vintage, British-era cottage into their summer home, right next to the school. Though the rest of the family asked him to also move to Dehradun, Rituraj stayed put in Noida. When the whole organization needed to be on its feet and get on with the work, he couldn't stay put within a bubble. He was alone at his Noida residence when he caught COVID. Giving him company was one member of his staff.

Whenever he got the time to visit his family in Dehradun, he would first quarantine himself for one week post COVID test in a guest house, spend a couple of days with his family and then travel back to Noida. That's what he did when everyone in Dehradun, including R.K., were down with COVID. Rituraj took care of the family. 'He did everything, fed us, gave us medication. He stayed with us till we recovered and then he went back,' says Pallavi. 'We were glad to have recovered and everyone was fine but overall, as a family, it was a dark time for us.'

Back in Noida, worried about his family and his SIS team, Rituraj spent his alone time reading books. He began reading one book a week, jotting down notes. Separately, he used the time to write. 'I had to keep my brain busy with something. So, that actually became a good learning period. I read about very random things and I read a lot and scribbled a lot—this idea, that idea.'

In all, Rituraj, the Sinha family and the larger SIS team had survived a crisis that could have broken them. They didn't just survive, they emerged stronger. To top it all, since the pandemic, SIS's place in Great Place to Work rankings has only got better. It's consistently ranked among the top companies in the country across categories—for women, mega employer, nation builders and for building a culture of innovation. In 2025, was ranked ninth in the country for mainstream Great Place To Work category. The citation said: 'For inspiring trust among your people, instilling pride in them, creating an environment that promotes camaraderie, and delivering a great workplace experience for all you employees, making your organization one of India's Best Companies to Work For.'

The certification comes like a cherry at the top of a list of significant achievements post a period of turmoil.

22

THE FUTURE

It was a forty-minute masterclass in rallying your troops. Rituraj Sinha was addressing 1,000 of his colleagues from India and overseas who had gathered in the giant auditorium of Delhi's Yashobhoomi Convention Centre, said to be the largest in Asia. It was 3 May 2025, the second day of SIS's annual conference. This year's conference held additional importance as it coincided with the end of the company's Vision 2025 plan and the start of the next five-year phase.

As the giant screen behind him flashed numbers showing the growth in SIS's revenue and margins from 2020 to 2025, Rituraj chided the gathering. 'We have underperformed. Do you agree with me?' he asked. The reply was feeble. He asked again. This time, the 'Yes, sir,' was loud and clear. 'Some of you may argue that conditions were not right, competition was tough. Let's discuss this. If anyone thinks these reasons are legitimate, raise their hands.' No one did. 'These could be genuine reasons. But can we do better?' he asked next. There was a resounding 'Yes!' Reminding them that they could indeed do better, Rituraj recounted SIS's growth from a Rs 22 crore company in 2002 to the Rs 14,000 crore it generated in the 2025 financial year.

THE FUTURE

By the time Rituraj finished his speech, the auditorium was alive and buzzing. In those forty minutes, the group managing director had made his men and women accept and acknowledge that they had come up short but at the same time had motivated and made them excited about the upcoming five years. Over the next few hours, the chief executive officers of various verticals and business units shared the targets for Vision 2030 and the big ideas that would guide them to those milestones. The targets were tough but the overall mood was buoyant.

'That was a fantastic session. It was straight out of an army boot camp,' a retired officer in the armed forces, who had recently joined SIS at a senior position, complimented Rituraj during the tea break. Later, at the end of the day, Uday Singh made a significant observation in his closing remarks: 'Anyone who has heard our chairman speaking in the past, and now having heard Rituraj the past two days, would appreciate the fact that the succession planning at the top of SIS is complete.'

The significance of that statement was not lost to the gathering. In the history of SIS, this was the first annual conference when the chairman was absent. R.K. was in Singapore, recovering from a stroke. In the past, it was R.K. who would make the inaugural address of every annual conference. This time, it was Rituraj. While everyone felt the founder's absence, they took confidence from the son's presence and his words.

For all practical purposes, Rituraj had been firmly in the saddle at SIS for a while. Uday Singh had hung up his boots in April 2018, handing over the reins to Rituraj. R.K. in these years had increasingly spent time away from the daily affairs of SIS and had been engrossed in his pet projects. This included helping his daughter-in-law Pallavi in taking an entrepreneurial plunge with Adya Organics. The startup specializes in products based on millets, a cause close to the patriarch's heart.

This meant that Rituraj now had multiple challenges. First, he had to ensure a smooth transition to a post-Uday Singh era. It wasn't easy to let go of Uday Singh. When he reached the age of sixty, the retirement age was increased to sixty-five. As he neared that age, sometime in 2015, Singh shared the desire to move on. On Rituraj's request he agreed to stay back, not in an executive role but as a director on the board of the company. Both agreed that Singh would step down as the chief executive officer of SIS after the IPO in 2017.

This was the second time in fifteen years that SIS was undergoing an important leadership transition. Moments like these could haemorrhage a business or turn out to be an opportunity. R.K. had done the first transition successfully by bringing in Uday Singh and Rituraj to take over him at the top of SIS. The decision, as we have seen in preceding chapters, proved to be a masterstroke. Now it was up to Rituraj to decide, of course in consultation with R.K. and Uday Singh, on how to execute this transition.

The SIS of 2018 was markedly different from that of 2002. From just one business, SIS had seventeen separate business units. Geographically, it was widespread in India and overseas. While it had gone deep in the core security business, its other two big verticals had also scaled. Even in these two businesses, operations had expanded quickly. The change in scale made one thing clear—while Uday Singh's shoes were big to fill, the SIS of today needed multiple shoes. Rituraj knew that SIS now had to chart its future course not as one business but as multiple businesses under the same ownership.

'So, we split the business into four groupings. The security group came under Tapash, cash logistics under Oscar. Dhiraj initially managed the facility management business but later Shamsher took charge. And Murli took charge of the international. Dhiraj was now the Chief Executive Officer of SIS India, the listed entity,' says Rituraj. Each vertical now had its own leadership team.

Each of these verticals have a lower rung of leadership that consists of functional heads.

A similar transition is also seen in the Group Management Committee, which among other things also decides on SIS's vision for the next five years. This is made up of five to seven of the most senior executives at the company. It was the third GMC that prepared Vision 2030, SIS's version of a Five Year Plan. The first one was prepared way back in 2010. Now, with Vision 2030 set in place, Rituraj and Dhiraj Singh are already thinking of the fourth GMC, which will decide the 2035 Vision. In other words, Rituraj and Singh have both the long-term and short-term maps of SIS firmly in their visions and, equally importantly, have already identified the next set of top leaders.

In effect, in this whole exercise of leadership transition, Rituraj hasn't tried to look for another Uday Singh to replace the original. This is acknowledging the most basic of human facts—no one person is like the other. No two people are the same. While Dhiraj Singh is as much a professional as Uday Singh, each came with their own passion and convictions. If Uday Singh was process driven, Dhiraj has been more entrepreneurial. 'He is the business incubator, value creation, deal-making and M&A type,' says Rituraj. There are no replacements and you shouldn't look for one. Rituraj used the opportunity to build a leadership structure that takes SIS forward.

A leadership and management structure as deep as this one was required to execute the vision that Rituraj has for SIS. 'In all these businesses, I see the opportunity to build multibillion-dollar security businesses across security, FM and cash. The vision is to allow these businesses to sort of stretch their legs and take their own shape. This is what the future of SIS looks like,' he says. The cash logistics business has already taken a step towards it. SIS Prosegur is preparing to be listed, the group's second IPO.

For each of these businesses to become multibillion-dollar operations, they need to compound in their growth. Not compound at a breathless rates that will inevitably lead to a collapse, but at a steady 15–20 per cent for the next ten years. 'There are two things that we need for that. Systems and people,' says Rituraj. And with the current crop at the top and the continued development and focus on tech within the SIS ecosystem, it appears Rituraj has set the company up for its next phase of growth. The importance of tech was reiterated multiple times at the May annual conference, with the company executing new software across functions such as billing, invoicing and guard operations. There is also SIS Ventures, which till now has invested in four startups that will give the company an edge in emerging technologies.

The focus on talent, systems and tech underlines what Rituraj wants—the institutionalization of SIS. That's in line with what entrepreneurs around the world do as their companies grow bigger in such a scale that it no longer can be dependent on just one individual. This will gladden both SIS employees and investors. It also leads one to a pertinent question: what role does Rituraj see himself playing in this vision?

Having grown up along with the family business, Rituraj knows that the glue that has held the organization together is its culture. The culture has been SIS's North Star, the guiding light. It's the reason, says Rituraj, why the company has survived over fifty years in an industry where scores of security companies open and close every year. 'I think the most valuable thing about SIS is its culture,' he says. 'So, for the last five, seven years I have been very focused on articulating the culture because one of the biggest things I worry about is the cultural mooring of this business as it grows larger.'

He cites the banyan tree, which adds roots even as its branches expand. 'As the sub trees become stronger, as they should, the main mother tree should not become weaker. They only make the mother tree also stronger. So, as the SMC business gets stronger and the SIS Prosegur joint venture gets stronger—it's good they are—it shouldn't mean that the cultural moorings of SIS become less important or less understood by them.' For the same reason, Rituraj has identified culture preservation and perpetuation as one of his main pursuits within the organization.

It's a challenge. Organizations often struggle to retain their essence as they grow. The two are strings that pull in different directions. Maintaining the core culture depends on continuity, whereas growth brings change. There are people who have been at SIS for over forty years. There are others who have spent just four weeks. Eventually, the number of newcomers will keep increasing in proportion. 'This balance is everything. We try to anchor our purpose around people and society and then there's the values. SIS is a social enterprise, the reason why the chairman started out. There are three values that we've always articulated—trust, people focus and service. So these values have to be protected, preserved and then you have to be constantly defining them.' Rituraj is leading this constant process of preservation and protection to ensure SIS doesn't get the big company syndrome, something that can impact agility and innovation within an organization.

How does Rituraj preserve the SIS culture? He doesn't have a magic wand.

'I don't know the right way to do it or the wrong way to do it but I think at every opportunity and every contact point, these things need to be reinforced. They don't understand everything at one go.'

He does this often when he is travelling. Like his father, Rituraj is also a wandering leader. The SIS GMD is constantly on the move, travelling up to 120 days a year. That's one in three days on the road, rail or in the air. Every time he lands in a new city, he calls up the branch or region head to join him on the car ride to his appointment. Even when he is travelling with family, often Pallavi and the kids hop on to a vehicle and Rituraj takes a separate car so that he can talk to his men. 'I spend that one hour with the manager talking to him about what's happening in his branch, what's new, what is the impact of systems, how is growth, what contracts did he lose, what are the customers saying, what's the guard saying, which competitor is doing well here. It's about everything. It's not a structured conversation about your targets, your KPIs but a general chit-chat.'

Rituraj loses no opportunity to speak to SIS's people on the ground—the guards and janitors. The joke in the Sinha family, often recounted by Pallavi, is about how one doesn't need to be worried if you suddenly lose sight of Rituraj in a mall, you would invariably find him talking to one of the guards. In fact, three years ago, it was a similar conversation that led to a decision that made a lot of difference to the lives of SIS guards.

One cold winter night three years ago, Rituraj was in Dimapur and was being dropped back to his hotel by his host. Next to the hotel was an outlet of a major retail chain. This company was a SIS customer and keeping guard was a SIS employee. 'He was closing the store and the store was shut at nighttime. I went to him and sat with the guy and had a hearty ten-minute chat,' says Rituraj. The guard didn't recognize the SIS promoter. During the conversation, Rituraj asked about how things were with his work. 'It's so cold. The senior officers go around with three to four layers of clothing and we have just got this SIS jacket and sweater and we feel cold inside and on our feet.' That's when Rituraj realized that the kit that every SIS recruit gets when he is hired didn't include thermal wear. When he got back to Delhi, he instructed his team to include a SIS thermal in every kit for guards who work in cold conditions. SIS worked with well-known textile manufacturers for six months before deciding on the thermals for different grades of weather. 'For extreme winters like in Punjab and Arunachal and for the kind that suits a place like Delhi, which has medium to extreme winters. So different types of warmers were made,' says Rituraj.

Every time he notices something, Rituraj is quick to send feedback. For instance, in Haridwar he came across a shabbily dressed guard. The branch manager immediately got a picture and a message from Rituraj. He also picks up new ideas. During a visit to the seva kendra to get his passport renewed, Rituraj was struck by the efficiency of the system and process that enable it to handle hundreds of applications a day. He asked his team to develop a similar system for SIS's recruitment drives.

The focus is not on just the financial metrics or KPIs, but also to reiterate the organization's goals of employee and client centricity, and the importance of upholding this culture.

That's probably the reason that SIS—an organization with nearly 3 lakh employees—doesn't have a chief human resources officer (CHRO). The CEO is the CHRO. 'In this business if the CEO is not the CHRO, he can't be the CEO. In my business, if the CEO doesn't understand his people, how is he going to get the business done? If he doesn't understand the culture, he can't do the business.'

There is the same sense of culture preservation and perpetuation in the way Rituraj mentors SIS's key leaders. He keeps core business discussion for the monthly and quarterly reviews. At all other times, he discusses strategy, big ideas that will improve operations. He reiterates the vision: 'So there's a set of big ideas that we will transform our pest control business from X to Y, maybe in size, maybe in profitability, maybe in geographical presence, maybe in production, maybe in terms of technology transforming it from the way they do it now to a completely different way. These are big ideas. Then, there's some ideas for improvement, like how can we fix the after-sales experience, how can we bring in more technology, how do we improve the satisfaction scores, how do we internally build talent to man more branches rather than hiring laterally.'

These discussions are an important follow-up after the whole organization is familiarized with the five-year plan and the annual business plans shared by the CEOs. 'When I sit with them,' Rituraj says, 'I'm talking more about how we are progressing on the big ideas that we discussed and improvement ideas bit by bit. Each business has different problems at different times. I'm more focused on that because, for me, I think ultimately the content of the service makes you a market leader or a failure. What happens with professionals is they are naturally more skewed towards numbers. Rightly so, but for me, service content is equally important.'

This evolution of his role in SIS marks a clear transition of Rituraj, from one who has keenly involved in the nitty-gritty of company operations to a promoter who drives the whole organization towards his vision and introduces big ideas. All this while, he has made sure the connection with his people on the ground is as strong as it was earlier. This helps in culture perpetuation and also provides him critical intelligence on the business. As with R.K., Rituraj also receives calls from employees across the ranks and makes sure their feedback is taken. That's also a challenge in an organization that has nearly 3 lakh employees. Now, this has been institutionalized. SIS employees have been given a number they can call to raise their issues. It's an automated number that uses AI to mimic Rituraj's voice to engage with the caller, build a conversation and also record what they have to say. Tech has taken employee engagement to another level.

Institutionalizing, creating a strong leadership, bringing in the best technology-led backend are some of the steps the likes of Sajjan Jindal,

Uday Kotak and Anand Mahindra did as they moved from executive roles to full-fledged promoter positions. Organizations which start as promoter owned and run develop to promoter-owned and professionally supported and finally to the third stage of promoter-owned and professionally led. JSW Group, Kotak Mahindra Bank and Mahindra & Mahindra Group have moved to the third stage. SIS, as Rituraj points out, is somewhere past the second stage and moving towards the third.

But hang on. None of the above three gentlemen were as young as forty-four—as Rituraj is today—when they made this transition. While it's true that he has already spent twenty-two years at the top of the company, he is still too young to think of the third stage at the moment. Yet, he is. What does he have in his mind?

SIS is a growth story that mirrors the transformation of India's economy over the last 50 years into the third largest in the world. Just like the Indian economy is at a critical juncture right now, the scenario is similar for SIS. As much as it has accomplished through two generations, technological focus, a unique culture and by professionalising management, the next 50 years are going to be even more complex to navigate.

For all its technological prowess, SIS will have to be even more nimble because the pace in which its customers operate and change, is getting quicker. The years between one generation of tech to the next hasn't ever been shorter. That nimbleness will be tough to achieve as its organization grows in length and breadth. Growth is complex, and this complexity often kills growth. This is where SIS's core culture will be further tested. Can the family culture, the founder's mentality perpetuate enough to remain vital as the businesses across verticals grow? That's within the organization. Outside, SIS needs to communicate and engage with its investors and revive its fledgling stock price.

Rituraj will keep these things in mind as he leads SIS to its next big goal—achieving the Vision 2030. The company had fallen short of its Vision 2025. While the pandemic played the big disruptor, and to its credit, SIS survived and also revived its fortunes in the aftermath, Rituraj wouldn't want to use that clutch. During his speech at the annual conference, the group managing director stressed on two things the company needed to accomplish in the coming five years—push for higher market share in each of the businesses and doing so by providing more and better solutions to customers.

To work towards a larger five-year goal, Rituraj has marked out some of the levers. SIS-Prosegur is prepping for an IPO, the second for the SIS Group. A big push will also come from M&A. Surprisingly for a company that had done fourteen deal in 10 years, SIS hasn't done any since 2019. That may change from 2025 onwards. In all, he wants SIS to be well positioned to capture all the opportunities that will be thrown up by a $10 trillion economy that India is expected to become over the next decade.

Rituraj has set up the organization towards this goal. Each of the business units have a well-defined leadership. Next rung of leaders has also been identified. At the group level, Dhiraj Singh has his priorities laid out. SIS is today a professionally run, promoter-backed company. However, the evolution is not done. There are two important milestones in the horizon.

Rituraj's vision for SIS leadership over the next 10 to 20 years has two important parts. One would be to completely hand over the operations to professionals and become a professional-run management. This would mean that promoters would take on a more board-level role, a natural transition seen globally when one company grows to become a sprawling conglomerate. The second part of this evolution is the transition within the promoters—from the second generation to the third. Both are sensitive, need extensive planning and need to be effortlessly done. Clearly, this is one of the biggest tasks ahead for Rituraj.

So how should the SIS of the future look? A services solutions multinational that is the biggest in each of its verticals in India and has expanded exponentially overseas; one that continues to be guided by the principles and culture that R.K. championed and Rituraj took forward; and a company that has finally been given its due by investors.

With so much to achieve, SIS is a journey well begun, with a lot to accomplish.

ACKNOWLEDGEMENTS

The SIS Story was a challenge in many ways. It is based on fifty-three conversations that were rich in detail. To comprehend this required hours of reading. The writing took many more rotations of the clock. The timeline was stiff. The book took shape in less than ten months.

Two things made it possible. One, the subjects. As you would agree after reading all the pages before this one, SIS has a rich legacy, an unusual story and an inspiring one at that. At the centre are its two extraordinary leaders, Mr Sinha and Rituraj. Thank you Mr Sinha and Rituraj for sharing your story with me. And a special thanks to your wonderful and warm family.

My gratitude to the leaders of SIS and those associated with the company for sparing time and sharing their own SIS stories with me. SIS's Ishant Saini played a big role in getting the logistics done.

Second, the book took effort and involvement from a lot more people who helped and supported me. Senior PR executive Amit Arora, Writer's Side founder Kanishka Gupta—thanks guys.

The team at HarperCollins are solid and thorough professionals. Thanks, in particular, to Sachin Sharma and Shreya Lall in bringing together the book.

ACKNOWLEDGEMENTS

I work at The Morning Context. My thanks to Ashish K. Mishra, The Morning Context's editor-in-chief, for backing the author in me.

This has not been an easy year for my larger family. We suffered a terrible loss. We have held it together. My gratitude to papa, mummy, sister and her family, and brother's family for constantly following up on the book's progress and encouraging me.

A book takes a fair bit of sacrifice from the family. My wife Sherin, daughter Amy and son Noah were equal partners with their patience and support even as I spent most of the weekends buried in the book. My gratitude and love to them.

The SIS Story is my second book, and a big milestone for me. Thank you, dear reader, for reading.

NOTES

Preface

1. Indian Defence Academy, 'How Many Soldiers in Indian Army', https://indiandefenceacademy.in/how-many-soldiers-in-indian-army/

4: A Bold Entrepreneur

1. Singh, Rajesh, 'What links coal mafia don Suryadeo Singh and the movie "Gangs of Wasseypur?"', Scroll.in, 6 January 2021, https://scroll.in/article/982819/what-links-coal-mafia-don-suryadeo-singh-and-the-movie-gangs-of-wasseypur; Mishra, Sandeep, 'Singhs Fight to Become Coal King in Dhanbad', 13 December 2014, *The Times of India,* https://timesofindia.indiatimes.com/home/specials/2014-assembly-elections/jharkhand-news/Singhs-fight-to-become-Coal-King-in-Dhanbad/articleshow/45498163.cms

ABOUT THE AUTHOR

Prince Mathews Thomas is a financial journalist with twenty-two years of experience. He has worked in leading business newsrooms, including *The Economic Times, Business Standard,* Dow Jones Newswires, *The Hindu BusinessLine,* Moneycontrol and *Forbes India.* He is currently managing editor at The Morning Context. In his career, he has written about leading business houses across industries, analysing their business models and management styles.

HarperCollins *Publishers* India

At HarperCollins India, we believe in telling the best stories and finding the widest readership for our books in every format possible. We started publishing in 1992; a great deal has changed since then, but what has remained constant is the passion with which our authors write their books, the love with which readers receive them, and the sheer joy and excitement that we as publishers feel in being a part of the publishing process.

Over the years, we've had the pleasure of publishing some of the finest writing from the subcontinent and around the world, including several award-winning titles and some of the biggest bestsellers in India's publishing history. But nothing has meant more to us than the fact that millions of people have read the books we published, and that somewhere, a book of ours might have made a difference.

As we look to the future, we go back to that one word— a word which has been a driving force for us all these years.

Read.